LAST WITNESSES

LAST WITNESSES

REFLECTIONS ON THE WARTIME INTERNMENT OF JAPANESE AMERICANS

EDITED BY
ERICA HARTH

palgrave
macmillan

First published in hardcover in 2001 by palgrave

First PALGRAVE MACMILLAN™ paperback edition: May 2003
175 Fifth Avenue, New York, N.Y. 10010 and
Houndmills, Basingstoke, Hampshire, England RG21 6XS.
Companies and representatives throughout the world.

PALGRAVE MACMILLAN is the global academic imprint of the Palgrave
Macmillan division of St. Martin's Press, LLC and of Palgrave Macmillan Ltd.
Macmillan® is a registered trademark in the United States, United Kingdom and
other countries. Palgrave is a registered trademark in the European Union and
other countries.

ISBN 1–4039–6230–8

Library of Congress Cataloguing-in-Publication Data
Last witnesses : reflections on the wartime interment of Japanese Americans /
edited by Erica Harth.
      p.   cm.
   Includes bibliographical references.
   ISBN 1–4039–6230–8
   1. Japanese Americans—Evacuation and relocation, 1942–1945.   2. Japanese
Americans—Evacuation and relocation, 1942–1945—Personal narratives.   3.
Japanese Americans—Biography.   I. Harth, Erica.

A catalogue record for this book is available from the British Library.

First PALGRAVE MACMILLAN paperback edition: May 2003

D769.8.A6 L37   2001
940.54'7273—dc21

                                                              2001021293

Design by Letra Libre, Inc.

First Edition: November 2001
10   9   8   7   6   5   4   3   2   1

Printed in the United States of America.

To my first-grade classmates at Manzanar,
and in memory of my parents.

CONTENTS

PART III
WHAT WE TOOK FROM THE CAMPS

PART IV
FROM THE PAST TO THE FUTURE

LIST OF PHOTOGRAPHS

ACKNOWLEDGMENTS

FROM THE EARLIEST STAGES OF THIS BOOK, my efforts have met with consistent encouragement, support, and help. I feel privileged to have worked with a group of contributors who have expanded my intellectual and emotional horizons and who have been unfailingly cooperative. Writers whom I did not know previously have become friends, even if in certain cases only via e-mail; with others, the friendships have been strengthened. For me, it has been a deeply rewarding experience to find such collaborative spirit and good will.

My thanks reach beyond the book's covers. Deirdre Bonifaz and Phyllis R. Stein helped me to get started on the project. Paul Watanabe gave me valuable guidance in the choice of contributors. My conversations with him and with Margaret Yamamoto have energized my work on the book. To Charlotte Sagoff and Anne O. Freed I owe much gratitude for their gifts of source material. Discussions with Dean Hashimoto, May and Tetsuo Takayanagi, and participants in the annual international seminar on American legal history held at Boston College have stimulated and refreshed my thinking on the internment. Thanks, too, to the many Brandeis undergraduates who have kept me on my toes with their questions and curiosity about this crucial episode of American history. The Marion and Jasper Whiting Foundation and Brandeis University provided me with financial support for archival research and preparation of the manuscript.

To encouraging and informative friends—Joseph Boskin, Juliet and Victor Brudney, Karen Klein, William Shay, and Ellen Schrecker, among many others—I am profoundly grateful. Dorothy Kaufmann gave me invaluable help through her reading of my work in manuscript. Thanks to Dave Wisniewski at Brandeis, to my indexer, Marcia Carlson, and to the editorial and production staff members at Palgrave/St. Martin's Press: Michael Flamini, Amanda Johnson, Rick Delaney, and Sabahat Chaudhary, for their ongoing interest, helpfulness, and patience.

And especially, I thank David H. Gallant for his limitless generosity in offering me editorial advice, logistical and emotional support, soul food, and countless other precious intangibles that have facilitated and enriched my task.

ERICA   HARTH

INTRODUCTION

ON SEPTEMBER 12, 2001, THE BANNER HEADLINE OF *THE BOSTON GLOBE*
read "New Day of Infamy." Comparisons of September 11 with the Japanese attack on Pearl Harbor of December 7, 1941, became commonplace. In the press,
articles started to appear with titles such as "War on Terrorism Stirs Memory of
Internment" (*The New York Times*, Sept. 24, 2001). Scary indications popped up
that civil liberties might be sacrificed to considerations of security. Two months
after the attacks on the World Trade Center and Pentagon, one poll revealed that
64 percent of the public believed that in wartime the president should have the authority to change or abridge constitutional rights.

If you're tempted to see the mass detention of ethnic Japanese after Pearl
Harbor as nothing more than history, you might want to think twice.* Suddenly
the need for historical memory has become more urgent than ever. The roundup
of hundreds placed in federal custody, the prospect of military tribunals, the sus-
pension of rules of confidentiality between lawyers and imprisoned terrorist suspects, the USA Patriot Act of 2001, the broadening of the FBI's powers of search
and surveillance, and other antiterrorist measures following September 11 constitute what Anthony Romero, executive director of the American Civil Liberties
Union, has called "the greatest challenge to civil liberties since World War II."

How much have we learned from the wartime internment of up to 120,000
ethnic Japanese, two-thirds of whom were American citizens, and all of whom
were guiltless of any act of sabotage or espionage?[1] The infamous Supreme Court

---

* For a chronological summary of the Japanese American internment, see the Appendix.

Korematsu decision of 1944, for example, which in effect upheld the constitutionality of the internment, is now a staple of law school curricula. It illustrates what can go wrong in approaches to vital constitutional issues. Yet since the terrorist attacks, *Korematsu* has been given a new lease on life.

Fred Korematsu was one of three young Japanese American men who deliberately challenged or resisted the government's orders of 1942 relating to internment: the imposition of a curfew for Japanese Americans living in what had been declared military "exclusion zones" on the West Coast; evacuation and removal to "assembly centers" (temporary holding pens) and later to "relocation centers," or concentration camps.[2] All three test cases reached the Supreme Court. Korematsu, a young welder, was so determined to avoid internment that he underwent plastic surgery to alter his appearance and doctored his draft card. He just wanted to stay with his caucasian fiancée. He was apprehended on a tip. The Supreme Court, six to three, endorsed the military's claim that internment of the ethnic Japanese was a necessity. Later the argument would prove bankrupt because of the government's deliberate suppression of evidence that there was in effect no military necessity for the internment. In the 1980s, Korematsu's conviction was overturned in Federal District Court, as were those of the two other resisters, Gordon Hirabayashi and Minoru Yasui.

One of the three dissenters in the *Korematsu* case, Justice Robert Jackson, warned that the Court's decision would create "a loaded weapon ready for the hand of any authority that can bring forward a plausible claim of an urgent need." Prophetic words.

In early December 2001, lawyers supportive of the Bush administration's antiterrorist measures started to brandish the weapon. *The New York Times* reported that lawyers in support of the administration had charged critics of its policies with ignoring "Supreme Court precedents that approved such extreme wartime actions as the internment of Japanese Americans in World War II" (December 12, 2001). In a sidebar to this article were sources cited by supporters of the administration, one of which was *Korematsu*.

The fact is that the 1944 *Korematsu* decision was implicitly discredited not only by the vacating of Fred Korematsu's conviction forty years later, but also by the passage of the Civil Liberties Act in 1988. This act, the culmination of the Japanese American community's national movement in the 1970s and 1980s to redress the injustice of the internment, was accompanied by a national apology. The act set out provisions for $20,000 in reparations per individual former internee and a Civil Liberties Public Education Fund. Ten years later, Fred Korematsu was awarded the Presidential Medal of Freedom.

To cite *Korematsu*, then, in support of administrative antiterrorist measures at the beginning of the twenty-first century is to return to the mentality of

1944. It is to say that when national security needs are perceived as paramount, ethnicity will suffice as a ground for suspicion of disloyalty. It is to place the stamp of approval on what Justice Frank Murphy in his dissenting opinion in *Korematsu*, called the "legalization of racism."

Suspicions of the Japanese Americans' disloyalty were based on a systematic conflation of ethnic Japanese in this country with the Japanese enemy abroad. The enemy was sneaky and untrustworthy; it didn't look like "us." Consequently, the ethnic Japanese in this country were judged to be the same. Acting on this racist assumption immediately after Pearl Harbor, the FBI rounded up some 5,000 Issei (first or immigrant generation) and Nisei (second generation, born here, and so American citizens). Over 2,000 among these suspects were sent to remote Justice Department detention camps for an indefinite stay, even in some cases for the duration of the war. The people pulled in were generally community leaders, heads of civic associations, men in the import-export business, and so on. Husbands and fathers would just disappear and were often not heard from for months. Frightened families waited for their turn, some keeping a packed bag in readiness.

For most Americans, however, World War II evokes not images of concentration camps on the home front but rather nostalgia for better days, when there were good guys and bad guys, when right was right and wrong was wrong. After September 11, the temptation is to recreate this moral battle in a new struggle against what President George W. Bush has called an "axis of evil." We forget that we who championed freedom and democracy abroad in World War II incarcerated almost an entire ethnic population—accused of no crime other than its ancestry—at home.

Only in the past fifteen years or so have we even begun to own up publicly to this dishonorable side of our role in the Second World War. Now, when the threat of terrorist acts brings a new challenge to the preservation of our civil liberties, it is imperative to take another look at our history in order to reassess both the past and the present.

Even after the publicized national redress movement of the 1980s, after sixty years' worth of documents, histories, art, literature, media coverage, film, and video on the subject, the American public is still largely uninformed.[3] The mass detention of Japanese Americans may well be the most documented and the least known miscarriage of justice in our history. Historian Roger Daniels notes that the internment "violated fundamental values of American democracy in the guise of fighting a war to preserve that democracy. . . . It was the first and so far the only time that the American government has violated, en masse, the rights of an ethnic group, the second- and third-generation Japanese Americans, to which its Constitution had given citizenship."[4]

How has all the material on the internment so long available to the general public managed not to penetrate the national consciousness? Certainly it is a story that we would rather not hear. Not only does it tarnish the image of our victory in World War II; it also clashes head-on with fundamental and enduring American values: the rule of fairness and equality, which allows you to remain innocent until proven guilty; the crowning of hard work by success. The Japanese Americans incarcerated in 1942 were held guilty until proven innocent, and the hard-won success of the older generation was smashed to bits by years behind barbed wire.

As it is today with Arab and Muslim Americans and immigrants, the issue was the supposed loyalty of the ethnic Japanese. Some individuals in this population could well be disloyal, the army and the government claimed, so you might as well lock up all 120,000 of them, "enemy aliens" (the immigrants, legally ineligible for naturalization until 1952) and "non-aliens" (the citizens) alike.

Political myths surrounding the issue of loyalty are among the most potent in this nation. We speak of loyalty to our country as if we know what we mean. But in looking back to the war years, we find that even the most basic questions about loyalty have yet to be satisfactorily answered: How do you determine loyalty? Who or what decides if you are loyal or disloyal? What do you do if you are arbitrarily declared disloyal? The fate of Japanese Americans during the war years hung on such questions, which resonate somberly today.

The sway of myth over public consciousness can go only so far in explaining the lack of large-scale education about the wartime internment. For myth to keep history at bay, certain concrete conditions have to facilitate the continuing ignorance.

First, the number of ethnic Japanese living in the continental United States before removal to the camps was minuscule—at its peak about two-tenths of 1 percent of the total population, hardly sufficient to constitute a "yellow peril." Immigration from Japan, already severely curtailed by the "Gentlemen's Agreement" of 1907–1908 between the United States and Japan, had been completely halted by the United States in 1924. The vast majority of ethnic Japanese lived in their own enclaves on the West Coast. So although racism and economic competition had combined to ignite severe animosity toward members of this group in the region where most of them lived, until the internment persons of Japanese descent went largely unnoticed by the rest of the country. Most Nisei*

---

*   Nisei: second-generation persons of Japanese descent, born in the United States and therefore citizens; Issei: the first-generation, immigrant group; Nikkei: all persons of Japanese ancestry.

werc under voting age, so they had no political clout. The Nikkei were a population that, in a very concrete sense, did not count. After Japan's attack on Pearl Harbor of December 7, 1941, ethnic Japanese suddenly found themselves in the unwelcome spotlight of President Franklin Delano Roosevelt's Executive Order 9066, which excluded them from specially designated military zones. Public Law 503, of March 21, criminalized violations of regulations governing the exclusion zones. This measure got through Congress with very little discussion and a great deal of indifference and ignorance.

Second, both the Roosevelt administration and the general public were preoccupied with what they considered the more pressing concerns of the war. The relative numerical insignificance of the evacuated group combined with the racism that identified the enemy with both Japanese immigrants and Japanese American citizens made it possible to sweep the whole matter under the rug.

Third, several historical opportunities arose for the general public to bask in a sense that the case of the wartime internment was closed. Japanese Americans, through their military service in World War II, were generally judged to have "proved their loyalty." Never mind that the suspicions leading up to internment turned out to be groundless; for the ethnic Japanese to gain acceptance as loyal meant literally to go through a test of fire. The all–Japanese American 442nd Regimental Combat Team performed so heroically in battle that it became the most decorated unit of the war. Despite racist attacks on returning Nisei in uniform, it is generally agreed that the 442nd's performance went a long way toward gaining widespread acceptance for Japanese Americans after the war. Monica Sone, one of the early memoirists of the camps, dates the formation of the 442nd as the "turning point" in the story of the internment: "It was the road back to our rightful places."[5]

Further opportunities for the general public to close the chapter came in the 1970s and 1980s. On February 19, 1976, the anniversary date of Executive Order 9066 in the Bicentennial year, President Gerald R. Ford rescinded Roosevelt's order. In the 1980s, we had the Civil Liberties Act and the reversal of the Supreme Court's convictions of Gordon Hirabayashi, Fred Korematsu, and Minoru Yasui.[6] Few people are aware that in these reopened cases the courts ultimately did not declare the internment unconstitutional but made their decisions on narrow grounds. Moreover, because the reopened cases did not reach the Supreme Court, the original decision in *Korematsu*, which endorsed the internment, remains on the books.

The demographic and political history of the ethnic Japanese in the United States and the historical markers that have invited a certain complacency about closure can help to explain the near blackout of information in our schools, colleges, and universities, a blackout that prevailed even through the redress movement of the 1970s and 1980s. It is true that much more information has been disseminated on the West Coast, but even there it has been surprisingly limited. Only now, at the turn of the century, does the wartime internment seem to be slowly edging its way into the curricula of schools and colleges. The redress movement and the rise of ethnic pride and multiculturalism in the 1960s and 1970s, along with increasing waves of immigration from Asian nations, finally seem to be having their effects. The growing interest evidenced in our educational institutions coincides with new recognition of Japanese Americans and their role in World War II. On June 21, 2000, twenty Nisei received (most posthumously) the nation's highest military award, the Medal of Honor, for their heroic service in the armed forces during World War II. The ceremony followed an extensive review by the army of many instances in which Asian Americans were passed over for the award to receive instead the second-highest medal, the Distinguished Service Cross. When Norman Y. Mineta, President Bill Clinton's nominee as secretary of commerce, was sworn in on July 25, 2000, he became the first Asian American Cabinet member.

Even as we applaud the increased presence of Japanese American history in the nation's educational institutions, it is worth adding a word of caution. If, during World War II, what to do with the Nikkei became known as the "Japanese problem," the more recent social and demographic developments have tended to create a segregated educational niche for the internment in college and university Asian American Studies programs. Long ago, however, Morton Grodzins said of the internment that it is "less important for what it did to Japanese Americans than for what it might do to all Americans."[7]

Grodzins' statement was not meant to belittle the catastrophic effects of the internment on its victims. Instead, it suggests to us over sixty years after the internment both that the mass removal has implicated and affected all Americans—although not equally—and that the story of the internment will not be over until we take full responsibility not only for the injustice but for the precedent it set. This volume of essays takes the two suggestions as basic premises. As we look at the internment across several generations, we see a dynamic of history that is ever evolving through the interaction of past and present. Voices of Japanese Americans and Americans who are not of Japanese ancestry tell us that the story involves us all.

Much of learning about history is "unlearning"—unlearning the myths that inevitably seep into any account of the past but which the conscientious historian, aided by the passage of time, attempts to confront. *Last Witnesses* is meant to contribute to the difficult process of unlearning. As the range of writers represented here demonstrates, this process can take several generations. Only with the maturing of the Nisei generation and the coming of age of the Sansei* was a national redress movement able to get off the ground. The success of this movement was a major eye-opener, especially for the Japanese American community. The general public unlearns more slowly.

The former internees among our contributors have had to find individual modes of addressing their own experiences of the internment and of living with them through the social transformations since the war. For writers of the younger generations, the first step has often been one of startling discovery. Only after this initial shock have they tried to reorder their feelings about their families, their lives, and the country of their birth. Those of us who were white children in the camps have some sober reckoning to do about the myths and meanings of Americanness and about our individual and family's civic responsibilities. Other contributors to *Last Witnesses* have realized that having no personal or family connection at all to the internment does not mean a lack of emotional or political connection. On the contrary, coming face to face with one of the most significant betrayals of American ideals casts a new light on our fundamental values.

The elusive problem of loyalty, deeply connected to the issue of racism, underlies the mythology surrounding the internment. The charges of disloyalty that sent 120,000 guiltless ethnic Japanese into concentration camps were taken up among the internees themselves. As often happens in instances of racism and injustice, myths that originated outside the targeted group got imported into the victims' consciousness, where they festered and intermittently erupted into disastrous internecine conflicts. The internalization of blame and guilt is so important to an understanding of the problem of loyalty among Japanese Americans that it is worth a brief exploration of its history in camp politics and in the long-term effects of the internment.

This history begins at least two decades before the internment, with the formation of the national Nisei civic organization, the Japanese American Citizens League (JACL). In 1919, a group of earnest young Nisei started the association's forerunner, the American Loyalty League. It was a time of general nervousness about disloyalty in an early Red Scare, set off by the Bolshevik Revolution and political opportunism at home. In November of the same year, the American Legion at its first convention passed one of what was to be a series of resolutions calling for the exclusion of Japanese immigrants from the

---

*   Sansei: third-generation persons of Japanese descent.

United States.[8] Attorney General A. Mitchell Palmer's raids on radicals in 1919–1920 resulted in the roundup and deportation of 249 aliens, the best known among whom was Emma Goldman. After Japan's invasion of Manchuria in 1931, a year after the JACL proper was founded, both Issei and Nisei had legitimate cause to fear for their own future. So began the JACL's long and tragically unsuccessful effort to ward off potential retribution directed at its constituency. In 1934, the organization at its third national convention passed a resolution to "cooperate with and support any organization or governmental agency to expel [sic] and deport from the United States such undesirable alien communists who are found guilty of subversive acts toward our nation regardless of race, creed or nationality."[9] As advocate for a then powerless ethnic group subject to widespread discrimination, the JACL had to walk a fine line between proving loyalty through "assimilation" and seeking social justice, a balancing act that failed tragically during the war years.

At the time of evacuation, the JACL pledged cooperation with the authorities, in the firm belief that only by adopting this policy could Japanese Americans give evidence of their loyalty and avoid even worse treatment. Early in 1943, in connection with the army's recruitment of Nisei volunteers from the camps, a long questionnaire was distributed to all adult internees. Questions 27 and 28 supposedly had to do with loyalty but in effect created a trap.* If you were Issei, you had to choose between statelessness (yes to number 28) on the one hand and "disloyalty" on the other. If you were Nisei, a yes to number 28 might imply disloyalty anyway (if you "foreswear" allegiance to the Japanese emperor, you presumably once did pledge allegiance to him), since by Japanese law all Japanese Americans automatically held dual citizenship. Answering no landed you in the camp at Tule Lake, California, which became a "segregation center" for the so-called disloyals.

When conscription was reinstituted for Nisei in 1944, a draft resistance movement sprang up almost spontaneously within the camps. It got started at the Heart Mountain camp in Wyoming, where Kiyoshi Okamoto had formed a Fair Play Committee to agitate for the Nisei's legal rights. In May 1944, a federal grand jury in Cheyenne indicted 63 of the draft resisters from Heart Mountain and sentenced them to three years' imprisonment. A total of 315

---

* Here is the original text of the two questions (later, number 28 was rewritten to be more understandable to Issei):

number 27. Are you willing to serve in the armed forces of the United States on combat duty, wherever ordered?

men from all the camps refused induction, and 263 of them were convicted. In 1947, Harry Truman granted a presidential pardon to all those convicted.[10]

The resisters of conscience and the "no-no boys" (those who answered no to the two loyalty questions in 1943) were spokesmen for what historian Roger Daniels has called the "left opposition."[11] In addition, a more generalized discontent and dissidence lurked beneath the daily routine of camp life. It burst forth in occasional dramatic episodes, such as the so-called Manzanar riot. On December 6, 1942, at Manzanar, military police fired into a crowd of demonstrators, killing two young men and injuring ten other internees. The demonstrators were protesting the arrest of Harry Ueno, a cook who had tried to organize a kitchen-workers' union and who had accused officials of the civil agency that administered the camps, the War Relocation Authority (WRA), of embezzling evacuees' sugar and meat supplies. Ueno had been charged with leading an assault on fellow internee Fred Tayama, an allegation that was never proved.

Fred Tayama was a leader of the JACL. The organization had disapproved of all resistance and opposition among internees. In the crises over registration, segregation, and the draft, JACLers consistently pushed for demonstration of loyalty, even to the point of sacrificing ties to family and one's own life. Many internees came to see the JACLers as collaborators or informers (*inu*). History seems to have come full circle in John Tateishi's essay, "Memories from Behind Barbed Wire." Tateishi, currently the JACL's acting executive director, discusses his feelings as a child in Manzanar when he saw his father and Harry Ueno, his father's good friend, being led away to jail together.[12]

Decades after the last camp closed in 1946, the JACL found itself once more the center of a controversy about loyalty, this time over the inscriptions on the National Japanese American Memorial to Patriotism in Washington, D.C., formally dedicated in 2000. One of the major issues was the inclusion of a quote from the Japanese American Creed written in 1940 by Mike M. Masaoka, an important leader of the JACL. The creed concludes with a pledge that has become emblematic of the JACL's desperate wartime bid to certify its constituency as loyal Americans:

(* cont.) number 28. Will you swear unqualified allegiance to the United States of America and faithfully defend the United States from any or all attack by foreign or domestic forces, and forswear any form of allegiance to the Japanese emperor, to any other foreign government, power or organization?

> Because I believe in America, and I trust she believes in me, and because I have
> received innumerable benefits from her, I pledge myself to do honor to her at
> all times and all places; to support her constitution; to obey her laws; to re-
> spect her flag; to defend her against all enemies, foreign and domestic; to ac-
> tively assume my duties and obligations as a citizen, cheerfully and without
> any reservations whatsoever, in the hope that I may become a better American
> in a greater America.[13]

Ironically, the Constitution that Masaoka pledged to support was violated
in the internment; defending the United States "against all enemies, foreign
and domestic" in fact invited Japanese Americans to inform on or fight against
members of their own families. For these reasons among others, inclusion of
the creed on the Japanese American National Monument became problematic.

Pro- and anti-JACLers still confront each other over such issues. Despite the
unifying effects of the redress movement—a movement led by the JACL itself—
and recent efforts to heal rifts within the Japanese American community even by
figures as prominent as Hawaii's Senator Daniel Inouye, a distinguished veteran
of the 442nd, the hurts do not seem to go away. At its biennial convention in July
2000, the JACL adopted a resolution to recognize the wartime resisters of conscience and to apologize to them for having failed to acknowledge their civil right
to protest the forced removal and incarceration of Japanese Americans in 1942.
The vote for apology was not unanimous, and it followed an impassioned discussion within the organization. (The public ceremony of apology was finally held
almost two years later.) At the same national convention of 2000, the JACL officially endorsed the National Japanese American Memorial to Patriotism and the
inclusion of the quote by Masaoka.

In their award-winning documentary *Rabbit in the Moon* (1999), Emiko and
Chizu Omori feature as heroes Harry Ueno (the friend of John Tateishi's father), resisters of conscience, and other dissidents—people who have not tradi-
tionally been accorded a prominent role in documentary and fictional
portrayals of the internment. (John Okada's 1957 novel *No-No Boy* is a major
exception in the literature.) These are the people who did not say "*shikata ga
nai*" ("it can't be helped"). In her essay, "The Making of *Rabbit in the Moon*,"
Chizu Omori points to the intensity of the debate—a renewal of old controversies—generated by the documentary. The problem is that resistance and dissent still raise the specter of disloyalty, a threat so dire that the prominent
public official Norman Y. Mineta once said, "I think that the stigma of being
accused of disloyalty was even worse than being sent to camp."[14]

Behind the controversies lies a continuing perplexity over the meanings of
loyalty. Does loyalty to one's country supersede loyalty to family? Who was

more loyal to the principles of American democracy, internees who went out to combat or resisters who were not willing to fight until their rights as American citizens were restored? To whom the glory, to the veterans or the resisters?

These questions may strike a familiar chord in readers largely unfamiliar with the history of the internment. Similar issues have bedeviled our history, from the rise of McCarthyism only a few years after the internment, and on into the Vietnam War years and our own times. Allan Austin ("Loyalty and Concentration Camps in America: The Japanese Precedent and the Internal Security Act of 1950") follows the preoccupation with loyalty that connects the internment with the Red Scare of the 1950s. The legislation of 1950, which Austin discusses, contained a "concentration camp clause" that in effect would have allowed the government to practice in the future the very type of detention that it had used in the case of Japanese Americans. At the close of the 1960s, with political, demographic, and generational shifts that proved empowering for Japanese Americans and other "minorities," the JACL, in a notable turn of its history, took an active role in the initiative that culminated in repeal of the Internal Security Act (1971).

Questions about loyalty and the internment will not be settled until all of us come to realize that the problem of loyalty originated not with any one faction within the camps but with the American government itself. For it was the government that created and defined these categories, at times with cynicism and conscious deception, at others with a dubious grip on reality. It is to our government that we must look for responsibility in the debacle of 1942. It was the government that placed the burden of proof of loyalty on innocent people—a burden of proof based on the racist assumption that ethnic Japanese in this country must have harbored disloyalty. The repeal of the Internal Security Act, as Austin argues, has not settled the matter. Until we get a clear statement from the judicial and legislative branches of the government that the internment was unconstitutional, we will not be able to put to rest our fears that it could happen again.

At the turn of the century, World War II recedes to an ever more distant past, and historical memory turns to memorializing and monument building. In locations as diverse as Santa Fe, New Mexico; Pietrasanta, Italy; and Washington, D.C., monuments to the internment, to Nisei military heroes, and to Japanese Americans will commemorate a troubled past. These monuments, especially the Japanese American Memorial to Patriotism in Washington with its attendant controversies, have concretized the problem of myth, history, and memory. What do memorials and monuments ask us to remember? What part history and what part myth? Valerie Yoshimura ("The Legacy of the Battle of Bruyères: Reflections of a Sansei Francophile") ponders the role of memorials in remembering and preserving the history of the 442nd. If we do not seek palpable ways to preserve the history and the heritage of the internment, we risk falling prey to all kinds of myth-making.

Commemoration, however, runs its risks and perils. Activist leader and former internee at Manzanar, Sue Kunitomi Embrey ("From Manzanar to the Present—A Personal Journey"), tells us that the struggle to get Manzanar designated a state historical landmark in the 1970s led to public outcry over the use of the term "concentration camp" (a term used by Franklin D. Roosevelt himself to designate the American camps) on the plaque at the front gate. Decades later, a proposal to set up another plaque marking the site of a Justice Department internment camp in Santa Fe provoked similar opposition there. But despite controversies, commemoration continues. At another camp, Heart Mountain, an Interpretive Learning Center is now scheduled for construction. And at the dedication ceremony of the Japanese American National Memorial to Patriotism in Washington, D.C., on November 9, 2000, the Clinton administration announced its intention to purchase land in Wyoming, Utah, and Arkansas in order to protect the sites of the camps in those states.

Public commemorations, however, do not necessarily succeed in counteracting old myths. During the war years we were told that the camps were for the internees' protection against possible acts of hostility directed against them. And that all who were removed let themselves be led to the camps with a docility, patience, and forbearance that are summed up in the expression, *shikata ga nai*. Many Issei, it is true, adopted this attitude of philosophical resignation. But often as not, Toyo Suyemoto suggests in "Another Spring," the traditional refrain barely muffled the hurt and impotence of resident aliens who had been subjected to American racism for decades. Outside the Japanese American community, there are many who still do not question the army's claim that "military necessity" had to override any hesitation to imprison nearly an entire ethnic group. The postwar effects of the internment on the Japanese American community, we have also been led to believe, have been largely benign. Camp inmates, barred from returning to the West Coast until the exclusion orders were lifted in 1945, resettled throughout the country and so became more assimilated than they would have been had they not been forcibly uprooted from their homes in 1942. Since the 1960s, Japanese Americans have come to be seen as a "model minority" (having achieved the American Dream the hard way).[15]

Years pass, things change, and other things stay the same. Both within and beyond the Japanese American community arguments and differences drawn from the mythology of the 1940s are gone over as vehemently as if they dated from yesterday. Two of many incidents can serve as examples of how old myths and hatreds endure:

1. A World War II veteran in Bishop, California, grumbles about the development of Manzanar (one of the two concentration camps in California) as a National Historic Site. "'My objection is it's not being recognized truthfully,'" says Mr. W. W. Hastings. "'The Japanese were free to come and go—all it was was an assembly center. They were escorted there not to keep them under control, but just to protect them. It did have a loose barbed-wire fence, but I saw them sneaking out all the time to go fishing'" (*New York Times*, June 20, 1998).

2. In June 1982, Vincent Chin, a young Chinese American man went out with some friends in Detroit for a bachelor celebration before his wedding. Two white auto workers, Ronald Ebens and his stepson, Michael Nitz, attacked Chin with a baseball bat and bludgeoned him to death. Apparently the two men had mistaken him for Japanese and so decided to blame him for the slump in the American automobile industry at the time. (We can't help recalling that *Life*, several weeks after Pearl Harbor, ran a photo feature on "How to Tell Japs from Chinese," or that Chinese Americans at the time sported buttons reading "I Am Chinese." Would that Chin had had such a button.) The two killers were sentenced to three years of probation and each fined $3,870. Subsequent legal action and an FBI investigation resulted in acquittal for both men.

Silence and myth help us to avoid confronting the deepest meanings of traumatic historical events. Years of silence in our textbooks and in public discourse have been matched by the silence of the Nisei, whose reluctance to talk about their wartime imprisonment, at least until the redress movement, is well known. Poet, human rights activist, and former internee Mitsuye Yamada and her daughter, Jeni Yamada, in their set of essays, "Legacy of Silence," track the effects of this silence across several generations of their family.

Since the redress movement, especially since the 1990s, considerable interest in the internment has been sparked by a burst of creative works on the subject, notably David Guterson's best-selling novel *Snow Falling on Cedars* (1994) along with the movie made from it (1999), and Philip Kan Gotanda's play *The Sisters Matsumoto* (1998). In opening up new questions about art, history, politics, and audience reception, these and other artistic creations have expanded debates on how to transmit the legacy of the internment. Playwright Rosanna

Yamagiwa Alfaro joins the debates in her reflections on "internment plays" ("Ethnic Expectations: The Politics of Staging the Internment Camps").

A not inconsiderable number of Issei and Nisei went into the camps believing in American ideals and went out of them sorely disillusioned. We hear little of them. Art historian Robert Maeda ("'Isamu Noguchi: 5–7–A, Poston, Arizona'") gives us a rare glimpse into the experience of one such person, the celebrated sculptor Isamu Noguchi, who went voluntarily from the East Coast to the camp at Poston, Arizona, where Maeda was incarcerated as a child. Noguchi found to his dismay that getting himself out of camp when he wanted to leave was quite another matter from being let in by request. Even now, after the Vietnam War years and repeated violations of what we still consider our most basic values, we do not want to acknowledge the kind of disillusionment that affected internees. It is easier to focus on the so-called secondary gains that enabled Japanese Americans to become a "model minority."

Bearing witness, a complicated act with its own dangers, can nonetheless make room for history to displace myth. The greater the diversity of voices that join to bear witness, the fuller and more complex the history becomes. Myth tells a simple story; history is contradictory and incomplete at best. Now, at a distance of several generations from the internment, we are beginning to fill in more and more silences. Three of us who were white children in the camps talk about our parents' roles as administrators there, about ourselves as young witnesses. We children of WRA administrators rethink our parents' connections with the strangely complex agency—"both jailer and advocate"[16]—that tended to regard itself as humane, benevolent, and constantly under siege by bigots and zealots. Indeed in 1943 it was investigated by the Dies Committee (House Un-American Activities Committee), and it was frequently attacked in the Hearst press. Through which lenses do we view it? With one set, the WRA itself was a casualty of the home front, an organization forced into unpleasant war duty. With another, it is the accomplice—even if at times unwilling—of a major crime perpetrated against an ethnic group.

George Brown ("Return to Gila River") ponders the ambiguous functions that his father may have assumed as community analyst in the Arizona camp. The community analysts were in the main anthropologists recruited by the WRA to study the incarcerated population. Neither spies nor objective scientists, they joined the roughly half of the nation's anthropologists who were contributing to the war effort, many of them in intelligence agencies.[17] When novelist Marnie Mueller ("A Daughter's Need to Know"), who was born in Tule Lake, sits down to fictionalize her late father, a conscientious objector who directed the consumers' cooperative enterprises at that camp, she must first surmount a mass of conflicting emotions. A chance twist in my mother's career brought me to Manzanar's first grade ("Democracy for Beginners") and offered me lessons on the workings of American democracy that have stayed with me through a lifetime. Doubts about our families and ourselves are hard to avoid as we look at the ironies of our situation as whites in the camps.

Unlike myth, the core of which is handed down from generation to generation, history is dynamic. As the years pass, discoveries are made; new stories emerge while old ones are discredited. We are all living repositories of history, and as such we interact with our past, which is bound to change as our world sweeps us along in its transformations. The McCarran Act of 1952 granted naturalization to those Asian immigrants previously denied it. A once tiny population of Asian descent has grown to such proportions that the number of Asian Pacific Americans has doubled in every decade since 1960 and is expected to reach at least 20 million by 2020. Donna Nagata ("Echoes from Generation to Generation") looks to the future and speculates on the importance of the internment for Yonsei* and Gosei* in an increasingly multicultural society. As a Yonsei and a product of this diversity, Stewart D. Ikeda ("Mixing Stories") confronts the effects of his family's checkered history. Patrick Hayashi, another contributor who was born in a camp (Topaz, Utah) and who was later to become a senior admissions officer at the University of California, Berkeley, brings his past to bear on the controversies of the 1990s over affirmative action. From a distinctively sympathetic perspective, he considers the effects of these controversies on the lives of young minority students with whom he has worked ("Pictures from Camp").

Like all the other essays in this collection, "Nineteen in '98," by Jason Kohn and Cara Lemon, two white undergraduates of Hayashi's students' generation, was written before the events of September 11, 2001. In its youthful, optimistic confidence in our immunity from historical catastrophe since World War II, this dialogue on guilt, responsibility, and the lessons of history has taken on a new poignancy.

All the contributors to this volume have necessarily had to reflect on how to write about the internment at a distance of sixty years. As the last witnesses to the mass removal and detention are about to leave the stand forever, we ask ourselves what stories we want to make known now. How do we begin to think about the implications of the internment for the era of the "war on terrorism?" What strains of American life run through and beyond the wartime history?

---

* Yonsei: fourth-generation persons of Japanese descent; Gosei: fifth generation.

How can unlearning and coming to speak on the internment help us to further the causes of social justice and human rights in the twenty-first century?

The Janus-eyed moment of passage from living to historical memory is at once a privileged and a critical one. Witnesses leave both a legacy of the past and a trust for future generations. The Nisei Student Relocation Commemorative Fund (NSRC), founded in 1980 by a group of Nisei living in New England, exemplifies this moment. Board member Glenn Kumekawa explains the NSRC's mission as a "payback" for the National Japanese American Student Relocation Council, a wartime volunteer organization that enabled some 3,000 Nisei students to relocate from camp to the various colleges and universities that would accept them. The NSRC in turn now offers scholarships to Southeast Asian students.

Through our stories and memories, we witnesses and writers want to help keep historical memory alive, to urge no relaxation of vigilance. The threats posed by Pearl Harbor in 1941 and the attack on the World Trade Center sixty years later are undeniable. But what is the appropriate response at home? How do you preserve civil liberties in critical times?

The authors of these essays make an implicit compact with the young: you will read our stories and hear our voices—but not in silence. If the history of the internment is to influence the future, you must constantly renew it with dialogue, reflection, active engagement with the issues, and conscience. Only by honoring this trust will you succeed in making the event outlive its witnesses and outwit the eternal return of myth.

NOTES

1. The figure of 120,000 represents all Japanese Americans incarcerated during the war, not only those removed to the War Relocation Authority's camps in 1942 but also those held in Justice Department internment and isolation camps, Hawaiian ethnic Japanese brought to the mainland for detention, and births during the period of the internment.

2. Although today "internment camp" is the common term for any one of the ten relocation centers administered by the War Relocation Authority (WRA), it more properly refers to the generally smaller camps, like the one at Santa Fe, in which aliens rounded up by the FBI (usually Issei community leaders) were imprisoned. Unlike the inmates of the relocation centers, the aliens interned in Justice Department camps had the right to an individual hearing once detained, after which some were released, generally to the relocation centers. Internment of aliens, Roger Daniels has pointed out, "has the color of law" (as quoted in Mitchell T. Maki, Harry H. L. Kitano, and S. Megan Berthold, *Achieving the Impossible Dream: How Japanese Americans Obtained Redress* [Urbana: University of Illinois Press, 1999], 5), unlike the imprisonment of citizens, which is completely without legal and constitutional basis. Maki et al. make an important linguistic

distinction between incarceration (in the relocation centers) and internment (in the Justice Department camps), even though, of course, aliens not taken by the FBI were incarcerated along with citizens in the centers. "Internment," however, is the widely recognized term for the historical event. I use "internee" for any individual imprisoned in the WRA or Justice Department camps. I have not standardized usage throughout the volume.

3. *Farewell to Manzanar* (1973), by Jeanne Wakatsuki Houston and James D. Houston, as of this writing is still in print. Miles and miles of archival material have been open to the public for decades at several major libraries, including the National Archives in Washington, D.C., and the libraries of the University of California at Los Angeles and Berkeley. Studies of the internment got underway as early as 1942, almost as soon as the West Coast population of Japanese Americans was "relocated" to ten concentration camps and many smaller prison camps. The WRA, the civil agency responsible for administering the ten "relocation centers," appointed "community analysts" (usually trained anthropologists or sociologists) as resident observers in each camp. Several of these analysts collaborated on a final report for the WRA (1946), which was later published as a book, *Impounded People: Japanese-Americans in the Relocation Centers*, authored by Edward H. Spicer and his colleagues (Tucson: University of Arizona Press, 1946). The Bureau of Sociological Research, headed by Alexander H. Leighton, conducted research at the Poston camp in Arizona under the auspices of the Office of Indian Affairs, which resulted in Leighton's book, *The Governing of Men: General Principles and Recommendations Based on Experience at a Japanese Relocation Camp* (Princeton: Princeton University Press, 1945). And finally, Dorothy Swaine Thomas, a sociologist at the University of California in Berkeley, directed a large, ambitious, independent research project, the Japanese American Evacuation and Resettlement Study (JERS), which enlisted the help of many internees themselves and eventuated in three books: Dorothy S. Thomas and Richard S. Nishimoto, *The Spoilage* (Berkeley: University of California Press, 1946; Dorothy S. Thomas, *The Salvage* (Berkeley: University of California Press, 1952); Jacobus tenBroek et al., *Prejudice, War and the Constitution* (Berkeley: University of California Press, 1954). In addition, Morton Grodzins published an unofficial JERS study, *Americans Betrayed: Politics and the Japanese Evacuation* (Chicago: University of Chicago Press, 1949). On the JERS project, see Yuji Ichioka, ed., *Views from Within: The Japanese American Evacuation and Resettlement Study* (University of California at Los Angeles, Asian American Studies Center, 1989). These inaugural studies laid the groundwork for volumes of research to come.

4. Roger Daniels, *Prisoners Without Trial: Japanese Americans in World War II* (New York: Hill and Wang, 1993), 107.

5. Monica Sone, *Nisei Daughter* (Seattle: University of Washington Press, 1979), 201. The memoir was first published in 1953 by Little, Brown.

6. On the Supreme Court cases that were reopened, see Peter Irons, *Justice at War: The Story of the Japanese American Internment Cases* (New York: Oxford, 1983); and Peter Irons, *Justice Delayed: The Record of the Japanese American Internment Cases* (Middletown, Conn.: Wesleyan University Press, 1989).

7. Grodzins, 1.

8. See Roger Daniels, *The Politics of Prejudice* (Berkeley: University of California Press, 1962), 86.

9. See Bill Hosokawa, *JACL in Quest of Justice* (New York: Morrow, 1982), 83. For the history of the JACL's founding, see Hosokawa, 20–32.

10. *Personal Justice Denied: Report of the Commission on Wartime Relocation and Internment of Civilians* (Seattle: University of Washington Press, 1997), 246–47. Frank Abe's documentary on the resisters, "Conscience and the Constitution," was released late in 2000. See the associated Web site, http://www.resisters.com. See also Eric L. Muller, *Free to Die for Their Country: The Story of the Japanese American Draft Resisters in World War II* (Chicago: University of Chicago Press, 2001).

11. Roger Daniels, *Concentration Camps: North America Japanese in the United States and Canada During World War II* (Malabar, Fla.: Robert E. Krieger, 1989), 128–29.

12. For concise accounts of the episodes of dissidence and resistance discussed here, see Michi Weglyn, *Years of Infamy: The Untold Story of America's Concentration Camps* (New York: William Morrow, 1976), 132–51; Daniels, *Concentration Camps*, 104–29.

13. As quoted in Hosokawa, 280.

14. As quoted in Maki et al., 70.

15. According to Roger Daniels, the sociologist William Petersen coined the phrase "model minority" in 1966 to apply only to Japanese Americans. Since that time the usage has become generalized to Asian Americans. See Daniels, *Prisoners*, 82, 107–108. For the more generalized usage see, for example, Ronald Takaki, *Strangers from a Different Shore: A History of Asian Americans* (New York: Penguin, 1989), 474–84.

16. *Personal Justice Denied*, 157.

17. See David Price, "Anthropologists as Spies," *The Nation* (November 20, 2000), 24–27. The WRA evidently sought the analysts' reports as a tool of social control. The counterpart in the Office of War Information (OWI) to the WRA's Community Analysis Section was the OWI's Foreign Morale Analysis Division. At least two of the cultural analysts of Japan (John Embree and Alexander Leighton), whose work was meant to help in developing psychological warfare against that country, also worked for the WRA. On the work of the cultural analysts of Japan, see John W. Dower, *War Without Mercy: Race and Power in the Pacific War* (New York: Pantheon, 1986), 124–39.

PART I

PARENTS AND CHILDREN

TOYO SUYEMOTO

ANOTHER SPRING *

TWO SMALL KEEPSAKES THAT I HAVE TREASURED from the internment
years have deep personal significance for me. They were the creations of two Issei
men: my father, who was an artist, and an adult student in the Basic English
evening class I taught in the Topaz internment camp. Each testifies to the Issei
generation's ability to find beauty in the bleak life that the evacuation and imprisonment imposed upon them.

The first memento my father gave to me. It was a knothole, two and a half
inches wide and one and seven-eighths inches high, which had fallen out of the
horse-stall door as the wood dried during the months we were held at the Tanforan Assembly Center in San Bruno, California. I wondered at his interest in the
knothole, as he turned it over in his hands.

The day before our family was evacuated from our Berkeley home, Father had
somehow managed to include in the baggage his old wooden box that contained
worn paintbrushes and tubes of colors along with some canvas boards. Perhaps the
box arrived at the Tanforan Assembly Center because he placed the painting equipment in his blanket roll, which was less subject to inspection than were suitcases.

So it was that the fallen knothole could serve as my father's canvas. After close
inspection of the oval knothole, he soon leveled off the bottom to make it stand on
a flat surface. On both sides of the knothole, he painted a view of the Tanforan center. The tiny detailed paintings show, on one side, the end of our barracks and a
portion of the road that led to the grandstand. On the other side is a view of the
green fence that separated our barracks from real houses outside our enclosure. A
sentry-tower, one of many that the military had erected to keep close watch over

*   With gratitude for the assistance of Susan B. Richardson, collaborator and friend.

the internees, is shown among telephone poles. The details in my father's minia-ture on the knothole continue to amaze me, and I remember the gentle, learned man who used to tell me that beauty lies in the eyes of the beholder.

The other memento was brought to me by a shy Issei man who held it be-hind his back before he could offer it with his whisper of "For you, *Sensei* [teacher]." We bowed to each other, and I marveled at the brooch, no larger than two and three-quarters inches by two inches. It was a lapel pin he had made by twisting navy blue crepe paper into a fine strand and then weaving a minia-ture basket filled with small flowers composed of tiny shells gathered from the sand of our Topaz camp. Topaz was located in Utah on the dried-up bed of Lake Bonneville, once a large body of water formed in the glacial period, and the shells dug up by the camp residents were mute reminders of life that had existed centuries ago. The tinted shell flowers formed a graceful arrangement, depict-ing even lilies-of-the-valley fashioned from minute shells the size of pinheads. The ingenuity of using shells, some colored with fingernail polish and whatever else he had on hand, seemed remarkable. I was awed by his ability to shape the loveliness he had retained from his Japanese background.

I was always aware that our parents' generation—the Issei—had had to cope with prejudice and discrimination from the time they settled in this country. Denied citizenship until after the war, they were aliens; the Nisei—their chil-dren and born citizens—were labeled "non-aliens." Both generations were de-prived of homes and livelihood, yet with the deference characteristic of their Japanese culture, the Issei continued to obey government dicta. In the camps, they continued to approach life with dignity and patience.

Taught as children to show allegiance and loyalty to one's country and family, the Issei passed on this tenet of honor to their children. Thus the Nisei learned not to question the authority of their parents, their teachers, even their playground instructors. We bowed in deference to the elderly in our neighbor-hood on chance meetings. Mother's repeated admonition was, "You are a Suye-moto. Behave well with that in mind."

My large family—parents, eight brothers and sisters, and my six-month-old child—stayed together during the three and a half years of internment, a period imprinted on our consciousness. The rigors of camp life stand out sharply in our memory in contrast to existence before and relocation after the war, when we Nisei were able to resume interrupted education and careers, and our once-active Issei parents retired from participation in business and com-munity affairs. My son Kay knew nothing before that period of camp life. Later, in his teen years, he would recall people and events from Topaz; the dominant figures of his childhood were clearly his Issei grandmother and grandfather. From them, he absorbed a deep understanding of courage, honor, and acceptance of what had to be.

It was their sense of *gaman* (patience or endurance) that gave the Issei strength in the face of these events, a sense that they hoped their Nisei offspring would also apply to their camp existence. The Issei mothers I came to know at Tanforan and Topaz exemplified *gaman*. Like my own mother, they were intent on education for their children and on preserving the unity of their families. As I looked into their faces and talked with them, exchanging chitchat as we met in the mess hall, the laundry room, and the latrine, I could imagine the turmoil they had experienced in preparing for the evacuation and removal to the barren internment camp. There were occasions when I would hear murmurs about camp life being *fuben na* (inconvenient) or *nasake-nai* (unfeeling or cold-hearted). Yet among these Issei women, there was acceptance of our situation. Their courteous gestures and speech did not seem *kokoro-bosoi* (forlorn and hopeless).

When the evacuation began, our family had half a day's notice that we were to leave on the morning of April 27, 1942. Since we were permitted to take only what we could carry, the order limited us to about two suitcases per person. Because one of my brothers offered to carry it for me, I added a duffel bag of baby clothes and diapers. Buses monitored by soldiers took our family from our home in Berkeley to the Tanforan Assembly Center, located in the San Bruno racetrack south of San Francisco. At the intake gate, adults and young people were searched for contraband, and Father had to explain why he had a small pocketknife in his pocket. Mother submitted quietly to the search of her pockets and purse.

After the questioning, we were assigned to a horse stall near the boundary fence. The horse stalls had been whitewashed, but they still had straw and horsehair between the planks of the walls, and they retained the smell of the animals throughout. The horse stall was drafty, and Kay—then six months old—developed pneumonia and had to be sent out of camp to the San Mateo hospital for treatment. Later, in the Topaz internment camp in Utah where the climate was more severe, Kay developed pneumonia again. After that, throughout his childhood and adolescence, he suffered from chronic asthma, the condition that caused his death at age sixteen.

As it turned out, families were kept together, but when the evacuation order first became known, Mother had gathered the family together to tell us that as aliens, she and Father might be separated from us. However, we were to remember that our ties and loyalty were to the United States. Mentally, Mother had been preparing herself for such a separation. Stoic and accepting of the conditions imposed on her family, she was trying to prepare us too for such an eventuality.

Nonetheless, she was not prepared for the kind of treatment given to a native-born American citizen in army uniform. After the evacuation began, all Japanese were forbidden to enter the Pacific Coast Area Number 1. My brother Roy, who had enlisted soon after Pearl Harbor, was stationed in Wyoming, and he did not know about Executive Order 9066. By the time he was granted a fifteen-day furlough to visit Oakland and Berkeley, our family was already confined at Tanforan. Since we did not know about his intended visit, it came as a shock to overhear a radio broadcast in our neighbor's barracks one spring morning that "a Jap spy in United States uniform had been apprehended in Oakland," and that his name was Roy Suyemoto! The San Francisco newspaper I was able to get from the canteen verified the news. In spite of his United States Army uniform, the Oakland police deemed Roy too potentially disloyal to be allowed in Area Number 1, and they turned him over to the military police for return to his post. He was nineteen years old then, lonely for his family. Mother's reaction to his arrest was, "How could they suspect Roy? He was raised an *America-jin* [American person]."

My father came to this country as a teenager in about 1905 to attend American schools. After graduating with degrees in engineering from the Universities of Nevada and California, Berkeley, however, he was unable to find work in his chosen field of mining engineering. At that time the Japanese were not hired for professional work. During my childhood in Sacramento, my father was a life insurance agent. In the community, he also served as an interpreter for other Issei when they had to consult a doctor or a lawyer.

My mother was not a "picture bride" as were some of the Issei women; Father had become engaged to her before he left Japan. Like my father, Mother was well educated and had finished normal school in Japan. Theirs was an unusually long engagement during which they kept in touch by letters. Mother came about ten years later, and she and my father were married in California in 1915. They lived many years in Sacramento, where I went from grade school to high school and then through junior college. As my siblings and I approached college age, the family moved to Berkeley to be near the university that Father had attended.

Father, himself fluent in English, wanted his children to speak without an accent. Therefore, unlike many of our school friends who spoke Japanese with their parents and who attended Japanese language schools after the regular public school day, Father had somehow decided against his children following these practices. At home, he and Mother conversed in Japanese, but Father usually spoke to us in English and acted as our interpreter. We children could understand Mother's polite Japanese, but our speaking vocabulary was limited. We soon learned, however, that Mother could understand very well what her offspring were talking about—even when we used slang!

Toyo Suyemoto's father, Tsutomu Howard Suyemoto, when a mining engineering student at the University of California at Berkeley, about 1911.

Toyo Suyemoto's mother, Mitsu Hyakusoku Suyemoto, Japan, about 1902 or 1903.

Because of their interest in reading—Father in English and Mother in Japanese—we children grew up in a world of books. We were introduced early to the public library in Sacramento. The Saturday mornings of my childhood were exciting; Father would take me to the corner of our block where the streetcar stopped and then ask the conductor to let me off at the public library blocks away. When I came home, he would check to see what books I had brought back and even suggest what titles I should look for next. When he advised me to read Dickens's *A Tale of Two Cities*, I complied—though I balked when he pointed to Harvey's study of the circulation of the blood.

Mother was the one who told us about Japanese literature that we could read in translation. She had a phenomenal memory and could recite from Japanese dramas she had seen in her youth. It was she who surprised me when I was in junior high school by asking whether I knew a play called *Hamlet* by Shakespeare. I was surprised even more when she proceeded to recite the well-known soliloquy "To be or not to be" in Japanese. Mother often reminded us that reading would enlarge our world. She would remark that because we were still young, we could see only what was framed by a window that limited the view. As we matured, she said, we would eventually gain a broader perspective and knowledge in the unexplored outside.

As we children grew older and acquired Americanisms that must have differed greatly from Japanese tradition, we sometimes questioned our parents or even protested their decisions. Our parents tolerated our barbarisms, and they were good listeners. Mother would sit in our midst and hear us out even when we suspected that she would not be persuaded and that her final comment would be contrary to ours.

Our education, therefore, was given a high priority by our parents, a value shared by most Issei parents. Because of their own educational background, my parents expected us to study hard and do well in school. Mother would say she had given us a sound mind and kept our bodies properly nourished, so we should not shirk our responsibility to study hard and earn top grades. A grade below an A was not acceptable. Mother would question us closely when we failed her expectations. She did not accept excuses, and at times when we made vehement explanations as to why the grades were not topnotch, she would calmly look at us and quietly ask, "Have you stopped to look to yourself as to why you have not done better?"

When we reached college age, my parents did not impose demands on how we should prepare for our careers. Each one of us was able to practice free choice in selecting a major. As an undergraduate, I attended Father's university in Berkeley from 1935 to 1937, where I majored in English and Latin. I was the only one of the children who selected the humanities; those who followed me decided to study medicine or related medical fields such as bacteriology, hospital dietetics, and social work when they resumed their education after release from camp in 1945. Oddly enough, I too gravitated toward medicine for a time. After relocation out of camp, I became a librarian for the College of Nursing at the University of Cincinnati in Ohio; later, however, after receiving my master's degree in library science, I moved on to become an academic librarian at Ohio State University.

When the internment wrenched their children from their homes and disrupted their schooling, the Issei parents were very concerned about the continuation of their children's education. Although some public schools in

California had accelerated the curriculum before evacuation so that the Japanese students could gain credit, others nonchalantly dismissed the students without any attempt to help them. In Tanforan, no provision had been made for instruction, classrooms, or school supplies, and the young people were at a loss without regular classes and organized activities. Parents were troubled.

A group of us college-educated Nisei responded to their concern. Once we had settled in, we contacted one another and held a meeting at which it was proposed that we start a voluntary high school with each of us teaching our specific majors. Posters announcing our project appeared around the camp. On the day set for registration, we all were surprised by the turnout. There were five hundred students who wanted to enroll! The parents were very pleased by our undertaking, and when I would meet any of them in the mess hall, they would express their deep appreciation for our efforts.

Our Tanforan school was held in the large open area within the racetrack grandstand, once the room where pari-mutuel bets were placed. Traces of the betting windows remained visible. There were no interior walls in this space at all, not even partitions between the classes, and mess hall picnic tables served as desks. But the students accepted what had to be, even as their parents did.

We Nisei positioned ourselves within the grandstand to teach our specialties. To my left, one friend taught civics; to the right, another taught history; straight ahead, yet another had a class in public speaking. I had the class in English. I suspect that the students seated on the outer edges of my group paid more attention to what was being discussed in the adjoining class than to our own class.

A Stanford graduate, Henry Tani, assumed the position of high school principal. Soon after the school was under way, Henry called for a school assembly out on the grandstand seats. It was a clear, sunny April morning, and we could see people strolling around the racetrack. Most of the teachers were from the University of California, though several came from Stanford University. After some announcements, Henry introduced the faculty, first those from Berkeley and then the ones from Stanford. The students, aware of the rivalry between the two universities, were quiet as the names of the Californians were called, but when the Standfordites were introduced, a clamor arose with applause and foot-stamping, as if the students were rooting for the "underdogs." I remember thinking how American their action was.

When the business of the assembly was concluded, Henry announced that the students were to return to their "classrooms" and continue with their subjects. All the five hundred young people stood up. To this day I do not know who started the singing, but the entire group began to sing in harmony, "God Bless America." Deeply moved, I turned to the Protestant minister who was seated beside me and saw that he too was touched by their singing. He muttered, "Those blessed kids." We noticed that the strollers on the ground, mostly Issei, had paused to listen to the young people.

Many years later I acquired Charles Kikuchi's book, *The Kikuchi Diary*, which details his four-month stay at Tanforan and his observations on the settling in of the displaced Japanese. Kikuchi wrote about camp politics, the residents, their social gatherings, and even the garden in the infield of the racetrack. He also reported on the high school, and in an entry for June 14 he wrote:

> Physical facilities are sad and the teachers are not so good. . . . The teachers
> have to yell to get attention and compete with their neighboring teachers. On
> top of that the classes have to be chiefly lecture due to the lack of textbooks.
> The High School students are much more noisy than the others and already
> Toyo is having difficulty in controlling them. She is so tiny and timid that she
> should stick to writing sentimental poetry. (133)

It was true that I had not taught large groups before, and occasionally rowdy boys protested my assignments. There were three especially who banded together in causing trouble, and I finally had to evict them from class. One of them, perhaps the ringleader, did come to me several days later asking for permission to return—probably at the urging of his parents—and when I allowed him to join the class, he gave me no further trouble.

Later, at Topaz, I taught not only English and Latin classes at the high school, but I began teaching Adult Basic English classes in the evenings as well. I noticed a marked difference between the Issei and the Nisei in their attitudes toward me as a teacher. The Issei students were always polite in bowing and talking to me in the classroom. By contrast, the Nisei high school students did not like homework and would greet assignments for work to be done at home with mutters of "waste time," an expression common among young people equivalent to "why do it?" Still, there was enough carry-over from their training at home that ruled out most rebellious outbursts, and I remember good experiences in those high school classes as well.

After six months in Tanforan, my brother Bill, a graduate student in bacteriology, was sent with an advance sanitary engineering crew of 214 to the more permanent camp in Utah, and we knew our departure from the California site was imminent. Leaving Tanforan was difficult. We had become accustomed to the routine of camp life, to the waiting in line at the mess hall, at the post office, at the canteen. We had come to know our neighbors from the other side of the bay. We were familiar with the curfew and the surveillance check by camp police in the evening and the headcount by the Japanese area manager—who frequently seemed confused by all the little children visiting in and out of our family's barracks. We had become oriented to communal living and the lack of privacy even in the latrine building with its doorless, uncurtained stalls. On the other hand, preparations for departure from Tanforan were much simpler than those for our first move: we had less to pack.

My family's Tanforan barracks were close to the departure gate, so we were able to bid farewell to friends who left before us. People came from all corners of Tanforan to see off acquaintances with bows and polite gestures, a formality rather strange in such a rough environment. The Issei were more subdued in the exchange of greetings than their children. The uncertainty of another move to a distant state caused them anxiety.

The journey from California to Utah on a rickety train was wearisome, and Mother was not able to eat after being rocked back and forth on the train. As the train lumbered on, the landscape became drear, devoid of the greenery familiar on the West Coast. The Issei, who once had gardens or extensive farms, faced the sight of vast empty land where the sage grew and tumbleweeds rolled. Farmers who had just finished the spring planting of crops on their land stared out the train windows. Some of them, who had had to sell their prosperous farms at three dollars an acre, said little to one another, holding on to their recollections.

Adjusting to the Topaz camp after our arrival on October 3, 1942, was not easy. However clean and new our barracks looked compared to the Tanforan horse stalls, they were far from the place we once called home. We arrived in Delta, Utah, and were taken by buses to the Topaz site where we were greeted by a band of young Boy Scouts playing "Hail, hail, the gang's all here" on their brass instruments. The Scouts carried a banner that read "Welcome to Topaz, the Jewel of the Desert."

When we stepped down from the buses, we sank almost ankle deep into fine dust. As soon as we were registered, my family was directed to our barracks in Block 4, close to the camp's hospital. We were assigned there because several members of the family were considered medical personnel: Bill would work at the hospital, my sister Hisa was assigned to the medical laboratory, and my sister Mae would be in hospital dietetics.

As we entered our barracks, we found the floor covered with a thick layer of alkali dust. Any movement raised white swirling clouds. We could not bring in our luggage until the dust was removed. There was no furniture, just army cots and two mattresses leaning against the unfinished walls. Along with our neighbors, we managed to borrow brooms from the block manager. With scarves tied over our heads, the women, Issei and Nisei, readied the rooms for occupancy. That first night, when we set up the cots, we allocated one mattress to Mother, the other to baby Kay. The rest of us—Father, my sisters and brothers, and I—made do by layering coats and sweaters on the cots, but we soon discovered how cold Topaz was at its high elevation. Instead of the usual nightgowns and pajamas, we went to sleep huddled in our outdoor clothes. Later in winter, milk bottles left on the windowsill would freeze and pop their lids.

We had to cope with frequent dust storms. It was almost fascinating to be indoors with all the windows closed and yet see large, suffocating puffs of dust blow in over the sills. Once the wind abated by evening, there would be a flurry of activity—shaking out blankets, pillows, and clothing, sweeping and mopping floors, doing extra laundry. As they must have done in former homes, the women and their older children cleaned their quarters systematically. The mothers made an efficient bucket brigade.

How much we children took our Issei parents for granted—our fathers and mothers who had grown up in Japan and had come to America to make a living and raise families! For the Nisei, our parents had simply always been there, caring for us, worrying through the Depression years, yet managing to keep us housed, fed, clothed, and educated. Now, amid the disruption of the internment, the Issei tried to maintain normality by fostering the family and community ties of prewar years in continuing to show respect for elders and courtesy toward all others.

I had learned even in childhood years the reliance of the Japanese upon one another, a reliance that extended beyond the family circle. In our Sacramento community, *Nihomachi* (Japanese town), I never heard of a Japanese having to go on welfare. I know that Father served as treasurer for a group of Issei men with families who contributed monthly dues to a community fund, even from meager wages. The fund was distributed to families in need, without publicity. Even now, in my mind's eye, I can see Father sitting at his oak roll-top desk calculating the accounts on his *soroban*, or abacus.

I suppose that helping one another in the community was derived from the sense of *giri* (duty or obligation), of *on* (a debt of gratitude), and of *on-gaeshi* (repayment of favor) that we children absorbed by precept. In the years before the war, a modified form of *on* and *on-gaeshi* seemed exemplified at the New Year, when families exchanged gifts, which entailed not individual presents but the giving of a hundred-pound sack of rice, a wooden tub of soy sauce, or a large wooden box of noodles. In camp, of course, we were unable to carry on this tradition of gift-giving other than to mark the holiday with the exchange of New Year greetings in Japanese, but the sense of responsibility to one another remained.

Mother and Father made decisions about their children's upbringing that might involve customs foreign to them but that nevertheless helped instill Issei values. Christmas was not generally considered as important as New Year's in our community, yet in their accommodation to the new culture, my parents celebrated Christmas for us as joyously as any holiday. From the time we were in grade school, my parents sent us to the Japanese Baptist church rather than to the impressive (and convenient) Buddhist temple because they felt that we would receive better discipline and teaching there. My siblings and I had an unbroken attendance record at Sunday school because of Mother's routine of waking us up on time, making breakfast, and dressing us in our Sunday best. Father did his part, too; dressed in suit and tie, he always attended our Christmas pageant and program.

Although not Christian herself, Mother had a Japanese Bible (a Bible that she took with her when we were evacuated from Berkeley), and she knew the passages we learned in church. To make sure that I had attended the service, Mother would ask what the minister had preached. Therefore, I would always try to catch a key word I had not understood so she could explain it to me. One Sunday, I heard a word, *dotoku-teki*, which made no sense to me. When I came home and reported it to her, she said, "Oh, ethics"—and proceeded to deliver another half-hour sermon of her own on the significance of *dotoku-teki*.

Our parents' discipline and *gaman* (ability to bear the almost unbearable) enabled their children also to tolerate their years in Topaz. Mother quietly accepted the inconveniences of camp life without the complaints her offspring would voice. She would say to us, *shikata ga nai* (it cannot be helped). Since we had no running water in the barracks, she made sure that by evening there was a bucket of water covered with a towel in our room for drinking. This saved us from having to go half a block to the latrine building for a cup of water. We saw other Issei parents doing similar tasks in adjusting to restricted living.

Mother's calm poise showed itself soon after we settled into the Topaz barracks. Because of the size of our eleven-member family, we had been allotted the two larger rooms in the middle of the barracks. Mother allowed the boys to take over one of the rooms, and though we had use of the space during the day, it was their domain at night. In order to go from one room into the other, however, one had to go outside first. Mother tired of having to do that whenever she wanted to summon my brothers, so she had Father cut an entry through the intervening wall where she hung a curtain. The boys banded together and asked for an audience, protesting "invasion of privacy." She heard them through, but as usual held to her decision: "That is all right, but Mama right."

For Mother, decorous behavior was not to be taken lightly or *pokan-to* (blankly or absent-mindedly). With little entertainment on hand, the shower rooms in the latrine building became favorite gathering places for young people. The latrine building was located quite a distance from our barracks. After dinner in the mess hall, my youngest sister Masa would often get on her pajamas and robe, gather up towels and soap, and saunter over to meet her friends for a gab fest that might last till late in the night.

Mother did not approve of her children "staying out" in the latrine building without parental supervision. Like other mothers in camp, she felt that discipline and respect for parental control were being ignored by the children. She would send me, the eldest, to see whether Masa was still with her teenage girlfriends, and I would usually find them chatting and laughing together. If she had already showered, Masa would take my appearance as a signal to return to the barracks with me.

One night, my two youngest brothers were not back from their showers though it was almost midnight. When Mother asked where the two could be, I told her that I had heard their voices through the fiberboard wall that separated the men's and women's shower areas. With a determined look she began pulling on her cardigan sweater. I realized what she was about to do, and I exclaimed that she was not allowed to enter the men's side. All she said was, "I shall bring them back." And soon she returned to our barracks with two sheepish-looking boys who said fervently, once they were in the room, "Please don't ever do that again." After that, she never had to remind them to be home on time.

Except for those attending the high school, the rest of my siblings worked at various positions—bacteriologist, medical laboratory technician, hospital dietitian, or teacher. When Father applied for a job, he did not tell the interviewer that he had a college background, and he was given the job of tending the furnace of the latrine building. He kept a close eye on the coal pile in front of the building during the winter, because whenever there was a coal shortage, he would find the pile diminishing.

I told Father that he should have stressed his college education on his job application. His matter-of-fact reply was that while I had to work steady eight-hour days, he could—between times of feeding the furnace—come back to our barracks to work on an oil painting.

Mother refused to apply for a job, as she was busy taking care of my son, so she did not receive the clothing allowance that working internees received. The rest of us tried to be aware of her needs since she never asked us for anything. When she ran out of toothpaste, she would bring back some table salt in the palm of her hand for a temporary dentifrice.

When the stress of teaching both day and evening classes became too much, I applied for the position of librarian for the Topaz Public Library; I worked in the library from December 1943 until June 1945. I continued to see my former students among those who came regularly to read and study. The library collection had been started with a nucleus of books donated to the Tanforan Library and later shipped to Topaz. Many of the books were old, but after a few new titles had been obtained, we started a rental collection; new books were loaned at five cents a week. As fees accumulated slowly, we ordered new books. We could purchase only a few titles at a time, but our steady readers always looked forward to my posting fresh title-covers on the wall near the circulation desk. The government provided funds for the purchase of periodicals and several newspapers, so the camp residents were able to stay abreast of current events.

Toward the end of the three years, the government began to put pressure on internees to relocate out of the camps. As the relocation program accelerated and people began to move out into the world they had earlier been forced to leave, camp services had to be curtailed. When the library had to close, I put the rental books purchased by readers on sale for nominal prices. Many were sold, and I was able to donate two hundred dollars to the high school scholarship fund.

As more and more people departed, including members of my own family, the blocks became desolate. Our Block 4 mess hall was closed, and we had to go to another several blocks away. We again saw friends off at the departure gate, this time with greater hope for them and with promises to keep in touch. Indeed, to this day, I still hear from some of the students I taught in those high school classes.

It was, I believe, the steady encouragement of Mother and Father throughout internment, as well as during our childhood, that enabled us to become what we are today. It is not the New that we hold as a prized pebble in our palm, but a crystallized piece of the Past our parents gave us. The Issei taught us Nisei the meaning of their life, and, as I wrote in a 1935 poem, it was "A heritage, it seems to me, / Well worth a life to hold in fee."

In the early days of Topaz, I complained to Mother of camp life, about the restrictions placed upon us by the government, about the uncertainty of the future. She listened to me patiently until I finished my diatribe. Then she said with certainty, "Spring will come again."

I burst out, "But it won't be the same spring!"

"No," she continued, "not the same spring, but another spring, a new spring."

Like the beauty created in the midst of barrenness by my father and by my Issei student, my mother's words testify to her generation's vision and hope. Perhaps a poem I wrote many years later on the anniversary of her death best expresses my mother's spirit and the bequest of the Issei to the rest of us:

Wisdom
(MHS)

The wisdom of a thousand years
Spoke in your level gaze
That learned to measure length
Of days
By continuity of spring,
Serenely you could see
No brittle leaf outlives
The tree.

MITSUYE YAMADA

LEGACY OF SILENCE (I)

ON OUR TELEVISION SCREEN IN THE LIVING ROOM flashed a short clip of Japanese American families being herded into trains with armed guards watching, another short clip of rows of barracks in the desert. A newscaster's voice announced that it was twenty years since the residents of Japanese ancestry in the Los Angeles area had been put into camps in 1942, soon after the attack on Pearl Harbor. My husband Yosh said to the children, "Your mother was in one of those camps."

My oldest, Jeni, who was about eleven years old then, looked at me with tears welling up in her eyes and said, "Mom, how come you never told us?"

The newscast went on to other momentous matters of the day. Jeni's younger siblings were noisily romping about in the living room, but not noticing that I was on the verge of tears myself, she persisted with her questioning. It was her accusatory tone—"How come you never told us?"—and the look in her eyes that had me scurrying through my mind to find a reasonable answer.

"I don't know why," was all I could manage.

I was thinking: It isn't as if I were keeping it a secret. It just didn't seem important enough. The subject never came up. Nobody ever asked me. An immediate facile answer might have been that I was always too goal-oriented to indulge in reflection, too busy with more "important" things to do during those years, such as attending classes, studying, working for my tuition, getting my degrees, getting married, and taking care of a husband and four children.

When I was growing up, my parents never brought up subjects that they felt would "burden" their children. As a result, my brothers and I never thought that our parents had financial or any other kind of problems. Even as the talk of the worsening relationship between the governments of Japan and the United States dominated the news media in the 1930s—and the subject must have been the topic of conversation among the Issei—they never expressed their concerns to us around the dinner table. It seemed to us that their only concern was that we go to school and study hard.

It occurred to me when Jeni asked, "How come you never told us?" that my silence was a legacy handed down to me by my Issei father. I remember angrily directing the same question at my absent father during those panic years after Japan bombed Pearl Harbor. I was shocked beyond words when the utilities companies called, warning us that the telephone, gas, and electric services would be shut off unless we paid our bills. How come he never told us that the utilities bills had to be paid every month? My father had been arrested by the FBI the afternoon of December 7, 1941, along with many other leaders of the Japanese community on the West Coast, and was held on suspicion of espionage during most of the war years. After his arrest, we were too preoccupied with daily money matters to pay attention to the mail that was piling up on his desk. The one person in the family who silently took care of all our needs was no longer with us. Our not knowing about monthly utilities bills was only a temporary inconvenience at that time, but it represented a terrifying question that I did not deal with until decades later: What else was he keeping from us? The unspoken question led me to send for my father's FBI file in 1980 under the Freedom of Information Act, years after his death. (The FBI's suspicions about my father, as about all the other Japanese immigrants to this country, proved unfounded.) The more immediate lesson I learned from my father was the parents' role of protecting their children from the unpleasant realities of life. As they were often heard to say, *Kodomo no tame ni:* for the sake of the children.

The newscast report of the forcible removal of the Japanese from the West Coast and actual film footage of the camps brought forth images in my head that had been long buried, but they did not encourage me at that moment to disclose fully my feelings about my internment experiences to my older daughter.

Jeni, now a mother of three growing sons, and I, a grandmother five times over, are both actively involved in community affairs that have been shaped by our past, the most prominent part of which was the internment experiences of the Issei and Nisei in the family. Much has been written about the collective silence surrounding these experiences for many decades. Jeni has been determined to break that silence among members of our immediate family—her siblings, uncles, aunts and cousins. In contemplating the "why" of Jeni's original question, I have learned that there was a combination of factors that contributed to my own silence.

Many of us who had kept silent all those years about our own war experiences should reflect on why we did so. Did we feel, as our parents did, that we did not have the right to speak out? Our parents, like nearly all Asians, were ineligible to become United States citizens through naturalization until the passage of the McCarran-Walter Act of 1952. They must have felt that they were denied the right to full citizenship through some fault of their own. Our parents, who were born and raised in Japan, may have accepted the "forever foreign" status to which they were relegated in this country. I, on the other hand, who, unlike my three brothers, was born in Japan but lived in the United States from the age of three and a half, never felt comfortable being treated like an outsider. As a teenager growing up in Seattle, Washington, in the prewar days, I often complained to my father about certain slights I experienced in school, and his cautionary words were always, "If you ever want to become an American citizen, keep your nose clean. Don't do anything that might seem un-American." I carried this warning with me throughout the war years as I traveled about the country. It acted like an internal barometer that made me check my tongue, even when I felt misunderstood by those around me.

I remember only too well that day in 1955 when I became an American citizen after having been a resident of the United States for twenty-eight years. What should have been a celebratory event became an occasion for me to feel more unwelcome in the country than I had ever felt before. In the interviewing room at Brooklyn College where I was about to be sworn in, the immigration officer asked, "Are you willing to bear arms in defense of this country?" There was that question again, I was thinking, the question to which we had to answer yes in order to receive permission to leave the internment camp. Then I thought about the rumors I had heard during my graduate school days only a few years before, that HUAC (the House Un-American Activities Committee) was ordering the University of Chicago to fire the professors who had refused to sign the loyalty oath. Suddenly I was aware that the officer was barking at me, "Whatsa matter? Why do you hesitate? You don't wanna defend your country?" I answered lamely, "Well, since I'm a woman, would I be asked to do that?" He mellowed a little, and said, "If you was a man, would you?" I felt like saying, "Not really," but I knew that this was not the time to argue about pacifism.

I came out of the interviewing room a little shaken. There were several lines of people waiting to be processed. An officer was shouting at a confused couple, an Asian woman and man, "Can'tcha read English? You stand over there! I said in that line!" I quickly found my own line. After we were all "processed," we were marched into a large room for the swearing-in by a judge who gave a short speech about American citizenship being a privilege and not a right. He closed his talk with an instruction to all of us newly sworn-in American citizens. As if he were sharing something confidential to the several hundred of us standing before him, he leaned over the lectern and said that the United States was open to all well-educated, good people trained in high professions. If we had relatives or friends of this caliber, we should encourage them to join us and become American citizens. My immediate reaction was, how about the home countries? His speech was having the opposite effect on me than what he intended. Although I had no intention myself of going back to the Japan that was recovering from the horror of the atom bombs and struggling to get back on her feet after the devastations of the war, the judge's words made me protective of what I considered to be my parents' home country. It made me realize that Japan, more than ever, needed well-educated, good people trained in the professions to help with reconstruction.

On the subway ride home from Brooklyn College, I confided my thoughts to my friend Heka Davis, who had come with me to be my sponsor and witness. Was there something wrong with me? Why wasn't I feeling as jubilant as my father and mother had felt after they gained their citizenship? Why was I feeling resentful that I was being treated as if I were not worthy of this honor? My friend laughed. Of course, she said, my reaction was natural, because unlike my parents, I had grown up here and had always felt American. She said, "Just think how very American your reaction is. Americans all think that citizenship, like a lot of other things, is a right." My friend, herself an immigrant from Europe during the war years but now naturalized, said that in spite of her slight German accent, she could still pass as just another one of those Americans who "own" this country. What would have happened, she speculated, if I had acted on my impulses and scolded the officer who was shouting at the Asian couple standing in line? Would he have exploded? Would he have charged that I was being un-American, speaking in such a disrespectful manner to a United States government official? On the other hand, I asked her, what would have happened if *she* had spoken sharply to him? He might have dismissed her as an ill-mannered woman, or, she added, she might have reminded him of his mother, or his wife! And we both laughed.

I knew then that I would never take my American citizenship for granted, that I have never felt and will never feel that I "own" this country in the same way that a white, native-born American does. I was no longer an alien at that moment, but I was acutely aware that in 1942, the evacuation orders posted on telephone poles referred to the American-born Nisei not as American-born citizens but as "non-aliens."

Jeni was four years old the year that I became an American citizen, and she already had a self-assured sense of herself. She was growing up in a New York suburb without any awareness of her difference. When a playmate called her a stupid not-white, she came running to me complaining, "Mommy, Andy called me stupid." Seven years later, she was trying to sort out in her mind why the Japanese Americans were removed from their homes during World War II, and why her mother had kept it a secret from her through all these years. Jeni, a Sansei, somehow understood that these matters concerned her personally in a deeply disturbing way, but at the time of the newscast she could only ask the more immediate questions, such as "What was it like? and "Did you have enough to eat?" How could she know that they were the wrong kinds of questions? The only possible response was, "Really, it wasn't *that* bad."

Hers were not naive, childlike questions. I'd heard the same ones years before from returning veterans at New York University in 1945. I was in my junior year there after completing two years at the University of Cincinnati. After leaving Minidoka in 1943, I wanted to turn my back completely on the war and my internment experience. Living at the University of Cincinnati dormitory as just one of the girls almost let me be a teenager again. I consider those years at the dormitory with seven other roommates some of the happiest memories of my college years. My contact with the United States military was confined to serving food to and bantering with air force trainees taking courses on the campus. In Cincinnati, the only person who knew about the camps and was interested in hearing about them was a conscientious objector who was in Cincinnati for a brief furlough from the conscientious objectors' camp in Trenton, North Dakota. (He was visiting his sister, who was my boss at the cafeteria.) On the other hand, New York University was teeming with young men taking advantage of the G.I. Bill, which allowed them a free college education. They were a group of eager, politically aware New Yorkers who were bursting to know everything about events at home that they might have missed during their absence.

I was startled when the veterans at NYU asked me if I had been in "one of those camps." They said that when they were overseas and expressed outrage over the shocking revelations of the Holocaust, the Europeans often taunted them by saying, "But look what you Americans did to your Japanese." The veterans had no idea what their hosts were talking about. When they returned, they discovered that no one had heard anything about the concentration camps in the United States. But these veterans too asked me only about the *conditions* of our incarceration, as if that was the only issue: "What was it like?" "Did they feed you enough?" "Were you tortured or anything?"

During those years, the news of the horrors of Hitler's Nazi death camps was filling the newspapers daily. Most of my fellow students in the small circle of friends that met every day in the campus cafeteria were of Jewish descent. In this context, when asked, "What was it like?" one could only respond, "It wasn't that bad." Such questions set us up to make comparisons as to the level of suffering that was involved, and silenced us because, as Emiko Omori states in her documentary, *Rabbit in the Moon* (1999), "It wasn't bad enough."

Nevertheless, Jeni's direct questions opened the door for me. I resurrected a box of notes that I had kept in camp but had hardly looked at through all those years. I rummaged through my notes as well as through my memory, and I realized that I needed to write explanatory narratives attached to the cryptic and often disorganized notes I'd written in camp. But there were too many distractions—a child's illness, preparations for schools. Life went on. While I was trying to decide what kind of notebook I should write my memories in (cloth-bound? paperback? loose-leaf? spiral?), I had a respiratory attack and about a month later was diagnosed with terminal emphysema by a family physician. I now had a more compelling reason to tell my story in writing. While confined in bed, I wrote in my journal in fits and starts, but my anguish over the possibility of being forgotten by my children after a premature death kept me from concentrating on the task at hand. During the hours I spent in bed, I dawdled by reading the *New York Times* and the *Los Angeles Times* almost from cover to cover, ending with the obituaries.

During one of those obsessive daily readings of the newspapers, I came upon a small item in an inside page of one of the papers about an organization that was calling for people to write appeals for amnesty on behalf of forgotten prisoners throughout the world. Amnesty International, as the organization came to be called, reported that there were thousands of people in prisons throughout the world because their political or religious beliefs were unacceptable to their respective governments. There were descriptions of the prisoners, many of them teachers, writers, and editors of newspapers. Members of Amnesty were encouraged to write letters on behalf of these prisoners, who were called prisoners of conscience. Feeling trapped in my bedroom with the air purifier humming away, and dependent as I was on the huge oxygen tank that stood next to my bed, I empathized with the situation of the prisoners. I wrote to the address given in the papers and received a packet of materials with descriptions of the cases, complete with model letters and names and addresses to which our letters should be sent. Some of the escaped or released prisoners' graphic descriptions of the torture to which they were subjected and of the conditions in the prisons were too horrible to contemplate. For this reason, I did not consciously connect their experiences to my own internment experience. Their situations in totalitarian governments seemed far worse than mine in our democratic United States. I became completely immersed in the task of writing the appeal letters. Like Scheherazade, I felt compelled to keep the letters going, as if my own life as well as those of the prisoners depended on them.

Seven years later, when a lung specialist found that my illness had been misdiagnosed, I continued my involvement with Amnesty International and went on with my life. I started a new career as an English teacher in a community college. It took me a few years to break out of structured lesson plans. Teaching my students to write compositions creatively out of their own hearts gave me the impetus to return to my own writing. Also, the controversy in the academic world over what constituted THE American culture during the 1970s and 1980s was energizing and led to my need to write about my own heritage as a Japanese American in white America. I resurrected my camp notes for a second time.

With my participation on panels held for schoolchildren on the subject of the camps and the publication of my book, *Camp Notes and Other Poems* in 1976 by the Shameless Hussy Press, I fully convinced myself that I had finally "dealt" with the experience. At a book signing, when a young Sansei came up to tell me that she hoped to use my book to open a dialogue with her mother about her time in camp, a subject about which they had never spoken before, I felt a certain satisfaction that simple disclosure had done its job. I thought that with disclosure we were finally recovering from what seemed to be our sense of shame over this so-called blemish in our lives. But there still remained my inability to talk to my own children about what the Japanese American internment meant to me and to them as the children of survivors. This silence served only to bury even deeper the psychic injuries that resurfaced from time to time in emotionally disruptive ways without warning. Two such incidents come to mind.

In 1980, during the filming of *Mitsuye and Nellie*, a film about the experiences of Asian American women in this country,[1] Nellie Wong, a San Francisco poet, my younger daughter Hedi, and I were sitting on wooden planks at the Minidoka camp site in Idaho discussing what had happened there some thirty-six years before. I found myself embarrassed by unexpected tears. At one point, we were talking about how I had always tried to protect my four children from being exposed to racist incidents when they were children. Nellie had to prod me for an example. I said that, for instance, I never gave my children money to go to the neighborhood store to pick up small items or to buy candy for themselves, as many of my friends did. I did not want them to be yelled at by the storekeepers or to be called "Japs" by them. Hedi said, "I know now why you felt a need to protect me." And tears flowed, right there, with the cameras still running.

Before this discussion, Hedi had commented that when she had first moved to a new school and saw an Asian girl in her class, she saw that the girl was different, and she thought, "Oh, I'm different too." Hedi was eighteen years old at the time of our visit to the Minidoka camp site, exactly the age I was when our family was incarcerated there. In her gentle, young voice, she was spontaneously confessing that as a young child she had understood what exclusion meant and understood, at last, why I felt I had to protect her and her siblings. Her admission was touching and disturbing at the same time.

Twelve years later, during the fiftieth-year commemoration of Executive Order 9066 at UCLA, I was sitting in the audience weeping quietly while everyone else around me seemed to be listening attentively to the speaker, Congressman Robert Matsui. When I felt that I was becoming too conspicuous, I stumbled over the feet of people seated near me and left to do my sobbing alone in the restroom. It was 1992, and the country was just recovering from the aftermath of the Gulf War. Matsui had just told the story of a young Yonsei girl fully dressed in her Girl Scout uniform, standing outside a supermarket with other troop members urging shoppers to buy their cookies. One of the shoppers brushed her aside saying, "No thanks, I only buy American." On hearing this story, a revulsion welled up inside me. I was back in 1943, in an encounter with a stranger in downtown Cincinnati a few days after I left camp. I was walking around in this strange town enjoying my new-found freedom, feeling comfortably invisible and anonymous. Suddenly a fellow pedestrian called me a "dirty Jap" and spat on me. At the time, I was living in a hostel established by the American Friends Service Committee to accommodate Nisei who were leaving the camps. When I returned to the hostel, though I felt my face still burning from the incident, I did not stop to talk to the group of Nisei who were gathered in the living room with Arthur and Kate Brinton, the Friends couple who managed the house. I went straight to my room and took a nap. Having slept off the unpleasant experience, I got up, had dinner at the house and went to work at the University of Cincinnati cafeteria the following day. Our parents' legacy of silence—"for the sake of the children"—had been a curse rather than a blessing.

I hope that the Yonsei Girl Scout was not as deeply affected by this encounter as I was by mine in Cincinnati. She went home and told her Sansei parents, who in turn told their friends. The story reached the ears of Congressman Matsui, who put a political spin on it and recounted it to a gathering of mostly Japanese Americans at UCLA. The young girl will probably not weep over the incident thirty-six years later.

What I found most painful about the her story was the realization that in a flash we can return to the "square one" about which Jeni writes in her essay. I was weeping over the incident because I knew that it was not an isolated one but a form of nonviolent hate crime to which our children are subjected all too frequently. I knew that such actions could not be legally prosecuted. Still, they do damage not only to the recipients of such attacks but to our society as a whole.

We need to ask questions beyond "What was it like?" The assumption behind such questions is that as long as we are treated decently, we have nothing to complain about. If we continue to think in these terms, we will come to conclusions such as the one that was handed down by a judge in Gordon Hirabayashi's case in 1981, when Hirabayashi was demanding that his wrongful conviction during World War II be vacated by the courts forty years later.[2] Initially his appeal was turned down, because Hirabayashi, by that time a respected professor at the University of Alberta, had not, it was said, been "grieved enough" as a result of his incarceration. Fortunately for us, and of course for Hirabayashi, Judge Mary Murphy Schroeder, a circuit judge for the United States Court of Appeals, reviewed the case and in 1987 made the stunning ruling that when any American's civil rights are violated, that person is lastingly grieved. No matter how many years have passed, a wrong is still a wrong.

We have for too long thought in terms of relative justice, comparing the weight of the suffering (who suffered more than whom?), and along with the rest of the country, we have indulged in voluntary amnesia about the internment camps. In too many ways we have been complicit in the silence that has been forced on us. And so the silence has left our children to sort things out for themselves and to wonder, "What else are they keeping from us?" I would change our parents' saying, *kodomo no tame ni* (for the sake of the children) to *mago no tame ni* (for the sake of the grandchildren). I learn from my daughters' examples in their more open ways with their children. The greatest lesson we can teach our children is awareness of the world around them. Jason's words (quoted by Jeni in her essay) give me hope that the legacy of silence is gradually being broken.

I also cling to the conviction that small actions on our part can yield small changes. In June 1975, I saw in the news that a tent city had been constructed to house several thousand Vietnamese who after the fall of Saigon were evacuated by the United States Marines to Camp Pendleton, California, just fifty miles south of where I lived. Because I had just finished my teaching for the academic year and was free for the summer, I drove down to Camp Pendleton and volunteered to teach English to the Vietnamese. My class was held in a tent with picnic tables originally set up for dining purposes. I walked up and down the middle aisle between picnic tables where the men sat (no women responded to our call), so crowded together that it was difficult for them to write. The second day of our sessions, three marines in their heavy combat boots tramped in noisily, saying, "Excuse us, ma'am" as I stepped aside to let them pass through to the other end of the tent. Five minutes later, another group of marines trooped in, and then another. I finally called after them, "Can't you see I'm trying to conduct a class? Why are you guys walking through here?" They answered, "To get to the other side," and laughed uproariously. At lunchtime, I stood in the long line of refugees with trays. The marines served out food, all the while making loud, crass jokes at both the men and women, who responded with smiles because they thought the marines were being friendly.

The next day I went to file a complaint with the commanding officer before reporting for class. I told him that the situation the refugees found themselves in was bewildering and humiliating enough. I found his marines' adolescent behavior extremely offensive and requested that they treat our guests with respect and dignity. The C.O. apparently acted on my complaint with lightning speed. By the time I got back to the tent city a few minutes later, several marines waved at me through the tent opening in a conciliatory manner and called out sheepishly, "Hiya there, Teach!" Even in an institution as seemingly intransigent as the military, change can happen. Inch by inch.

NOTES

1. Allie Light and Irving Saraf, *Mitsuye and Nellie, Asian American Poets* (USA, 1981).
2. Gordon Hirabayashi had refused to be evacuated in 1942 with the rest of the Japanese community in Seattle, Washington, and he was convicted of violating military orders. He served his sentence, but in 1981, Aiko Herzig-Yoshinaga, a Nisei working as a researcher for the Justice Department, discovered crucial evidence showing that the military and the Justice Department had suppressed documents that directly refuted the government's claims of Japanese American disloyalty. Hirabayashi's case, along with those of Fred Korematsu and Minoru Yasui, were brought before the courts by attorneys who used the writ of *coram nobis* to overturn the three resisters' wartime convictions.

Mitsuye Yamade in majorette boots and her mother, Hide Yasutake, at Minidoka,
Spring 1943.
Inmates were forbidden to have cameras in the camps. The two photos from Minidoka
were taken when a Nisei enlisted man came to visit and brought the camera with him.

Soldier friend, Mrs. Yasutake, Mitsuye, and her brother, Joseph, at Minidoka, Spring 1943.

JENI YAMADA

LEGACY OF SILENCE (II)

I am four years old, playing outside a stone castle. I see another child my age with dark hair, bangs, and chin-length hair, in a lacy drop-waist dress and ivory stockings that sag slightly, creating hairline folds below the points of her tiny ankle bones. We play. Suddenly in the way of dreams . . . everything changes. The sun vanishes. There is a chill in the air. A wicked witch approaches. We scream. We struggle to open the large wooden castle door with iron hinges, rivets and a large heavy handle. Together we pull as hard as we can, trying desperately to work the door open before the witch comes. The door groans open slightly. An unseen interior source throws an amber bar of light onto the pavement.

Swiftly, the other child slips her small body into the crack of the open doorway. I have a sense of exhilaration. My friend and I are going to escape from the monstrous witch. But before I can translate thought into movement and move through the open doorway, the door slams. A moment of confusion turns to disbelief. The other child has betrayed me, abandoned me. I awaken, the child's face vivid in my mind's eye. Her face is of a child in a photograph on our living room mantel. She is my mother at age four.

In the morning—the morning after the dream—I lie in bed trembling with rage and hurt. I struggle with the themes. Abandonment. Exclusion. Secrecy. Somehow, between sobs I try to articulate the dream to my mother. I am angry. I cry and push her away. I still remember her bewildered voice, "But Jeni, it was only a dream!"

I think about the legacy of silence.

I was born in the 1950s, after the Japanese internment camp era had ended. I didn't live the camp experience. But I didn't escape it either. Events that happened in my mother's life before my birth shaped her shaping of me. Only now have I begun to see fully the profound impact of my mother's wartime experiences on my own life.

When I was very young I had an awareness of internment camp, but not of the details. Mom said nothing about it and then just a little. "It wasn't that bad," she insisted, "Actually we were safer there." There was so much left unsaid. Unexplained. There were only passing references to camp. "Grandma knitted this skirt in camp," Mom might say, or (to her mother), "Remember those white majorette boots I had in camp?" As a child I loved to explore her beautiful wooden jewelry cabinet. It had small diamond-shaped knobs, tiny drawers, and a center compartment door that scrolled open like a rolltop desk. Once, as I was pulling the little drawers in and out, enjoying the *scritch-scratch* of wood sliding against wood, she told me that this cabinet had been made "while we were in camp." *Camp.* A word that conjures up summer: sports, swimming in the lake, and munching on s'mores around the campfire. But not in our family.

Mom says I found out about the camps one evening when a brief newscast about them was aired on television. This was in the early 1960s. Perhaps it was the twentieth anniversary of Pearl Harbor and the camp era. It might have been the first time in my life I had seen images of people, Japanese people, being loaded onto buses and trains, and of people living in the camps. Mom says I turned to her, tears brimming, and said, "How come you never told us?" All the references to the camps I had heard all my life had not included the details about the discomforts, the humiliation, and the loss of freedom.

In 1942 my mother, her mother and three brothers were interned in Minidoka, Idaho, one of the ten concentration camps (or so-called relocation centers). My grandfather had been arrested by the FBI and then was detained in a series of United States Department of Justice internment camps. He was separated from the rest of the family throughout the war years.

When my mother left camp in 1943 and settled into college life in Cincinnati, she would sit around in the residential halls with her friends and talk about boys. It was as if the war weren't happening. No one ever brought up the Japanese internment camps. My mother was struck by something Emiko Omori said in her documentary *Rabbit in the Moon*. Emiko said that it wasn't that internment camp was so bad, it wasn't bad enough. "That's just it," my mother confirmed, "It wasn't bad enough."

Immediately after leaving camp, I was so busy trying to make ends meet that I had no time to think about what we'd been through. I do remember being asked about

the camps when I went to NYU in 1947 but always in the context of the Holocaust. All
my friends were Jewish. You were made to feel apologetic, almost, about complaining of
our "treatment." But I do remember being annoyed during one of these discussions by a
remark, "Well, at least YOU weren't gassed or anything."

In the decade following her camp experience, Mom not only went to college
and got her master's degree. She met my father, got married, and began having
children. She weighed seventy-seven pounds on her wedding day. Her hair was
dark and short with curls arching across her forehead. She used two shiny metal
clips to shape her bangs into curls. Her cap-sleeved white satin wedding dress
with the pinched waist accentuated her thin frame and waiflike appearance.

I was born in Chicago. A year later we moved to New York. Mom and Dad
lived the fifties lifestyle and had babies, one after the other. I was the first. Soon
after I was born, Mom lost three babies, then had three more. She buried her
memories of the camps and threw herself into a new life.

Mom hand-painted curtains, sewed dresses for me, and baked apple
turnovers and lemon cream puffs. Sometimes she would take up a blue-ruled
notebook and write. Occasionally she'd sit at an unobtrusive distance from my
playmates and me and record the magical dialogue of our preschool world. On
other occasions, Mom would ask me to dictate stories spun from my own childish imagination. I gladly obliged, offering tales of lost girls and dinosaurs. I
loved my Ginny doll with the brown-rooted hair and blue eyes.

Some of the earliest memories I have are of living in Queens in an apartment house built in a U shape with sour-smelling hallways, brick-red metal
doors, and hordes of children in the quadrangle outside. In the courtyard, parents shouted after their children in many languages: German, Spanish, and English. We were children of immigrants and of struggling young parents. Later
my family moved on to white, middle-class suburban neighborhoods (first in
New York, then in California), where a lot of the time I felt normal. I thought
of myself as a happy child in a happy family.

When I first started school in the suburbs of Long Island, New York, I was
the only Japanese American child in my class. In fact, I was the only Japanese
American child in my entire elementary school. The only other child of color
was a black girl with straightened hair whose name was Sheila or Sherry. I don't
even remember talking to her. Did we studiously avoid one another to prove
we were each capable enough, normal enough to be friends with the fair-haired
girls in the class? Perhaps we didn't want to be seen together. Perhaps we didn't
see any similarity between us at all.

Jeni Yamada, about 1955.

I'd been an outgoing preschooler, but by the time I was in first grade I was shy. I knew certain people disliked me immediately before they even knew me. "What are you?" they asked, slightly accusingly, upon meeting me. I knew that somehow it wasn't the best thing to be Japanese. "I'm an *American*," I'd insist. At school it was not uncommon for children to run up and scream "Jap!" You're a Jap!" "You bombed Pearl Harbor!" I didn't know what Pearl Harbor was, but I knew it was a bad thing. Somehow I was associated with it. "Why," I remember thinking, "do I have to be left-handed *and* Japanese?" When I was growing up, people talked of Japanese things as cheap and of poor quality. We had to distance ourselves from anything Japanese in order to prove that we were true Americans. Loyal Americans.

My parents didn't speak Japanese to me when I was young. Maybe it was because Japanese was the language of the enemy. I turned away from my cultural past. I didn't like the sound of the Japanese language and the smell of Japanese food. My favorite foods were hamburgers and french fries. The concept

Jeni Yamada and her mother, Mitsuye, March 1957.

of multiculturalism and ethnic pride had not yet taken hold. We dissociated ourselves from our histories. Even though my face was Japanese, I didn't feel Japanese. I didn't know how to *be* Japanese.

I think I know how an adopted child feels. I was severed from my history in a significant way, like a child adopted from a foreign country. Somewhere along the way I lost the language and much of the culture of my forebears. When you lose these key elements, you lose an important thread of continuity. Until recently I felt more at home in the company of people of European background than with other Asian people.

I'm at the supermarket. I see a small, dark-haired, dark-eyed child with skin the color of my own, sitting in one of those shopping cart seats. She is being pushed along by a tall, fair-haired woman with porcelain skin. The mother is turned away, scanning the shelves for just the right orange juice. I'm standing in front of the milk carton display when I turn, and the child and I lock gazes. She searches my face and I hers for something we have both lost. Then momentarily, the child's mother turns around and breaks the spell. She eyes me just a little warily. We move our separate ways. As the cart passes, the child turns around in her seat to look back at me just one more time.

When I found out about the camps, I was shocked. I was horrified. I was ashamed. The news program was probably the first time I'd seen photographs of people being herded across bridges, down streets, onto buses, onto trains, tags tied to their buttonholes and flapping in the breeze. I have no clear recollection of the show itself, but I do remember following my mother around, asking her questions. She didn't seem to want to talk about it. It was something in the past, something she had put aside.

Did I talk about it to anyone outside the family? Did I mention it to my Caucasian friends? Did I comb the library for more details? I don't think so. By now my parents had moved from New York to California. I threw myself into our borrowed, white middle-class identity. I wanted to be just another junior high and high school student. I didn't want to feel different. My parents avoided living in Japanese and Japanese American communities. We didn't need that. We didn't want to "cluster." As long as our Caucasian neighbors and friends weren't threatened, they wouldn't threaten us. It was a good strategy. I felt like part of the white community in which I grew up, at least some of the time.

In high school, one boy I dated always met me away from his house, always lied about his whereabouts to his parents when he was with me, and always made sure he got home by curfew. Finally he admitted that his father would "kill" him if he knew his son was seeing me. I raged, "What right does your father have to judge me? He doesn't even know me!" I didn't give the boy himself enough credit for rejecting his father's prejudices. Other boys in high school wrote things in my yearbook like, "You little Oriental Flower." For the most part, Jewish boys were more open-minded about dating Asian girls. Was it because, like me, they were Other? I felt comfortable and accepted among Jewish friends.

Because of the silences in my family, silences about the family history, there were gaps that I needed to fill in other ways. I knew our family had experienced the camps, but I knew so little. I searched for details in other people's histories. I lived other lives in my dreams, feeling a resonance with Jewish culture.

I am in a museum gazing at a painting of European peasants in a field. Momentarily I am sucked into the painting head-first. I am a Russian peasant cowering behind sacks of flour, trembling at the approach of the Cossacks.

I am being herded into a bus headed for a death camp. I am standing naked in a shower stall among many others. The man with the long silver scissors glinting in the dim light is cutting my hair, pulling and tugging this way and that.

Eventually I married a Jewish man. Jewish people I know have a strong sense of membership and their culture. There is a powerful pride in their heritage. I was hungry for that. My husband and I agreed to raise our children Jewish. I decided to convert. After studying the religion, I went through the final rituals of conversion in an immersion ceremony on a California beach a few months before our first son was born. I rationalized that this was not alien to my own background. I'd been a religious skeptic for years. My father, a scientist (who was born in Hawaii and so was not interned), didn't participate in organized religion. My mother raised me Episcopalian, but by age twelve I'd rejected the concept of original sin and was questioning the tenets of Christianity.

In marrying a Jewish man I didn't have to abandon my own ethnicity. My husband and I talked about the similarities in our background; there was the immigrant status, the emphasis on education, and, of course, the camp experience. There were differences too. For many Japanese Americans, being in the camps was a mark of shame. It was as if association with the camps tainted you and gave you a hint of criminality. I understand that some Jewish survivors feel guilty for having survived the camps when so many others died. But many do not seem to feel guilty or in the wrong for *talking* about the camp experience. The willingness of many Jewish survivors to talk about and document their camp experiences contrasts sharply with the Japanese Americans' tendency to remain silent.

During the time that I was coping with the intensity of pre-adolescence and then adolescence, my mother was undergoing her own transformations. Once her youngest child was of preschool age, she began casting about for intellectual stimulation, reading and studying. At one point she began leaving books around the house. In the bathroom one day I discovered Germaine Greer's *The Female Eunuch*. I ran to the dictionary to look up that strange word, "eunuch." Later I discovered Betty Friedan's *The Feminine Mystique*. Interchanges between Mom and Dad began to change. Dad used to sit at the table and bark, "*Ocha* [Tea]!" After a while he didn't do that anymore. Mom began campaigning for various causes. Equal rights for women. Fair housing. Human rights. I watched and listened. I may not have understood it then, but something was changing in my mother.

Something was changing in me as well. In high school I began to challenge my teachers. A physiology teacher argued one day that an unmarried pregnant girl should be made to bear her child. She should have to "pay for her mistakes." I stood before him and raised my voice. "Why is forcing a girl to have a baby a good 'punishment' for her? Why shouldn't the father of the child be held equally responsible?"

Mom says that she was always taught by her parents not to complain, not to speak out. Somewhere along the way she changed operating principles. Somehow Mom went from, "Whatever happens happens, don't complain, don't whine, just *gaman*," to "I'm not going to take it anymore."

Once my mother made the transition from Japanese daughter to activist, she began to write and talk extensively about many things, including her camp experience. It became okay to acknowledge that what happened was a violation of human rights, of our ethnic group, and of our family. In turn, it was finally all right for me to be angry about it. It wasn't until my mother broke the silence and admitted her anger that I was able to explore my own anger.

Chicago. I was born in Chicago. I began to understand the significance of this fact only a few years ago when I began giving lectures on the Japanese American internment to junior high school classes. When people were first allowed to leave the camps they were not permitted to return to the West Coast, where many of them had lived before the internment. The government still had suspicions about the Japanese. It wanted to ensure that these people would not engage in any intelligence operations on the coast. People had to move inland. Many Japanese Americans are from Chicago. Until recently it didn't occur to me that this was a direct result of the camps. My parents might never have met if it weren't for the camp experience. My mother's father was head of the Chicago Resettlement Committee, an organization designed to help people reintegrate into civilian life. My father used to come to the Resettlement House. If it weren't for the camps, I would never have been born.

There were things I didn't understand about my family that I could understand only once I knew about the camp experience in more detail. Judging from old family photographs, Mom's family lived in big houses with nice cars and fine clothes. To my childish eyes they looked wealthy. Then why, I wondered, did Grandma work as a cleaning and ironing lady when she lived with us in the 1950s and 1960s?

Only after hearing more details about the family's camp and post-camp life experiences did I learn that Grandma and Grandpa, who *had* been wealthy before the war, had to work as domestics upon coming out of internment camp. Grandpa, with his Stanford University education, years of experience as an interpreter for the Immigration and Naturalization Service, and background as an insurance salesman, could not get a job. He and Grandma were employed as a butler and a maid for a wealthy family in the Chicago area.

I used to be shy. I'm not shy anymore. I try to teach my children to speak out. When you see something that bothers you, say something. Do something. Make a change to create a better world.

As a teenager I passed out grape-boycott leaflets, carried candles in Take Back the Night Marches, and protested the Vietnam War. Later I joined a group called Women Against Violence Against Women, which condemned images of violence against women in the media and advertising. I joined the American Civil Liberties Union and Amnesty International. The idea of speaking out about injustices against people of my own ethnic group didn't occur to me until much later. Like my mother before me, I thought that those slights and injustices seemed too minor to get upset about compared to the virulent racism against blacks in this country.

I want to spare my children from racism. One day at elementary school some "friends" taped a "Mr. Sushi" sign to my son Aaron's desk chair. Another day my son Jason and a friend of his decided to have a wrestling match. "I'll be America, you be Japan," the friend suggested. Still another time a few of Jason's classmates used their new-found awareness of internment camps as a reason to sneer, "Your family was in ca-amps, your family was in ca-amps."

I like to teach the history of the internment, to go into the schools to talk about racism and tolerance. When I give these talks I draw on family experience. I want children to understand that violations of human rights and of civil liberties don't just happen in foreign lands where tyrannical governments are in power. I point out that violations can happen in a democratic country, even here in the United States. Children are shocked to hear this. In this country human rights can be violated. And in fact they were. I don't imply that the camps were as bad as the European camps, but I think it important to note the similarities. Students want to know details. What did people eat in camp? What could you buy there? Where did people get their clothes? Were the guards cruel? Did people get killed? Was there an organized resistance movement?

When I talk about the internment, I show photographs of people registering for evacuation, walking to the trains, being loaded onto the transports, two suitcases per person. I show the archival photographs of life in camp. I also show photographs of my own family before camp, smartly attired, standing amid their home furnishings, or in front of their homes and cars. In educating others I learn so much.

When I think about what my mother and her family endured, I also think about how things have changed and not changed. Racism is not a black-and-white issue. Some of us have our advanced education, our titles, and our trappings of success. Sometimes we forget and we really believe that things are different, that we are perceived as who we are. Sometimes we are taken seriously. But sometimes something slaps us in the face with the fact that the world still sees us as the maid, the janitor, and the laundry worker. Something electrifying happens that takes us back to square one.

I once served on an antiracism panel along with several African American men and women. We shared square-one experiences. One black man talked about being a college professor and having someone who was walking down the hall of his department mistake him for the custodian.

I have had my own square-one experiences. I was once standing outside a hospital elevator with a group of other people I didn't know. I was a young doctoral student. I felt professional and self-possessed. As I was walking through the open doors of the elevator I realized in a fleeting moment that all of the people walking into the elevator happened to be Asian. One of the people already in the elevator, a Caucasian person, quipped, "Whoa, it's an invasion."

I once went to a friend's wedding shower at a Chinese restaurant. The crowd was primarily Caucasian. One of the guests approached me with a broad smile and held out her hand. Thinking she was extending a greeting, I held out mine. Into my upturned palm the woman pressed a handful of crumpled up napkins and garbage and said, "Throw this away for me, would you?" Only then did I realize that she had mistaken me for the restaurant help.

Throughout my life I have thought about the dream in which my mother and I played together as two four-year-olds. I think about the themes. Abandonment. Exclusion. Secrecy.

Why didn't Mom talk about the internment for so many years? Why didn't I ask more? We were just regular people living regular lives. Mom was busy doing her life and not dwelling on the past. There were hidden things that I sensed from an early age, but they were hurts that she chose not to share. She wasn't going to define herself along those lines. Neither was I. We didn't think about race all the time. I wanted to believe I was just another American girl growing up in the suburbs.

As I have learned more and more, I reinterpret. I believe that my mother kept a lot hidden not to shut me out or to exclude me. She was trying to protect us, her children, from the racism that she herself had endured. In addition, she was battling with the news (which later turned out to be incorrect) that she had a terminal medical condition. She didn't tell me about the poor prognosis at the time, but I do remember her emotional distance, her preoccupation with other things. If she didn't tell her story, it would be lost forever. Perhaps the notion that she might not be around much longer helped to give her the courage to speak her mind. Life is intricate, and there are many reasons why we evolve as we do. But I now know that it is voice, not silence that will ultimately protect us.

I have been collecting stories via e-mail from different family members, asking them to write their recollections of the internment experience. I ask the question, "What do you remember telling or being told about the internment camp history?" and my mother, uncles, aunts, cousins, and siblings have responded in an electronic discussion. Several uncles wrote that they had been *willing* to talk about the camps but didn't recall saying much. Another said he was frankly uncomfortable talking about it. When a number of Sansei cousins commented that their parents never said much about the internment camps, uncles and aunts responded that it wasn't that they wanted to avoid talking about it; it was just that their children hadn't shown much interest in the topic. Silences about the camps mean that there is a paucity of information for the next generation. While various family members are now working to fill this vacuum, we still have many gaps left.

Perhaps traditional Japanese attitudes have contributed to these silences, even in a family like mine, which is not completely traditional. One traditional notion is that one's fortune or misfortune is related to one's past. My mother has explained to me that the Japanese have the concept of *bachi* (divine punishment or curse). Basically, bad things happen to bad people. For example, the *hibakusha* (atom bomb survivors) were treated poorly by the Japanese because someone so unlucky as to be a *hibakusha* must have done something wrong in the past. Vestiges of such traditional attitudes probably still exist in the Issei and Nisei generations. To some extent, internment camp survivors may have maintained silence because they felt somehow responsible for their own misfortune.

Then again, one can't say that attitudes of the Japanese Americans are solely what contributed to their silences. To break silence and draw attention to the internment experience can be dangerous. Most Japanese Americans know that to bring up the internment camps, Pearl Harbor, or the atom bomb is to invite abuse. On September 29, 1999, there was a story in the media across the country that a memorial to Japanese Americans interned in Santa Fe was going to be built. United States veterans and others raised a hue and cry, protesting any such memorial. "They were the enemy," said one, "and they still are." During the redress movement, when the notion of giving $20,000 to each internment camp survivor was being proposed, there were vehement protests from the general public. And just a few years ago, when my mother was invited to an elementary school in California to talk about her interment camp experience, the teacher of the class was called before the school board to explain why she had invited "the enemy" to speak. Many Japanese Americans would rather not bring up the subject of the camps, knowing that as soon as such issues come to light, the masks of friendliness and good will on the faces of their Caucasian colleagues and friends may quickly fall away.

As I become more and more insistent that the history—not just the internment camp history, but the immigrant history—must be preserved, my own sons have sometimes complained that I am "obsessed" with these topics. They too want to fit in—and not feel different. I am not obsessed. I am making up for past omissions. Of course, like my mother and my Uncle Mike, two very high-energy activists, I don't want to fight battles for just my own ethnic group; that would be too narrow a focus.

In 1999, when he was in eighth grade, my fourteen-year-old son Jason needed to interview a social activist. By default (he'd left the report until the last minute), he interviewed me. I told him about the causes I've supported. I discussed human rights, women's rights, and civil rights. I talked with him about how living in the post–World War II era affected me, and about what it's like to be marginalized. I talked about how his father and I had invited a black South African man to live with us years ago when apartheid still existed. My oldest son Aaron was seven and Jason was only two. Subsequently, after seeing that life for blacks was just as hard here, the young man returned to South Africa. We corresponded occasionally. Years later he wrote that he had decided to take a homeless, white South African teenage boy into *his* home as a result of the kindness we'd shown him. After our interview Jason put pen to paper to express his feelings:

> I lived with P. when I was only two. And I still remember him. I remember noticing his peculiar way of wanting to stay down in our dark cement basement and not coming up very often. We had offered to furnish the room but he refused for one reason or another. I hadn't thought of P. for a long time, until last night. It was then that I realized that that was the biggest act of kindness I have ever had a personal connection to. And it taught me acceptance of others and how to deal with people who are different. I, of course, didn't know that was what I was learning then, but I realize it now. . . . When my mom began talking of the boy P. took in I was shocked and overjoyed at the same time. . . . Somewhere, deep inside my head, unconsciously, I was learning the skills and values that I hold today and will (hopefully) for the rest of my life.
>
> I had been tired with the women's rights movement. It seemed that every time I would talk to a woman in my family they would go off about injustices about women or other people and I got tired of it . . . but last night [in the interview with JY] I saw the purpose behind it. I saw the reason that my grandmother is constantly preaching about human rights, and it all made sense. It actually got me wanting to be a social activist even more so than before.
>
> When I started this interview I thought it was going to be pretty dull. Hadn't I heard everything my mom had to say? The truth is, I hadn't at all. I learned some things that she had been trying to teach me all my life . . . and I found that I was amazed with my mother's story.

In this essay I see Jason's emerging social awareness. His consciousness of himself as (part) Japanese American, and his awareness of our immigrant history and of our internment camp experience are also emerging. Just as my mother's internment camp experience affected her raising of me, so has my post-internment era upbringing affected my children. I did not grow up in a community of Japanese Americans, nor have I been able to raise my own children in such a community. As my own consciousness has evolved, I find it more and more important to reestablish the cultural link to our past. In recent years, through friendships and conscious effort, I've tried to provide my children with cultural experiences that they would otherwise have missed. Just last year, I began studying Japanese again, after a brief attempt in college. After a recent move to a mid-Atlantic town with no visible Japanese American community, finding a cultural connection for my family is all the more challenging.

Children in the next generation have to grapple with issues of identity. Many of these children, like my own sons, are biracial or multiracial. To what extent will the ethnic history be preserved and passed on by a generation that draws just part of its identity from the Japanese American experience? At this point my three children are deeply connected to their Japanese American heritage. I sometimes fear I know far too little. Perhaps I worry unnecessarily. In our family the Japanese internment camp experience has contributed to a consciousness and an activism that span the generations. We have only begun to move beyond silence.

DONNA K. NAGATA

ECHOES FROM
GENERATION TO GENERATION

DOES TIME HEAL ALL WOUNDS? With the passage of over fifty years, it is
easy to think that the internment has passed and that its wounds have healed.
Most of the physical evidence from the camps, the tarpapered barracks and
barbed-wire fences, are gone. Yet there are important ways in which the World
War II incarceration continues to affect the lives of third-generation (Sansei) and
fourth-generation (Yonsei) Japanese Americans today.

My essay itself can be read as an echo of this past. Much of my research was inspired by my own background as a Sansei whose parents and grandparents were interned. Like most of my generation, I was born after the war and did not face the
internment directly. Still, I have always sensed the importance of the camp experience. "Camp" was a pivotal point in time linked to my family history. It was a topic
that, as I was growing up, provided the backdrop to many of the conversations and
memories of the adults around me. The internment has been of interest to me
since high school, although I did not have an opportunity to explore this topic formally until I became an academic. Much of the work that I have done in the past
twelve years examines the intergenerational impacts of the camp experience over
time. A close-up view of some of these long-term effects will help us to appreciate
the diverse ways in which the past continues to affect the present and the future.

INTERGENERATIONAL EFFECTS AMONG THE SANSEI

What is an intergenerational perspective and how does it apply to the internment?
The intergenerational perspective on life events directly challenges the notion

that time heals all wounds. Family systems theory tells us that what happened in one generation reverberates in subsequent generations: "The trauma and its impact may be passed down as the family legacy, even to children born *after* the trauma."[1] Studies on the intergenerational transmission of trauma emerged through the observations of clinicians who were struck by the number of children of Nazi Holocaust survivors seeking treatment. Since that time, the intergenerational perspective has been applied to a wide range of populations, both clinical and nonclinical, including the children and family of war veterans, the offspring of the Turkish genocide of Armenians, and the Khmer Rouge genocide in Cambodia.[2]

In the late 1970s, social worker Nobu Miyoshi began to examine the Japanese American internment through the intergenerational perspective. Through her observations of family interactions, she noted that the camp experience emerged as the key symbol of a generation gap between the Nisei who endured the incarceration and their Sansei children born after the war.[3] Miyoshi's work and the literature on children of the Nazi Holocaust survivors helped provide a framework for my interest in developing an empirical research project to explore the intergenerational effects of the internment. In 1987, I began the Sansei Research Project. The project included survey responses from some seven hundred Sansei and in-depth interviews with thirty of the participants.[4] Its results offer us a picture of the multiple ways in which parents' camp experiences can affect the contemporary lives of the Sansei generation.

One of the major effects of the internment was a shroud of parental silence on the topic of "evacuation" and the camp years. In some cases, the silence was complete; Nisei parents never discussed the camp years with their children. In others, the silence took the form of muted conversations that Sansei described as "oblique," "evasive," and "superficial." In fact, less than a third of the respondents felt that their parents had ever discussed the internment as a central topic. More often, "camp" was mentioned very briefly as an incidental topic or a reference point in time. It was not unusual for Sansei like myself to think that "camp" referred to a summer or Scout camp when we were children! As we grew older and learned more about the internment and its significance, we asked more about our parents' past. Most of us, however, continued to encounter only minimal responses to our questions.

There was an important consequence of this lack of communication. The camps felt like a taboo subject, a painful past cloaked in avoidance, or filtered through positive memories. As a result, Sansei often felt confusion or frustration about what one interviewee called a "void" in their personal history. The absence of discussion signaled the presence of something too difficult for their parents to talk about. This phenomenon was similar to the intergenerational gap reported earlier by Miyoshi and has since been corroborated by others.[5]

Several of the Sansei Project interviewees indicated that they also carry feelings of unspoken sadness and anger for their parents. Having learned more details about the internment through books, films, and other media over time, these Sansei have had to balance their knowledge about the injustice of what happened with the inability to talk freely about the personal significance of the camps within their own families. For some, the suppressed feelings created a sense of shame and inferiority linked to their ethnicity. "I assume they [Caucasian Americans] are going to reject me because I'm Japanese since there was such rejection of my parents," reported one interviewee. Another Sansei described the impact in the following way:

> I believe the difficulty of communication has taken its toll. My parents' silence gave me no way to express the inexplicable shame I felt for being of Japanese ancestry. Inside, I believed that no matter how hard I tried to please others and to fit in (as they wanted me to do), I would always fall short.[6]

A related theme was the Sansei's sense of pressure to achieve. Although they recognized that Japanese cultural values had long emphasized educational success, many felt that their parents were especially eager to have their offspring "prove" their worth to a society that had questioned the loyalty of Japanese Americans. Academic achievement could demonstrate their strengths and commitment to being good citizens. In other cases Sansei noted that their parents urged them to get an education because the knowledge they gained could never be taken from them, even if another internment were to take place.

Most Sansei saw the internment as an important factor in contributing to the accelerated loss of the Japanese language and culture. Understandably most Nisei parents did not actively encourage their children's Japanese ethnic identity after the war. This reticence added another source of sadness and anger for the Sansei. They grieved not only for the unjust treatment and hardships endured by their parents, but also for their own loss of connection to the Japanese culture and language.

Several of the Sansei respondents chose specific careers or attended particular educational institutions in order to fulfill the unfinished dreams of a parent whose aspirations were cut short by the camp years. My research on the internment reflects another way in which the internment can shape a Sansei's career path. Other respondents, sensitized to issues of justice, chose to enter law, the clergy, or community activism in order to address concerns about civil rights or humanitarian efforts. For many, the internment has engendered a lingering skepticism about the United States government. Sansei, knowing the injustice of the camps, expressed discomfort in reciting the Pledge of Allegiance. Their knowledge reminds them of the fragility of their civil rights in this country and of what it means to be an ethnic minority.

Those who endured the camps sometimes refer to that time as the "lost years."[7] Indeed, the losses were numerous: lost freedom, lost education and careers, and lost earnings. Some also lost their lives. Gwendolyn M. Jensen reported that the suicide rate in camps was double that of the national population and possibly four times the pre-incarceration rates. Nearly 80 percent of those who died by suicide were men. In addition, her research found evidence of an increased risk for cardiovascular disease in former internees after the internment and that previously interned Nisei have died an average of 1.6 years earlier than their non-interned Hawaiian counterparts.[8] Data from my own research also showed that more than twice as many Sansei whose fathers were in camp died before the age of sixty when compared with Sansei whose fathers were not interned.[9] Therefore, losing a parent, especially a father, has been yet another consequence for some Sansei, and their fourth-generation (Yonsei) children are now missing a grandfather in their lives.

Some Sansei identified positive effects of the internment. Many drew inspiration from the strength shown by Japanese Americans in response to their incarceration. They admire the resilience of their parents and grandparents during and after the war and look to them as role models. Others recognize that their own existence is related to the internment, since their parents first met in camp. Finally, Sansei also see the internment as an important force that sensitizes them to all forms of injustice in the world.

On a broader level, the internment has created a range of "what if?" questions in Sansei's lives. What if my parents had never been interned? How much more outgoing, or prosperous, or healthy would they be? What family heirlooms would still exist to be passed down to me? How would my life as a Sansei be different if the camps had never happened? These questions loom in the background.

After analyzing the data from the Sansei Research Project, I was struck by the themes that seemed prevalent for so many of my generation: family silence, sadness about the hardships endured by parents, and a loss of connection with our Japanese heritage. Equally important was a sense of vulnerability. Although the Sansei as a whole have achieved significant levels of educational and economic success, they remain aware that neither success nor citizenship protected their parents from the incarceration. In fact, 44 percent of the Sansei respondents with two parents who were interned thought that a future internment of Japanese Americans was possible.[10]

SANSEI RESPONSES TO THE LEGACY

Not all Sansei see the incarceration as a central force in their lives, but it is clear that many do. The range of emotional legacies has, for some, found an outlet in activities dedicated to preserving and promoting the significance of the internment. Sansei were key in establishing pilgrimages to former camp sites and developing a Day of Remembrance each year on February 19 to mark the date when President Franklin Roosevelt issued the executive order that permitted the evacuation. Don T. Nakanishi has noted the important role that Sansei played in resurrecting the issue of the internment within the Japanese American community after decades of silence.[11] Sansei energy combined with Nisei activism to form the national redress movement in the 1980s. The success of the redress movement was important for the Sansei in strengthening intergenerational ties.[12] It also helped some Sansei by relieving their anger about the way in which the government had ignored this dark chapter in the history of civil rights.

In 1994, a small group of eight Sansei displayed a different response to the internment legacy. Together with former internees, they worked to dismantle two original barracks from the Heart Mountain, Wyoming, camp site and move them to Los Angeles, California. Once in California, the barracks were reassembled as a museum exhibit. While the Sansei in the group who were born after the war had a variety of personal reasons for participating in the Heart Mountain barracks project, they were united with the Nisei and other former internees in their overall mission to bring the barracks and the American concentration camps into the view of the broader public, "so that others might not forget."[13] Sharon Yamato's account of the barracks project reflects the power of that experience.

> As a Sansei, I longed for specific answers to my questions about how the internment affected my mother and father. What I found is that clear answers are difficult to come by, but that if we choose to take the journey, we will find them—along with mutual acceptance and lasting connections. I went to Heart Mountain to tear down some walls. Now, I gently embrace them.[14]

Some Sansei have responded to the legacy of the internment through their contributions to museum exhibits and public programs; others have gathered in smaller, more intimate groups to discuss and contemplate the incarceration's impact on their lives. One organization, formed in 1990, provides small groups of Sansei with a forum in which to share personal stories and to explore their family legacies. The project has also sponsored multigenerational family sessions to promote communication within families, particularly about the camp experience.[15] A separate, therapy-oriented group led by Satsuki Ina provided Sansei who had been interned as infants or young children with an opportunity to explore the powerful emotions engendered by that experience.[16] While most Sansei do not participate in organized programs to address the personal impact of the internment in their lives, the emergence of these programs reflects the fact that there are Sansei who have felt a desire to share their feelings about this issue.

YONSEI REACTIONS

We have seen how the internment can affect the Sansei generation long after their parents were freed from the camps. But what about future generations beyond the Sansei? Tina Kazumi Yamano conducted an intriguing case study that included an assessment of fourth-generation Yonsei perceptions of their grandparents' internment.[17] Through a collection of individual interviews with members of three generations (Nisei, Sansei, and Yonsei) from the same extended family, she explored the impact of the internment on those who lived through it and on their children and grandchildren. While the sample of six Yonsei in the study was small, Yamano's results suggest that the echoes of the internment can continue into the fourth generation of Japanese Americans. For some of the Yonsei interviewees these effects were reflected in a continued sense of anger over their family's incarceration during the war. A similar anger had also been expressed by the Sansei in my own research. Another Yonsei who expressed relatively little emotional response to the internment felt that this reaction itself had been shaped by her grandparents' matter-of-fact but distanced way of discussing the camp years. Just as the Sansei wondered about the degree to which the internment had affected their parents' personalities, there are Yonsei who see their grandparents' quiet reserve as having been shaped by negative experiences in camp.

The Yonsei in Yamano's study noted the same shroud of silence around the camp experience that affected the Sansei. While some of the Yonsei in her study were more inclined than their Sansei parents to ask their Nisei grandparents directly for more information about the camp years, the overall lack of discussion was marked. Interestingly, Yamano's research also found that the success of the redress movement failed to stimulate significantly greater levels of communication about the internment within the family.

Nonetheless, Yonsei could identify the significance of the internment in their lives. Like the Sansei, they take pride in the resilience of their grandparents. One of Yamano's participants also saw the internment as shaping his upbringing. "They raised me to see other people with open eyes, not to judge prematurely just upon race, nationality, or looks but look deeper into the person and see that one certain group of people are not bad."[18]

LOOKING INTO THE FUTURE

As the elderly Nisei grow older, the number of those who lived the camp experience grows smaller each day. What role will the internment play in future generations of Japanese Americans? While there is no clear answer, it is worth considering some of the factors that might influence a response to this question.

One important factor concerns the ethnic identity of the Japanese American community itself. If Yonsei and fifth-generation Gosei become increasingly acculturated and distanced from their Japanese American heritage, it is possible that the intergenerational echoes of the internment will fade, particularly once the population of former internees is gone and the power of personal testimony about that time fades. According to a report from the year 2000 in the *San Francisco Examiner* (September 11, A1, A11), the experience of the internment has become more and more remote with each generation. Today's Japanese American youth, reporter Annie Nakao points out, are less concerned about the camps and more focused on issues of interracial identity and pan-Asian pride. However, there are forces that could counter this trend. First, there are many Sansei who maintain an emotional connection with their parents' internment. Once the Nisei are gone, there are Sansei who will tell their children and others about the significance of the camps. Second, there is currently an increased emphasis in multiculturalism and ethnic identity among Americans.[19] Yonsei and Gosei growing up in such a social environment may be more rather than less likely to embrace their connection to Japanese American history.

Another factor that may influence the role of the internment in the future is intermarriage. Recent data from Los Angeles County in California show that Japanese Americans have the highest rate of outmarriage when compared to other Asian American groups, and the rate has increased with each generation.[20] Third-generation Japanese Americans were found to have an outmarriage rate of over 60 percent for females and over 50 percent for males. These statistics point to the fact that the Japanese American community has become, and likely will continue to be, increasingly heterogeneous. The number of multiethnic Yonsei and Gosei will grow as we move into the next century.

Does this trend indicate that the impact of the camps will fade? If future multiethnic generations do not identify with their Japanese American heritage, will they be increasingly less affected by the internment? Current literature suggests caution before assuming that this will necessarily be the case. For example, both monoracial and biracial Yonsei participants in Yamano's research saw the internment as important and relevant to their lives. In addition, researchers have found that there can be great variability in the degree to which biracial Japanese Americans maintain a sense of ethnic identity, and we cannot assume a necessary decline in identification with one's Japanese American heritage.[21] In fact, one study comparing levels of ethnic identification among mono- and biracial Japanese Americans found no significant differences between the two groups.[22] Finally, Amy Iwasaki Mass cites additional studies suggesting that interracial Japanese Americans "may be more aware of their Japanese heritage because they have to struggle to affirm and come to terms with their dual racial background."[23] This observation suggests that for some multiethnic Japanese Americans, there may actually be an increased likelihood of continued interest in the internment.

Within Japanese American communities, there is a range of opinion about the place of the internment in the community and its activities. Many consider it vital to keep the legacy of the internment alive, noting that the need to remain vigilant about civil liberties, constitutional rights, and racism is as applicable today as ever. Some individuals, however, wonder if it is time to focus more energy on current and forward-looking issues. In their eyes, particularly with the success of the redress movement and the declining numbers of surviving internees, it is important for the Sansei and Yonsei generations to identify contemporary concerns and to lead Japanese American communities into the future.

There are signs that radiating effects of the internment remain crucial to many Nisei and Sansei. A recent *Wall Street Journal* article, titled "Decades On, a Legacy of War Still Haunts Japanese-Americans," describes the ongoing tensions within the community over a need to recognize and honor those who resisted the government's induction orders during the war. The draft resisters, who refused to serve while imprisoned by their own government, numbered more than three hundred. Many were convicted of violating the Selective Service Act and served time in prison. At the same time, Nisei veterans considered serving in the armed forces to be a way of demonstrating their loyalty to the United States and many viewed the actions of the resisters as cowardly or disloyal. Controversy stemming from these wartime differences between the views of veterans and resisters continues within the community.[24] Some feel it is time for healing to take place between various groups, while others object to any form of apology. For younger Sansei and Yonsei, recent coverage of this ongoing debate is likely to reinforce the salience of the internment in their lives, generating questions about their families' responses during the war, their thoughts about what they might have done under similar circumstances, and where they stand today on the current divisions. As a Sansei, I am saddened that Japanese Americans must still grapple with the emotional consequences of events forced upon them six decades ago.

MUSEUMS AND MONUMENTS

Developments aimed at public education can also serve to keep the internment in the future consciousness of all Americans. Museums such as the Japanese American National Museum in California and the Smithsonian Institution in Washington, D.C., have displays devoted to telling the story of the camps. New monuments, such as the National Japanese American Memorial in Washington, D.C., are dedicated to the wartime experiences of Japanese Americans. These monuments will expose a broader range of the population to the internment's historical significance. Monuments at various camp sites also exist. Although they are located in areas away from the travel routes of most Americans, they carry important symbolic significance for future generations of Japanese Americans who can visit former camp locations and see for themselves the actual areas where internees were held.

Numerous educational projects have also been developed through the assistance of the Civil Liberties Public Education Fund created by the redress legislation. Increasing numbers of books, videos, and curricular materials are becoming available to educate future generations of Americans—regardless of ethnic background—about the incarceration.

At the same time, technology has put us in greater touch with international and national events. We immediately hear news about tensions with Japan or other parts of Asia as well as race-related crimes and intimidation within our country. Increased access to this information may also serve to keep the legacy of the internment alive, as we are reminded of the dangers that can arise when Asian Americans are blamed for tensions in Asia or for stereotypes and angry sentiments in the United States. Moreover, recent reports indicate that the number of racial hate incidents has increased on college campuses and elsewhere.[25] These issues will confront the Yonsei and future generations of Japanese Americans as they move through adulthood.

In the course of my work I have come to appreciate the intergenerational effects of the internment more than ever. The range of these effects has been far-reaching, touching upon family communication, ethnic identity, and community relations. I have been sobered by the stories of loss and inspired by the stories of resiliency. I have also realized the importance of educating my own children about the experiences of their grandparents and great-grandparents, in the hope of sensitizing them to what preceded them and of encouraging them to prevent future injustices. Time does not heal all wounds. Indeed, as Sansei in my own research have pointed out, it is critical that the wounds of the internment remain known. I hope that both Japanese Americans and non-Japanese Americans—whether through monuments, books, or other media—will continue to recognize the significance of the internment.

NOTES

1. Yael Danieli, "Introduction: History and Conceptual Foundations," in *International Handbook of Multigenerational Legacies of Trauma*, ed. Yael Danieli (New York: Plenum, 1998), 9.
2. See Danieli for discussion of intergenerational transmission of trauma among these and other groups.
3. Nobu Miyoshi, "Identity Crisis of the Sansei and the American Concentration Camps," *The Pacific Citizen* 91 (1980): 41, 42, 50, 55.
4. Donna K. Nagata, "The Japanese American Internment: Exploring the Transgenerational Consequences of Traumatic Stress," *Journal of Traumatic Stress* 3 (1990): 47–69; Donna K. Nagata, *Legacy of Injustice: Exploring the Cross-Generational Impact of the Japanese American Internment* (New York: Plenum, 1993); Donna K. Nagata, "Intergenerational Effects of the Japanese American Internment," in Danieli, 125–39.
5. Linda Carr, "The Japanese-American Internment: The Transmission of Trauma to the Offspring of the Internees" (unpublished diss., Columbia University, 1993); Nancy N. Kawasaki, "The Japanese-American Internment Camp Experience: Intergenerational Patterns in Experiences With Racism, Coping Strategies, and Psychological Symptoms (unpublished diss., Ohio State University, 1997).
6. Sharon Yamato, *Moving Walls: Preserving the Barracks of America's Concentration Camps* (Sharon Yamato, 1998), 38.
7. See, for example, Sue Kunitomi Embrey, ed., *The Lost Years: 1942–1946* (Los Angeles: Moonlight Publications, 1972).
8. Gwendolyn M. Jensen, "The Experience of Injustice: Health Consequences of the Japanese American Internment" (unpublished diss., University of Colorado, 1997).
9. Nagata, *Legacy of Injustice*, 142.
10. Ibid.
11. Don T. Nakanishi, "Seeking Convergence in Race Relations Research: Japanese-Americans and the Resurrection of the Internment," in *Eliminating Racism: Profiles in Controversy*, ed. Phyllis A. Katz and Dalmas A. Taylor (New York: Plenum, 1988), 159–80.

12. Yasuko I. Takezawa, *Breaking the Silence: Redress and Japanese American Identity* (Ithaca: Cornell University Press, 1995).

13. Yamato, 34.

14. Ibid., 39.

15. Annie Nakao, "Sansei Dig Up Buried Roots," *San Francisco Examiner*, Sunday, May 26, 1996: C-1, C-4.

16. Satsuki Ina, "Counseling Japanese Americans: From Internment to Redress," in *Multicultural Issues in Counseling: New Approaches to Diversity*, ed. Courtland C. Lee, 2nd ed. (Alexandria, Virginia: American Counseling Association, 1997), 189–206; Satsuki Ina, *Children of the Camps: The Documentary* (USA, 1999).

17. Tina Kazumi Yamano, "Brooding Silence: A Cross-Sectional Study of Informal Learning, Socialization, and Child-Rearing Practices in a Japanese American Family" (unpublished diss., University of California, Los Angeles, 1994).

18. Ibid., 193.

19. Peter I. Rose, "Of Every Hue and Caste: Race, Immigration, and Perceptions of Pluralism," in *Annals of the American Academy of Political and Social Science* 530 (1993): 187–202.

20. Harry H. L. Kitano, Diane C. Fujino, and Jane Takahashi Sato, "Interracial Marriages: Where Are the Asian Americans and Where Are They Going?" in *Handbook of Asian American Psychology*, ed. Lee C. Lee and Nolan W. S. Zane (Thousand Oaks, Calif.: Sage, 1998), 233–60.

21. Amy Iwasaki Mass, "Interracial Japanese Americans: The Best of Both Worlds of the End of the Japanese American Community?" in *Racially Mixed People in America*, ed. Maria P. P. Root (Thousand Oaks, Calif.: Sage, 1992), 265–78; C. W. Stephan, "Ethnic Identity Among Mixed-Heritage People in Hawaii," *Symbolic Interaction* 14 (1991): 261–77.

22. Mass, "Interracial Japanese Americans."

23. Ibid., 266.

24. Norihiko Shirouzu, "Battle Scars: Decades On, a Legacy of War Still Haunts Japanese-Americans," *Wall Street Journal*, June 25, 1999, A1.

25. Arthur Levine and Jeanette C. Cureton, *When Hope and Fear Collide: A Portrait of Today's College Student* (San Francisco: Jossey Bass, 1998), 75.

PART II

FAMILY SECRETS

STEWART DAVID IKEDA

MIXING STORIES

FALL 1993: HOW CRUEL TO FIND YOURSELF HERE: in America's Dairyland, this old yellow house where Georgia O'Keeffe once lived; on Lake Monona, where Otis Redding died. In the year of Mogadishu, Rabin/Arafat, Pacific Trade, Baltic Europe and Russia, sit on the first porch you ever owned, watch the light soft-shoe across the lake, and catch a whiff of history. Chain-smoke, scratch items on your "to do" pad. Stranded in Madison, this Puritan town, listen down the phone to a friend describing the Manhattan skyline outside his window as if to a siren on a sex line. Kvetch about the dearth of baguettes, adult movies, dim sum. "I feel very ethnic." Say a little sadly, "Have to go teach my first class now."

197_: "You know what you are?" Grandpa said, eyeing me closely. Six o'clock shadow and happy hour made his expression mischievous. "A mutt, that's what. A mongrel." I became a mutt in 1970-something, before I learned of history, geography, race or any distance that distinguished me from family, friends, and universe. It would have been Friday evening, cocktail time in the white Philadelphia suburb; since the divorce, my father's parents took unofficial custody of me on weekends, holidays, and vacations. Some little ghoul on the schoolbus had called me "Chinky chongy" or "Nip" or, most likely, "Spic"—to look at me, almost any slur would do. Even "mutt": an epithet, I now know, meant to desensitize—a *hapa*,* half-something and half-something-else, racially mixed, but with echoes of "alone, adrift,

---

* From the Hawaiian hapa haole, literally "half-white"; formerly a derogatory term.

abandoned." For him, divorce symbolizes all of America's moral decline: our short memories, lust for complaint, and inability to go the distance. This was before I'd ever conceived of a creature, much less myself, as Japanese American, before my university studies inspired a novel exploring that identity in the context of World War II and my research uncovered that era's central truism, *shikata ga nai*. I now think he meant: As a mutt, you're left to wander, sniff for scraps. Only family is reliable, and now you can't even rely on them. Now you will rely on me. It can't be helped—*shikata ga nai*—but it can make you strong.

Fall 1993: Drive fast to campus, like you do when you still have out-of-state plates and are convinced you're just passing through. Park the car. Be anxious. Head to your first day of work at the AASP, Asian American Studies Program office. Get a key and photo I.D., be hustled around, introduced to people. Feel not ethnic enough. Smile, make connections. Doubt these Midwesterners are as friendly as they seem and wonder what secret, sordid perversions lurk in them. Feign fascination by the copier, ditto, and facsimile—learn where to leave mail for franking. Be relieved an office is found for you to share, where you'll meet with the young people you will teach about what you do and think. A small room, furnishings traditional black tin, lined with an officemate's intimidating array of books and ancient computer. Slide wide the window curtains, crane your neck, stiff as a scarecrow, and stop breathing to prevent fogging the glass. Feel important to have an almost-unobstructed lake view. Wonder at the tiny rushing sloops below. Wish your grandfather could see. Open the new class roster addressed to Professor Ikeda. Feel you've arrived somewhere.

Pushing yourself out into the campus, climb, climb up past Abe Lincoln seated in bronze at the peak of Bascom Hill. Nervous, short of breath, have a smoke anyway. Notice the vibrant foliage, the rolling lawn, the predominance of red motor scooters and young blond people; feel astonishingly Japanese. Catch a whiff of cows from the nearby ag school. Wonder: How did you come here—to a place where they study cows? Do deep breathing, then pierce the building—down the hall, and pass: Dean of Students Office.

Order yourself not to sweat, but do so profusely. Stop by your room, 202, inflate yourself, rocky-jawed, massive chest, proud patrician brow upright—be John Barrymore waiting in the wings. Tilt your great profile higher. Radiate confidence, authority as you walk. "Good afternoon, class!" Too loud. Flop your writer's bag—a laptop computer bag, pockets for stories, floppy disks, and pencils—on the table and be aware it's not a professor's case. Grip the

biggest piece of chalk, feel powerful to screech on the blackboard as you write
your name.

Pronounce it for them, both ways. Eye-key-duh: the East Coast, *hakujin*
way, how you said it for twenty years. Ee-keh-duh: the California way, how an
AASP professor must say it. Figure they'll mangle it anyway; recall one is from
Nagasaki and feel ashamed, figuring *you'll* mangle it with your hopelessly
Philadelphian accent. Feel more WASP than Japanese. Say, pronounce it how
you like, but you must spell it right. Tell them of junk mail to "Stuart D. Arca-
dia" or "Steward Akita." Provide exotic cultural background: Akita is a Japanese dog. Say, professional writers check their spelling.

Observe the word you've written—"Ikeda"—and realize its inadequacy.

Winter 1990–1991: This quest for "Ikeda" begins in Ann Arbor, where I start
my career as fledgling writer and Japanese American in the University of
Michigan fiction MFA Program. It leads me back fifty years to World War II,
the mythical temporal space of Back Then—when our young country com-
mandeered so much of the map to become a superpower. It is 1991: Cole
Porter's on the charts again, and Grandpa has just received mixed news—he's
been diagnosed with pulmonary fibrosis, an irreversible lung disease; simulta-
neously, a $20,000 government check in reparation for his wartime uprooting
arrives. While health allows it, he will take Grandma to Alaska, the only state
they've never seen, to celebrate their golden anniversary, a tragic, final trip. Redress lifts a veil of silence from my own family, our history, as it has for so many
Yonsei, and I am bursting with questions and extremely pissed off. Cornering
Grandpa, narrative vampire that I am, I demand, "Okay, what's the story? *All* of
it, straight—the whole thing."

And because I am not yet a *good* writer, I imagine the story must begin with a
bang—with a dramatic spectacle of war. I start with Pearl Harbor. What was it like?

But it is 1991, and America commemorates its own golden anniversary on
the airwaves—replaying World War II on the Discovery Channel, then on
CNN, and I learn what it was like firsthand. One night, in Nicholas Delbanco's
fiction workshop, we're about to dig into a story when a cleaning woman rattles
by with a monstrous cart of janitorial supplies and a transistor radio. She knocks.

"Um, sorry to barge in," she says. "We've just bombed Baghdad. Thought
you'd want to know." She rattles off again.

That week, I dream of an elderly Japanese man and a white boy outfitting a
scarecrow on a farm; a gusty, westward breeze rocks the straw sentinel, and I
know it's the aftershock of Little Boy extinguishing Hiroshima. The curious

image spurs six years' labor on a historical novel in which I can explore all the questions I could never ask my family. That's where this starts.

190_: On the West Coast of North America there lived an ambitious boy who'd seen something of the world. Though he considered himself—in the language of his day—a "bird of passage," he died there, too. But I get ahead of myself. Born second son on an island to the Far West of California, he early on heard and believed the gospel—the promotional campaigns and recruitment posters promising adventure, a good living, and the free pursuit of happiness. Perhaps he heard that Chinese travelers called America the Gold Mountain, and with his older brother—the *chonan*, the eldest—just coming of age, young Shigeki Ikeda was a little short on that metal then. Restless, bored as a teenager can be, of course he responded to those posters, those invitations. Borrowing the fare, he sailed far into the east, reveling in the sea breeze, elated by his youth, strength, courage, and enviable good looks. After many long Pacific days he landed somewhere on America's oceanic skirt, maybe Angel Island. Upon docking, he leaped from the deck and was amazed as the ground gave way beneath his feet, not gold-paved at all, but soft and clayey.

But young, strong, and very good-looking, he would mingle, mingle, mingle, talk to some savvy fellows, meet some sweet girls, buy a map and decide which town would get to have him. En route to that town, however, he noticed his wallet deflating and took jobs, only temporary, slinging fish, selling vegetables, painting houses, mowing lawns. He worked as a "schoolboy" for a rich family while he went to business school, where he learned of laws prohibiting him from owning property, but learned too the American saying, "Where there's a will, there's a way." Degree in hand, he was led by his pioneering, entrepreneurial spirit through many odd jobs, and although he was now not so young, he was still strong and very good-looking, thus optimistic. Then one day, he walked down a broad Tinseltown boulevard, electric with anticipation, his wallet warm and thick as a corned beef sandwich in his pocket, flipping a shiny quarter in the air until he tripped. The coin fell tinkling at his feet. Bending to retrieve it, he saw set into the concrete pavement a handprint and beside it—like an X on a treasure map—a winking gold star. Hungry for a piece of this pavement, he had a think. He needed American children. Donning his one dress suit, he had a photo taken in a fancy borrowed automobile and wrote to an uncle of his need for a wife—a fruitful one. After months of letters, exchanges of fuzzy, deceptive snapshots, the match was agreed upon.

Or so I imagine. There's so much in this story that my grandfather does not or cannot say.

Summer 197_: It was actually a *hakujin*, my mom, who first spilled the beans about World War II. Like me, she'd overheard the rare, veiled references to "camp," and imagined canoeing and bonfires, like at the summer cabin on Michigan's Lake Houghton where she finally heard the story. Mom's memory is cloudy, but I imagine: She and Grandpa smoking filterless butts, drinking gin into the night, loudly yapping about It, waking everyone. I can hear him booming: "The *dumbshit* Californians locked us up in *horse* stables! But *I* wasn't gonna stay there," and "Your mother-in-law gets mad when I say this, but I think, Hell, the Japs asked for it, too. All stuck together in these communities, you know, they're sitting ducks. It's easy to get a *bead* on them." The way Mom tells it, my grandmother "flew out of the bedroom like a ghost." I see her in a knee-length nightgown, maybe that sparkly hairnet, her face pale with night cream. "Don't!" she hissed. "Just don't!" She's a tiny, graceful woman (I'm only five-six, and when we hug, her hair brushes my chin), but the way she said, "Don't!" the two drunken loudmouths in the living room listened.

For a long time, I listened, too. If history is the tale of the victors, then I fear many Japanese American losers consider our omission from the textbooks natural, logical. Trying to recover and restore those scraps strewn about the editing room floor, I often wondered: What does Grandpa think about our interest in him, in this history? That we gather round him like orphans starving for those details he and our country have spent years forgetting? Does he feel like a man who's offered a few bucks for an antique rotting in his barn: *What, you wanna buy* this *old piece of junk?*

My own cloudy remembrances of those Houghton summers are of cameras flash-bleached white, Canon, Nikon, that Japanese shutterbug gene bred into Grandpa's bones. His archives contain miles of Kodachrome, Polaroid, Super 8s recording the first smile, trip, haircut or Big Wheel of his first grandson. His face was round and wide as a sandwich plate then, hair cropped like G.I. Joe's, his belly soft-round as I pressed into it, climbing up to probe his nostril with my pinkie. His loud, restless sleep habits made my grandparents often take separate rooms, so there was usually space in his king-size bed for me to slip into at night after pinching his nose to stop his snoring. I remember him teaching me to shave with a toy razor and pee standing up; the fumes as he tanked up his Olds after driving hours from work in Delaware to pick me up on Friday; how he came to Parents' Day at school, endured my excruciating violin recitals; how he carved out rituals for my life . . . as if for an orphan.

1917: A feisty and fisty boy, Carol Ikeda was born second son in a litter of nine. The Ikedas made a formidable gang of toughs in the tiny town of Havre, Montana, and after a few schoolyard rumbles they made the *hakujin* be their friends or else. There was Albert, the *chonan;* then sister Yuri; and himself, Carol; then brother Bill; and after a respite, Dorothy, then Otto, Don, and Ted. Later came sister Sue, who was adopted by the "rich" man who led the minuscule Japanese Association there. The organization did little more than bolster small business or hold picnics on the emperor's birthday, but it did form a language school where my great-grandma, Asako Arai, taught Saturday classes—an offense that would warrant her FBI arrest in 1941. Still, Carol managed not to learn Japanese until forced by business in middle age. For those kids, as for me, Japan mostly took the forms of a trade issue and martial arts movies; they could barely follow the foreign dialogue of the imported samurai film screenings, where they sat in the back throwing popcorn, aping the sword fights and grunts.

Havre was a railroad town. The Ikeda clan lived in an old wooden boxcar on the Great Northern property. The boys slept sideways like sardines in one bed and used their dog, Brownie, as a footsie-warmer; the girls and folks had their own beds. The thin-walled boxcar was heated by a cast iron coal stove with a reservoir for heating water, enough to fill a large galvanized tub once a week. "In the winter it got so cold, Mom would stoke that stove up to warm us while we took our baths Japanese-style: the old man first, then the boys, then the girls, by age. Mom always got the dirtiest water, going last."

Winter 1990: Exactly how thick is blood, how determined heredity? I'm left to wonder what I'll pass on (besides bad teeth, bowed legs) along with the name of the C. K. Ikedas. My grandfather was an accomplished industrial chemist who could tell you the precise difference in molecular heft between H_20 and that conglomerate of corpuscles. To me, "acid" and "base" are what you hallucinate on and slide into before you're tagged out, but he tried to give me science, save me from a life of destitute artsy-fartsiness. Despite strong reservations and an essential frugality, he was in fact the one to pay my tuition to a performing arts school, where I began farting artfully.

Still, I'm part Asian, thus naturally scientific. My concern with heredity's chemistry has recently become more dire, as the origins of his pulmonary fibrosis remain uncertain. His doctor claims it's not hereditary and thinks it incredible odds that the same disease recently killed brother Don. I've no proof, but I suspect the culprit may be industrial chemistry practices Back Then. How the hapless experimenters baked untested materials in kilns, sucking in toxic vapors, protected only by goggles or maybe oven mitts. Thus speculating, I once joked in typical American fashion, "This smells to me of a lawsuit."

"No," Grandpa said, more serious than I had been, "the company took care of their workers. They were good to me." The Quaker overseer who offered him his first and last job after internment also helped with moving costs and a housing search.

Anyway, now retired in Arizona, my grandfather has rotten lungs, a gold watch, and many patents. If your home is in America and contains paint, carpeting, or fireproof materials, chances are you're surrounded by some of his work. I'm proud of his contribution to the world, and used to think it an adequate (albeit invisible) legacy. I was wrong.

Christmas 1990, he wants to bequeath something else to us, more enduring, and does it in a wordless manner my family regards as "Japanesey." Outfitting us like Green Berets with hiking boots, Nikons, Canons, and a heavy video setup, he drives my fiancee Tasha, cousin Keith, and me out to the ruins of the Gila River concentration camp. The only life in this desert wasteland is a tiny orchard of fruit bushes covered with burlap to protect them from freezing at night. Even in December, though, days are so hot that I am sweating as I bounce along shooting video footage: framing Keith on the site of his mother's birth, here in the makeshift hospital now reduced to a few concrete slabs sunken into the scorched dirt. There: sitting upended, bleached and half-buried like a dinosaur's skull, a porcelain toilet—from Back Then? The only testament to the Japanese American civilization that lived, loved, birthed, and died in this place is an awkward concrete monument atop a low crest. A horseshoe-shaped platform pointlessly semicircled by thick pillars bracing nothing, it looks like an abandoned UFO landing pad. The Pima and Papago residents of this reservation have made some use of this otherwise useless structure: empty rifle casings and shattered glass bottle targets litter its floor; its pillars are streaked with spiky, bored graffiti. Useless, except to make a mark: standing here, amidst the endless expanse of cactused nothingness, of dull, red-brown sameness, one can say at least, "I don't know where I'm standing, but I am standing somewhere." From the heights, you can still see the rows upon rows of foundation blocks outlining the barracks. So many. You had not thought there would be so many. The tape runs out.

Back at home, we opened a pack of audio cassettes, aimed the microphone at him, and pressed "record." "Okay," he said. "What's your question?"

190_: Shigeki first came to Montana as a rep for a Seattle oriental trading company that sold Asian foods to the railroad workers. In entrepreneurial fashion, he identified these lonely men's other hungers and devised a slew of "bright ideas to make him a millionaire." He tried photography (that bug again), built a darkroom and studio. He had only Japanese customers, though not for lack of imagination. In a brilliant stroke, he bought the chassis of a dead automobile, wherein his customers posed for prospective brides, wearing an air of American affluence. Too much overhead, too few Japanese, the enterprise failed. His restaurant project failed even faster.

The Nisei Ikedas' earliest secret fantasies—one cannot say "ambitions"— were to be railroad engineers. Havre's highest social stratum, those men had "*a lot* of money." Their children enjoyed elaborate birthday fests, with splendid party favors befitting the "top of the heap." Then there were the laborers who worked at the roundhouse and serviced the engines. A boiler-maker was a skilled man who could rivet and weld. On the crews, the flagmen placed torpedoes on both flanks of idle trains to anchor them in place. Then there were those at the bottom: the boiler washers. When the engines came in, they cleaned the ashes out of the fire box, cooled it down, then scrubbed the inside of the boiler, scraping slake from its ribs, unplugging the tubes of mineral deposits. The work called for small men, Chinese and Japanese. Finally, after several failed projects, as times grew lean and the family plain grew, a twenty-something Asako commanded, "You're going to get a *job* with the Great Northern," and Shigeki climbed under the heap.

Shigeki knew the destructive capacity of nine idle children. His "bright ideas" made Carol moan "because they just meant work for us boys. He was "What do you call them? A manic depressive. When he got these ideas, he'd work the hell out of Billy and Albert and me. We'd go along with the program, knowing pretty soon he'd get depressed and forget about everything, or go out of business. The downs would only last so long, but when he was up . . . oh boy!"

With a steady income, still Shigeki moonlighted. "He was going to make a mint raising rabbits to eat and sell. He had us build hutches underground in the dirt floor of the garage; we sectioned it off and dug holes, put a box down there where the rabbits could live. Rabbits are called bucks and does, but he always called them bucks and *sows*, and we never corrected him because he was always right. He'd put the 'sow' and buck in the pen for a couple of days, and we'd watch them fornicate. We fed them coarse bran from a hundred-pound sack (Pop thought, Hmm, if it's good for rabbits, it's good for us!—but we revolted). After a while, all these little rabbits popped out of the ground, ran around the garage, and we separated them from the mother. The problem was that after watching them grow, they became *pets*. When they reached a certain age, my mother would say, 'It's time to slaughter them,' and we had to decide which ones to eat. You had to hold it up by the ears and hit it in the back of the neck with an axe handle, an operation that can kill your appetite. Mom cooked them, but when we sat for dinner, Albert said, 'I'm not eating the bunny.' He got ham, so then I said, 'I'm not eating it either.' She said, '*You're* eating rabbit!' But we all refused, and that project failed, too."

But Grandpa admits, "Pop worked hard, you know. He worked in the shops at the railroad roundhouse from four to eleven at night, then got up in the morning and took in home laundry. After us boys picked up the dirty wash, lugging it home on a wagon for a nickel tip, he would boil and scrub it in suds in the basement. Mom pressed sheets, tablecloths, and linens in a commercial mangle. At about two in the afternoon, he'd take us out to the yard and hit us pop flies, then go to the roundhouse."

Shigeki Ikeda, I think, believed in American one-upsmanship until the end. When the war came and the FBI took his wife, he was easily convinced to join the advance crews who built their own prison in Manzanar, in exchange for first dibs on the best barracks for his family. It was his final failed enterprise. Through some mishap causing a family rift that has lasted fifty years, the other Ikedas were sent to Gila River. Shigeki did not complain, though. Yes, times were temporarily tough, but he did not plan to die here.

Winter 1990–1991: For us newly Nipponized, these wartime revelations spawn outrage, and outrage gives way to resentment: *Why didn't you tell us?* Then: *How could you sell out like that? Why didn't you revolt?* Our grandparents could say, "Well, you didn't *ask*," and "You weren't *there*," but they don't. Instead, they struggle to remember themselves at twelve, fifteen, twenty—the Jack Armstrong wannabes, the teenage lovers, the collegiates—and to relate just when they became burdened with alien parents and enemy genes and things started to go wrong. So we press them and press them until by the end of the millennium young Japanese Americans will sometimes say they're tired of hearing about the camps.

Yet, Christmas 1990, the camps are *all* I want to hear about—the only thing I really hear. I am almost disappointed to learn that Grandpa wasn't actually interned at Gila River with my grandmother. That he managed a release from the temporary camp at Tulare to start school and find a job, a home for his family, strikes me not as lucky or clever or just. Rather, it dulls the luster of my outrage, distorts my self-image as samurai-poet defender against an absolute injustice, my family's oppression. For my college studies and politicization have led me to conclude that the power of this story rests in what was done *to* Japanese Americans, not what they themselves felt and thought and did. There is great drama inherent in a fifty-year national lie and outsized racial violence, and I am not yet a fine enough novelist to see beyond the most obvious spectacle. As an older man and better writer, I will observe those minority students who enter my class like rabid wolves, still feeling raw, betrayed after taking intro lessons in the tale of the losers. Their poems are propaganda, their stories antiwhite wish-fulfillments, characters caricatures of victim-heroes. In critiques, I will gently say, "Yes, I see Japanese America in this story, but I don't see a Japanese American."

Christmas 1990, however, I too am thinking: *Screw the rabbits.* "Yes, yes," I say, impatient as a vampire at dawn. "Back to the evacuation. How many guards were there? Did they have bayonets on their guns?"

Now that redress has convinced Grandpa, like other Nisei, that he can at last speak without shame, it annoys him that I persist in asking the wrong questions. So he sets out to construct an alternate record to my novel, to tell his own story in his own, nonliterary way. He decides to transfer his gazillion old photos and films to video, doing a voiceover himself. We buy a top of the line, high-def dubbing VCR with floating heads, a slide easel, a titling machine, a sound mixer; hooked to multiple decks, remotes, and the stereo, these make the den an unnavigable jungle of patch cords. Thus he begins reliving his life again, rabbits and all. Although ten hours of tape barely make a dent in his archives and he finally gives up, I get to see many images for the first time, including their newlywed shots. How handsome! How dashing were his wide, double-breasted jackets, baggy pants, suspenders, black wingtips; his hair thick and wavy, cheeks high, chin strong. And my grandmother, in those fabulous shoulder-padded suit dresses, matching satin gloves snaking up her arms, a chic veiled bonnet, heels and those stockings with seams, hair flipped up like an Andrews Sister. They looked like movie stars then, and full of promise.

Spring 1942: At my age, the newlyweds hung on promises—made by Washington, by church, by Madison Avenue—of a better life to come. What did they have to lose? Any step away from California, where they met and married, must have been in the right direction. In April 1942, Grandpa's college mentor, the Nobel laureate Linus Pauling, helped secure his release from the Tulare stables to a Ph.D. fellowship at the University of Wisconsin. They planned that my grandmother, now pregnant and due in August, would follow once he'd settled in Madison. A hitch occurred, however, that remains between them to this day.

I imagine the young father-to-be rattling along on the train, stretching over two seats, thankful that no passenger will sit with him. Leaning heavily against the window, its shade pulled up showing only desert, he runs his palm over the worn vinyl onto a dog-eared copy of *Life*. He reads the Science section first, always that. He reads war news of Italy, where brother Bill—already in the service before Pearl Harbor—has insisted on promotion from sidelined mechanic to front-line paratrooper, and brother Albert will soon go for broke. I imagine he skips the review of a new Disney film starring that ridiculous, speech-impaired duck in a navy uniform. And what about the feature on the girls' beauty school, the Before and After photos like so many mug shots? All the young, fat-faced round eyes, lips painted into harlequin lines, blond bobs curled at the edge; on their knees, pins bristling in their mouths like daggers in the teeth of movie pirates, hemming each other's party gowns? Does he desire them?

"No," he told me. "Interracial dating was out. It was inviting trouble. You just didn't date white girls, though white guys asked Yuri out a few times." He *could* date other Asians, maybe blacks and Chicanos, but Asako forbade this and besides, who wants to belong to a club that will accept them?

"Every face," the *Life* article tells him, "has its own standards of beauty. The brown mascara that enlivens Betty's eyes would make Joan's look tired and narrow."

A technology buff, he also scans the ads, promises from GE and Philco: the toasters, fridges, and washer-dryers that are currently war *materiel*, but all well-earned and indispensable for the Atomic Age, after Victory. At prolonged station stops, he wrangles with vigilante telegraph-operators and petty station-masters on guard against an enemy invasion of Sacramento. "Who are you? You a Jap? You got documents?" Finding a bench in the empty concourse, he props his feet on the suitcase—maybe smokes a Lucky, nods to the colored shoeshine man ordered by the stationmaster to keep an eye on the Jap. He rises with his bags to approach a nervous redhead behind a concession counter. Keenly aware of his pitiful, shrinking store of small bills and coins, like a hemorrhage of currency, he opens and closes his fist inside his pocket, jangles the change—it will become a lifelong habit.

"Can you take my order, please?" he asks. The girl blinks at him, rooted to the counter. *It speaks.* He repeats the request. What to say? Loose lips sink ships, but she nods, decides to risk national security. Oh, fragrant Liberty! A medium burger strewn with sautéed onions, sizzling french fries, a frothy malted. Does he release a heroic, appreciative belch? Say *Itadakimasu* or Grace? He wipes his mouth with a paper napkin, then mangles it into a tattered, browned ball—also a future habit—his most annoying—and tosses the remains onto the counter. He will remember this Sacramento.

Spring-Summer 1991: I begin to feel my first novel going down the tubes, and feel punch-drunk with the realization that I don't understand my grandfather at all, not really, except in that irksome, roller-coaster logic that comes with love. It begins during the Gulf War.

I learn quite a lot about what happened to him during World War II through watching news of Operation Desert Shield on CNN. It begins when a newscaster announces that someone with enough brass has called for FBI surveillance of Detroit's sizable Arab American population. Grandpa thinks it a sound idea, and I fear he means it, just as he means it when he insists that Arab American soldiers who refuse to fight in the Gulf should be "locked up."

"How can you say that?" I howl. "How can you of all people say that?"

His brothers, he insists, had to make the same hard choices: They bought American, they fought the Japanese.

I can't let this ride because of The Note. In the sort of profound cosmic irony that drives people to religion or revolution or drink, our argument comes on the same week I first saw an actual copy of the national apology. Of some 120,000 former internees, half lived to see the 1988 Civil Liberties Act authorize $20,000 restitution; my grandparents were among the far fewer still who lived to see the mailman clap the postbox lid shut on that check and the accompanying modest memo. The crisp white half-sheet stationery gave no return address but "THE WHITE HOUSE, WASHINGTON." Simple type: a 10-point Courier, block format, left-justified. It's not everyday one gets a personal note from the President, and with such a limited target-mailing, it is worth reprinting here in its brief entirety:

> A monetary sum and words alone cannot restore lost years or erase painful memories; neither can they fully convey our Nation's resolve to rectify injustice and to uphold the rights of individuals. We can never fully right the wrongs of the past. But we can take a clear stand for justice and recognize that serious injustices were done to Japanese Americans during World War II.

In enacting a law calling for restitution and offering a sincere apology, your fellow Americans have, in a very real sense, renewed their traditional commitment to the ideals of freedom, equality, and justice. You and your family have our best wishes for the future.

Signed "Sincerely, George Bush," the President's script makes it appear more like "Guy Burl," and only future history can attest to its sincerity. Grandpa, however, thought it sincere enough to vote for Bush in his losing reelection bid.

"That's a concession," I say, "not an apology."

"It's symbolic," he says. "It's something."

His neighbors at Ahwautukee Retirement Village—playing poker at the rec center, putting over the golf course, or leaning over backyard fences—have been slow to renew their commitment. "It's not right," one told him. "Why should you get *all that dough?*"

"It's not enough," he replied, but he never told them the rest of the story—of lost homes and property, contracts and promises and psyches broken, of lives uprooted, wasted, and extinguished. I've met some of these friendly family men—veterans like my mom's dad, like George Bush, who occasionally reunite with their squadrons to recall their glory days. Some of them helped my research, doling out war stories as generously as sidewalk pamphleteers. I'm sure they take redress as another example of crybaby liberal abuse of the greatest country in the whole blammed world, but don't think poorly of my grandfather. As he wheezes off in his golf cart, they might shrug and say, "Aw, Carol's all right. Nice work if you can get it, though."

My grandfather is a real patriot. Before I was a skeptical global villager, he raised me to be a patriot, too. Not the gaudy kind—not Old Glory boxer shorts, styrofoam Miss Liberty crowns, or plastic mini-flags; but with the intensity of a man trying to convince himself that all's well, he often took me on excursions into Philadelphia's Old City, where I know every inch of Independence Mall—the Bell, the Hall, Betsy Ross's House. His penultimate vacation before the illness was a seniors' mini-course in Washington, where he and Grandma visited the Capitol, learned the intricacies of checks and balances and the circuitous route a piece of paper can make around that town. Today, in the jaded folds of academia, I am frequently ashamed of my impulses to patriotism—to be, when I let my guard down, a believer.

During my next visit, in the throes of now-Desert Storm, we patriotically spend our nights watching the fireworks on CNN. As is our custom, we sit with personal rice bowls of Chex Party Mix, which Grandma makes by the barrel. We watch the fancy new "smart bombs" gut high-rises with, the Pentagon assures us, "surgical precision." In my obsessive research of the war after the war to end all wars, I had found an ad for the B-17 Flying Fortress, the Ultimate Weapon of Victory. "Precision bombing will win the war!" its makers proclaimed. Equipped with the "incredibly accurate Norden bomb sight, which hits a 25-foot circle from 200,000 feet," some 330 of these careful planes carpet-bombed Dresden. Hailed as "the poorest targets yet developed," about 22,000 of these were downed before Victory. In my novel, a slightly fictionalized B-17 bombs a halfway-secured Pacific island, killing a beloved character in what today CNN calls "friendly fire."

"'Surgical precision,'" I say sarcastically. "Isn't that great?"

"Humph," he says. He says that he's not long for this world, and so doesn't really care, but thinks "we should just drop the bomb over there instead of dragging it out."

"What?" I yell. Maybe he's just feeling picked on, but I don't think so. He batters back my protests with (what it now occurs to me was a largely Asian) history. Korea. Vietnam. Cambodia. He's lived to see much, and the lesson he imparts to his grandson is: *shikata ga nai.* "There's nothing you can do about it," he says. "Drop the bomb: we'll lose a lot less lives in the end." With frightening surety, he says, "I've seen it all happen before, and mark my words: you'll see it happen again." Then, he adds, "If you live long enough." It's on the following day that I'll fly out of Phoenix and my grandparents will leave on their anniversary trip to Alaska where, amidst the icebergs and caribou, he catches a near-fatal pneumonia, driving his already weakened lungs into their accelerated, relentless deterioration.

Impatient with Desert Storm, I beg him to read my manuscript. He turns off the war and dutifully disappears with a red pencil and my book, which he returns the next day with unsettlingly few margin notes. "I can't help much," he admits. I can tell he doesn't like it. "I wasn't in the army, of course; Uncle Bill could help you there. You'd have to ask Grandma about camp."

Spring 1942: After Sacramento he heads to Montana, where sister Sue's foster family is in dire straits. A boycott has driven her father, the "rich" Japanese Association leader, out of business, into a borrowed shack and poor health, and Carol thinks they'd have done better in camp. Almost broke, he takes Sue out to buy her much-needed eyeglasses. From Montana, a heartline trip up and down the country's belly, and finally: Madison. He first sees Lake Mendota, so lovely in summer, with boaters, bathers, and picnickers. He feels he's arrived somewhere. He writes a note to Grandma of his plans to bring her out of camp.

Then, reporting at the university, he presents his papers and says, "I'm ready to start my fellowship."

"I'm sorry," he's told. "They declared the university off-limits to anyone of Japanese ancestry." Word of a new navy program had just come down from the Dean of Students Office the day before.* "You can't matriculate here. Stick around anyway. Maybe something can be found for you to do." ("Well," Grandpa says, "I stuck around about two weeks. *Nothing.* Nobody would *touch* me.") He then goes to Chicago, where sister Yuri lives exiled, and spends the summer seeking work, applying to other schools. One scholar at Penn State, shooting down the application, writes, "You don't have it so bad. Just think of all our boys who have to go to fight overseas in Germany." He could not know, of course, of the Nisei begging to enlist, and those soon to be drafted right out of camp; nor of how impossible it was for Carol to imagine short, gentle Billy being pooped out of an airplane into the smoke-filled clouds above Italy. Carol is himself nervous about being drafted, but this turns out to be unnecessary: his lonely wife writes from Gila River, and now he's a father.

Summer 1992: To be American is to accept the incursion of technology into the most intimate nooks of one's life. Exiting the flying metal tube after mere hours to find that Detroit has become Phoenix can still astound me, like an audience volunteer at a hocus-pocus show who has survived the magician's saw. I ride the airport moving stairs; the exit doors swing wide, open sesame; I don't take these things for miracles. The first time I see Grandpa's miraculous portable breathing apparatus—his "leash," we joke, in the manner that those in deepest denial make light of the horrific—is in August, on my birthday. On a bench outside baggage claim, I wolf down smokes and fistfuls of mints before the folks come to fetch me. "No smoking near the house," I'd been warned. "There's this new machine, this air problem."

When their bargelike white Buick pulls up, I cannot see through its tinted glass. Grandma steps out of the driver's side (I always forget how small she is) to open the trunk. I hug and kiss her, the way I've reluctantly learned to from Tasha's family, who are Soviet Jews, touchers, squeezers, hand-jivers and knee-patters; their kisses last for minutes, alternating between cheeks, wet and loud, as if afraid to miss a spot. My grandmother's cheek is very, very soft.

---

* Universities engaged in military research did not accept students relocating from camp.--Ed.

Opening the passenger door, I find Grandpa curled up uncomfortably, his hand resting on a foot-long, burnished steel oxygen tank set at his side like a lapdog. From its snout, a length of clear plastic tube hoops through his belt like Indiana Jones's bullwhip, then runs up his thin chest, bifurcating at his upper lip, nestling at last in his nostrils. Its noise shocks me—I'd expected a hiss, but this travel tank's regulator delivers air only every other breath: *whiss, click, whiss, click*. I swallow my alarm and the impending joke I feel compelled to make. I plant a big, beefy Jewish kiss on his cheek—it is scratchy; he says even shaving winds him these days—and let it linger. I don't look at his face for fear of seeing it redden.

Back at their low ranch house, I offer to lug the tank inside, but he's determined to go it alone as long as he can. The house is cool but bright with pure Arizona sunlight. It smells clean—Grandma makes certain to keep it dustless now. I follow Grandpa in and out again onto the back patio. He disconnects his portable tank, hooks up to a new umbilicus, several yards long attached to a machine in the porch corner; the size and shape of a plain basement dehumidifier, it clanks and gurgles, punctuated by a little muffled bell, and now my grandfather sounds like Darth Vader. Watching this ritual, already so natural to him, I'm made stupid with heartbreak and fascination.

"Pretty fancy piece of equipment you got there," I say. Technology: I'd imagined a new west wing, a great looming supercomputer, like a CAT-scan suite at a hospital. How can such a rickety tin can sustain life? "Um, what about blackouts?" The model Boy Scout is always prepared: a man who does his taxes early, opens college funds as soon as the rabbit dies, and who, as I learned that visit, had already arranged his own death, funeral, house sale, and future life-care for his wife. Backup tanks for several days sleep in every room—some lean and short as house cats, one massive as the cannons I played on when he took me to Valley Forge as a kid. By the guest room waits a collapsed, lightweight wheelchair "just in case."

We talk much that visit. Yet, he subtly makes clear I am still asking the wrong questions when, after hours of taped interviews, he sneaks off and breathlessly, secretly answers the *right* ones. I will discover this only much later, getting around to the transcriptions at home. Wearing my Walkman, I listen to his secret story to me, his wheezing so lifelike on Memorex. Finally I notice how animated he grows recalling a particularly memorable Fourth of July in Havre, when a stray rocket ignited the entire pile in one dazzling explosion. Not until transcribing the two dozen tapes do I see how deeply ensconced he was in the past, speaking pages of direct dialogue in character voices, even providing sound effects, banging on a table, clinking a glass, his descriptions lively with onomatopoeia.

Illnesses and accidents of the body are etched in his memory. The bright red quarantine sign hung on their door when Albert and Asako contracted typhoid. A battered Albert in the hospital, his leg shattered after being struck by a motorcycle. Or when Albert chopped off his finger trying to stop the blades of a neighbor's lawnmower, and Asako had run back with the weeping Carol, found the tip, preserved it in ethyl alcohol. Shigeki: his appendix rupturing, or being robbed and beaten in Chicago after camp.

For as long as I can remember, Grandpa's palette has been dull, his ear tin, maybe due to his hidden sinus and breathing problems. Yet, most of his boyhood memories are olfactory, culinary, and incredibly vivid—such as the infamous "gardening at night." Though he and Albert had briefly been Boy Scouts, they quit, disillusioned when their leader was arrested for theft. With such a model, they joined a band of little pirates, white and yellow, that was infamous among neighboring farms for its nocturnal raids, stealing chickens, corn, apples, tomatoes. Hauling the loot back to their forest campsite, they had royal feasts and afterwards drew straws to see who must share a tent with one awkward, stinky boy who always peed in his sleep. Early morning, they returned to town, stole milk from stoops, some sugar and ice from outdoor storage bins, and made ice cream behind the school.

"We were always hungry," Grandpa says.

With boyish glee, he recalls hiding with Billy in the putrid-smelling outhouse, trying not to gag or giggle as Yuri sought them nearby. He describes his before-school chores, collecting dirty linens for his folks' laundry service, hugging a newlywed couple's balled-up, sticky sheets and being overwhelmed by an alien musk. Or the thousand reeking fryer chickens he beheaded, plucked, and gutted for a living one year.

"Nothing tastes good anymore," he now says. "Can't smell a damned thing."

Winter 1993: So much of the story is lost, fragmented. Why did Asako immigrate? Was she a picture bride? With the rare distinction of having graduated from the Nippon Joshi dai-gakku, the women's college in Tokyo, and from a prosperous enough family, what could have drawn her across the Pacific to Shigeki Ikeda? How did such a woman, whom the mayor of Tokyo himself congratulated at graduation, arrive in this hostile land, where she was barred from becoming American yet punished for remaining Japanese, bounced around federal pens, then dumped in the desert? Later, she was relocated to Chicago, tired and old, so old that my only memory is of a shriveled munchkin—like the Jedi master Yoda—whom Grandpa had to carry several blocks from the parked car to the restaurant on her last Mother's Day. America: where she raised her litter out of a boxcar in the desperate Montana winters to be surgeons and chemists and businessmen, who saw her at last become American, like them, but hardly knew her at all. How can it be that the Nisei Ikedas, and her umpteen grandchildren and great-grand-children could never, ever manage to ask the one, true question: *Why?*

"Pop was kind of quiet," my grandfather says, shrugging. "And Mom: we were always curious, you know, but you just couldn't ask her those kinds of things. Then it was too late."

In the course of this writing, Tasha's Israeli grandmother, Sara, passed away. A tough, round woman as bellicose as Attila, alluring as a starlet, and proud as the most powerful matriarchs can be, she was an art collector, physi-cian, and lifelong Zionist who witnessed the rise and fall of both the Reich and the USSR. Mere months earlier, she visited during our first week in Madison. We sightsaw, hiked, tested local cuisine, swam every morning in Lake Monona. I suspect she knew she was ill. The news that she'd fallen into a brief coma stirred a flurry of phone calls and flight arrangements. I tried then, really tried to help Tasha rehearse the last scene, to guess what was important to say, to do.

"Tell her you're fine," I said. "Promise her you'll be happy," I suggested. "Tell her *we're* fine. Tell her we take care of each other." Maybe that wasn't im-portant, though. "Tell her you'll be a professor. Tell her you're good and smart and respected." Or, "Say nothing: it's enough to just be there." So we re-hearsed, but I'd lost Tasha in the eye of the hurricane, and really I was talking to myself. After I put her on the plane, I raced home to call my grandfather. I didn't want to scare him, but I had to tell him about Sara, because I wanted to say, "You did a good job. You led a good life. You've been a good man."

I couldn't say this, though, and perhaps I won't know why until I'm his age. What I can do is be of use, to write and leave a trace.

190_: En route to the fairground, little Carol chased the annual parade of cir-cus carts and animals and freaks down First Street, Havre's main drag. "We couldn't afford to pay our way in to see the show," he explains. "Instead, we'd work for the circus people—help them erect the tents, unrolling the canvas and carrying the small tent poles. We'd carry water for the elephants, horses, and other animals. At first, we'd take our tickets, go in for the matinee, then never return at night to finish our work, so the crew foreman began holding articles of clothing hostage. Well, after a few years of this, we all wised up. We made sure to wear our worst clothes to the circus."

December 1993: If redress permitted him to tell his story, and I badgered him to, his own body now demands it. It's been a record-setting, miserable winter here in Madison, and even in Phoenix, and I'm concerned. After Alaska, I admit I braced myself for a deathwatch, but his Boy Scout readiness paid off. A golf cart and the travel tanks let him play nine holes, go to movies and museums, dine out. But winter severely limits socializing since, with his steroid-weakened immune system, a mere sniffle or mild flu can be deadly. The "just in case" wheelchair now gets frequent use. The steroids also make him hyper, though, and one day he telephones me with an astounding proposition. Fueled by a long-standing, umm, *difference of opinion* with a relative who also meant to compile a family history, he has decided that *he* wants to work on a biography.

"She'll mess it all up, so I'm taking over," he informs me. "And I've decided *you'll* write it."

"Really?" Trying to convince him I won't starve as an artsy-fart, I had sent him copies of my first two post-MFA publications, both stories about young, contemporary, urban black characters. "These are good," he decided. "I wasn't crazy on that novel, but you've gotten a lot better." So having passed his test, I say, "It'll have to be honest—no holds barred."

"I know you won't be able resist taking your 'poetic license,'" he says. "So I'm gonna edit it."

February 1994: The process of helping each other peel the layers of years and habits is touchy. Each day with my own work and freelance deadlines, I sit at my computer and flip through files—my work or his? That book review or my family history? A resume item or an enormous home-made Christmas gift—and will next Christmas be too late? When I sit transcribing, the headset's sponge earphones warm over my ears, and hearing him talking, wheezing, talking, I know my fingers are in a race against his lungs. He's lost weight, he says. No appetite. Can't sleep.

"Take vitamins!" I prescribe over the telephone. "Don't entertain guests."

The deadline sometimes sits crushing my fingertips, unmoving, like the succubus that sits on my own chest on nights of uneasy sleep.

"Keep warm," I tell him. "Don't go outside. Don't forget to eat."

Compiling his memories, I divine thematic patterns of labor and hunger, going beyond typical immigrant education and work ethics to an ethic of survival. Beauty, wisdom, and even love are infrequent characters in his tales. Instead, the greatest compliment he can bestow is: "She had a hard life, but she worked hard. She put food on the table."

One prepubescent summer, he lied about his age to join a railroad extra-gang, netting a buck a day. They lived in boxcars and breakfasted on coffee, eggs, toast, sour-milk pancakes: "The food wasn't all that great, but there was a lot of it." He started as a waterboy but was too small to carry the full buckets. Then they made him a gandy dancer, shoveling gravel beneath the wooden ties or extracting bent spikes with a crowbar, until a division inspector spotted him and sent him home. Two summers later, he returned to work for three exhaust-ing months, and by the time he quit, school began immediately. He com-plained bitterly that he'd had no vacation at all, and Asako sniffed in her cool way, "Well, if you don't like that kind of menial labor, then you'd better get some education." And at fifteen, Carol "got ambition."

"I did it." The intolerance of the self-made man—like that of the reformed smoker—can be violent. Somewhere, sometime, someone told my grandfather, "Pick yourself up by your bootstraps, Jap!" and he did it. We argue about wel-fare, immigration: My ready-made liberal defenses are loaded and cocked on my tongue-tip—charges of class privilege, of displaced self-loathing—but fal-ter. Does the fact that he maximized a few acts of kindness from strangers com-prise collaboration with the Man? Where do brainwashing and repression end and his native, ethical disdain for the culture of complaint begin? And what privilege can I attribute to his skin—what doors opened to him as a yellow man, not brown or black?

Certainly not this door to the Dean of Students Office in Bascom Hall, a door I pass daily en route to class. Grandpa: how it must baffle you, to work your whole life to secure for me a privilege I now criticize—to ensure that this door would never slam on another Ikeda, a Jap, even as my work here in Madi-son sends me spiraling back to you, desperate to recover what remains Japanese American in me before it is too late. *What do you make of me?* I want to ask, but cannot, just as I couldn't quite muster the heart to dig in about the Arab Amer-ican soldiers, welfare, affirmative action, forced assimilation.

"I did it," he says, and I feel that to argue—to say, "At what expense?"— would be to say, "No, you've been had."

"What is a mutt?" asks the AASP professor—a question that must be an-swered in the light of, and not in spite of, love. My class discusses critical issues of authority, representation, political coalition, models of assimilation and cul-tural pluralism; we read Robert Olen Butler and the anthology *Aiiieeeee!*, ask-ing: is Asian Americanism a birthright or a sensibility? I explain that my maternal grandfather was a good man, a sports-loving country doctor of an old

WASP family, who spent the war bombing the Japanese in Burma, ostensibly to defend the very liberties denied to my paternal grandfather, also American, a good man, ousted from his home, stripped of property, and imprisoned *as* a Japanese. These men—in their work ethic, concern for propriety, and profound distaste for public displays of emotion, intimacy, sensuality, complaint, wealth, or anything else—often seem interchangeable, or at least harmonious. Mom's lines hail from the United Kingdom, some Irish and Italian. She delights to point out genetic quirks: "You're getting my double chin. You've got my cowlicks." My "Japanese chest" is bald but for a few sprouts of wirelike hair ringing my aureoles, my "Italian" nipples.

"Stew," Tasha often jokes, "is Japanese and WASP, but also Italian: he has passionate emotions, but can't express them." Very funny. True: I've inherited a double-dosage will to silence, and the resulting chronic, teeth-grinding jaw aches. Today, Mom said she'll kill me if I write about her in this essay ("A true WASP makes the paper only thrice: birth, marriage, and the obituary"); Tasha has forbidden me to write *certain* things. And how do I write what it meant to my newlywed grandmother that each envelope from the Midwest arrived already opened, stamped by camp censors, and without the train ticket that it was *supposed* to contain? How do I write what it meant to lie with her legs strapped open on the rough gurney in the desert prison hospital, pressing my aunt into the world feeling utterly alone, abandoned, betrayed, when all she will say to this day is, "He wasn't there"?

Negotiating the distances between Burma, Gila River, and Madison demands a kind of honesty, but I'm not eager to hurt or embarrass my family, and I've had to be clever. No wonder my old mentor Charles Baxter characterized my more confessional (and rare) autobiographical writings as "relentlessly theatricalizing, cavalier and distancing."

If it's a wrenching process becoming part Japanese American, equally difficult is coming to grips with being white in America. I reject the lie of the cultural schizophrenia supposed by white and yellow racists to lurk within the Amerasian—I reject utterly the chopstick versus fork dichotomy. Yet, the world demands: *you stand with us or against us.* Without feeling divided myself, I do often and increasingly feel alone, my empathetic capacities exhausted, and all around me I find new chasms widening between me and those closest to me, white and yellow.

Teaching, writing, living, I've had a special concern for engaging with non-yellows. With PBS TV show hosts who sniffle in phony, quasi-British accents that "There is no race problem in America." With politicians who would revive the Yellow Peril. With Ugly Americans who vacation in Japan, then insist, "*I*

know more about being Japanese American than you do!" With the feminist
poet who, despite repeated correction, remains certain that my course must actually be listed in Asian Studies. With the most well-meaning, progressive
scholars who can distinguish Asian from American but crow, "I *love* Asian
American culture!" But how can this be? Surely they don't love all of it, when
there's much there also to despise? A closer look sees a side of our history that
is in-fighting, kowtowing, appeasing, and often wishy-washy in relation to
other minorities. In short, it is American—good, bad, and ugly.

Above all, I have grown particularly wary of a white liberal impulse to kill
discussion with guilt: "Isn't it terrible what *we* did to the Japanese Americans,"
they say, not seeing that therein lies a story that for once isn't about what *they*
did, terrible or not. Wary, yes, for I too harbor white liberal guilt and its resentful flip side. It will tire. As Germany, when the opportunity arose, made clear it
won't keep paying old debts forever, the last of white guilt will exhaust itself,
and it will be time to be white again; by then, America will look *very* different,
and will we too rise to the occasion and knock down our own wall? An argument says we have far too many stories about being white, but I disagree—
these detail whiteness against a white backdrop or, recently, a black one. A time
will come for white to be a color and not, as a shy student of mine believed,
vacuity of color and culture.

I've been hard on my mother, who—in her die-hard 1960s hippie humanist
idealism—does not seem to conceive of racism in terms more gray-shaded than
backwoods, nineteenth-century Georgia lynchings. Yes, she has black friends,
marched for civil rights. Yes, she's a feminist, a self-made professional woman and
single parent who thinks we'd all do well to grow up, go to school, and act much
more Japanese. Still, she scoffs when I protest that the "model minority" stereo-
type invites resentment, scapegoating—not among a handful of extremists, but
regular old people. I can't convince her that Vincent Chin's is no isolated, temporary burp in the great legacy of the flower child, or that hate crimes, supremacist
groups, and separatism are waxing. "*You're* not Japanese, you're American," she
insists, "like Grandpa Ikeda," but to me this resounds of "white," or else assimilated like-white. "Right," I say. "I'm a Japanese American. I choose to be." She's
proud of her WASP heritage, good-doing Protestant aunt, gentle father, and the
family names that trail back through centuries of society pages to Philadelphia's
founding, and it saddens her that I veer away from this history. When I say,
"White Americans have an awful lot to answer for and think about," she thinks I
mean people like her, when really I mean people like me.

Above this chasm where acceptance hinges on assimilation and multiculturalism verges on separatism, there stretches a bridge as material as a gasp of

fear, and that is where I find myself standing these days. Many among my parents' generation so dearly wanted to bridge that gap that they sacrificed even their bodies to construct . . . me. How painful it is to face my mother—my standard of beauty, of woman, of American—and perceive a great blind-spot of her generation, the myth that love is color-blind. Like me, she's a believer; but like my grandparents', my parents' generation was had, too.

Fall 1993: Look at the word you've written on the blackboard—"Ikeda"—and realize its inadequacy. Chalk out the course title and try not to screech: "Topics in Asian American Studies 240: Creative Writing Workshop"—and realize its inadequacy. Turn, at last, to look at the class. Count the black-haired heads, the red and blond, and the face ratio, freckled pale to the shiny brown, clumped around the table. Hand out the syllabi and give them five minutes. Meanwhile, sit behind your writer's bag and try not to hyperventilate. So far, so good, tell yourself. No one's left yet. Be encouraged, feel like Sally Field winning an Oscar, maximize the momentum.

Tell them they must complete assignments on time. Realize you don't know what will happen if they lapse. You want to say: If you skip class you will not live up to your potential or tap the creativity you will squander as junior account execs and computer technicians; you will die without leaving a trace that you breathed and lived and loved in the face of imminent extinction. Recall you failed Yoga as a freshman acting major, dropping your GPA to a C. You're allowed only three absences, you say ominously. You *must* bring an excuse note.

"Why am I here, in Madison, Wisconsin, in this class, standing at this blackboard, talking to you?" you wonder, and feel nauseous to realize your lips have moved, your diaphragm compressed, and the question has floated out of you aloud.

Squirm as they look at you—expectant, hopeful, dubious. Why are they staring at you like that?

Oh, yes.

You are a teacher now. You are armed. You are ready to love them and help them tell their stories.

Spring 1994: For a chemist, my grandfather has been a surprisingly good collaborator—his margin notes on our transcribed interviews show a sensitivity to style; he returns edited manuscripts promptly and has an elephant's memory for dates. Each day his voice grows weaker, and merely tying his shoes exhausts him, but his zeal for research is impressive, and we've just begun an exchange of articles, stories, and poems, learning new things about the war era together. A lifelong consumer of Zane Grey novels and pulp mysteries, he's now developing a literary palette; he sends me the fiction contest issue of the *Rafu Shimpo* and I send him poems by David Mura and Garrett Kaoru Hongo, stories by Hisaye Yamamoto. We confer weekly by phone. He charts the ups and downs of his health. I bitch about the weather and Madison, then ask, "What's this word on page ten, 'meboshi?'"

And sometimes, like now, I will sit in my office at the university, read the word "Ikeda" on the door, then stare out over six stories onto Lake Mendota—dotted by isolated madmen with their ice-fishing huts, frozen and silent as if in prayer—and I am overcome by gratification and gratitude. At such times I suspect there is a cosmic scoreboard, and if the game goes well, if the cosmic goalkeeper is alert just a bit longer, Carol Ikeda may yet see the results of our work—as I read this now, it's impossible to say where his story ends and mine begins, what's real and what's true. And maybe all those unsaid things between us don't matter so much. For now, we're beating the clock, and we've got work to do.

"Oh, 'meboshi!'" he'll say, and his breathing momentarily blossoms with life again. "That's pickled plum, eaten with rice. Verrrry salty. That was my lunch when I worked on the railroad," he'll say, and I think he sounds happy.

MARNIE MUELLER

A DAUGHTER'S NEED TO KNOW

IT TOOK ME TWENTY-TWO YEARS TO WRITE AND PUBLISH my novel about Tule Lake Japanese American Segregation Camp, the place where I was born.

In 1977 I began a self-imposed sabbatical from a high-pressure job. Within two weeks of stopping work I had bought myself a typewriter and for no reason that I could discern at the time, I started to write fiction. I had never written more than letters and grant proposals. The words poured out with such intensity that the keys of my Smith Corona kept flying off and I would have to go to the typewriter repair shop around the corner to have them reaffixed. Page after page of forgotten stories of my family and our peripatetic, quirky existence emerged, as I documented our moves across America from one small farm community to another while my father organized farmers into cooperatives. One day a fictional narrative began to emerge of a white man's experiences in a Japanese American prison camp in Northern California. There were scenes of an army takeover of the camp and of a traumatized Caucasian child who is separated from her parents during the disturbance. There were more gentle depictions—a Nisei woman bathing her child in a metal washtub in her barracks. As I wrote, I felt my deep resonance with the material, but when I tried to go further, I got stuck. I knew nothing more about the camps, except that I had been born there. Angry and helpless at coming up empty-handed each time I attempted to advance the story, one day I exploded, yelling, "Damn it, this is my story. I have a right to know!"

Growing up in America after we had left the camp, I learned early on not to speak of where I spent my earliest years. Whenever I entered a new school, I was asked, Where are you from? Where were you born? Initially I was proud to answer, "Tule Lake Japanese American Relocation Camp in California." I was met with blank stares, even from the teachers, and not solely because I was white. The teachers denied that such camps existed, saying they didn't think I had my information right. After a couple of such shaming episodes I learned to answer simply, "I was born in California."

As the years went on and the history of the camps was never referred to in public school or at the university, I began to feel that what I'd been told by my parents, that I was the first Caucasian born in Tule Lake, was either a product of my imagination or an invention of my idiosyncratic parents to make our lives seem more exotic. By the time I reached high school, I'd become invested in the notion that I was an ordinary American kid with the blandest personal history to go along with my bleached blond hair and bobby socks. It must have been too difficult to be a girl so unlike everyone around me in 1950s America, too uncomfortable to explain a history that no one understood or wanted to know about.

From as far back as I can remember, I have kept secrets about myself and my family. As we moved from one conservative small town to the next, locales that were openly anti-Semitic, I caught on quickly, never telling anyone that my mother was Jewish or that my great-aunt was active in the establishment of Israel, concealing this piece of personal identity behind my father's surname of Elberson and passing for gentile. Nor did I want the other children to know that my father was a socialist, an organizer with the cooperative movement, and that he'd been a pacifist, which meant that he had refused to fight during World War II. I hid the facts that I barely knew my grandmothers because my parents were estranged from them, that my parents were "eggheads," and that by 1946 my hometown-birthplace no longer existed.

I was like a frightened, paranoid refugee whose past had been expunged when she'd passed over into America, except that in my case, as with 120,000 people of Japanese heritage, I'd gone from one America into another, an alien in my own land. I've wondered lately if my secrets and my terror of being found out and my determined creation of another "life" had anything to do with the silence and disbelief I met when I first tried to tell the story of my origins. Did the silence of my nation about this essential and personal detail of history and my own identity contribute to my extreme denial of self and my attempt to create a more palatable all-American girl? Add to the above the confusing issue of being born white within a Japanese American prison camp. All my life I've been told that I was the first Caucasian born in Tule Lake, a curious piece of information for a white American. Being white for me has meant being non-Asian, just as blacks, Asians and Indians in this country have been seen as non-white. If I had been born in any other town in the United States of America, my race would not have been mentioned in my birth announcement as it was in an old copy of a staff newsletter: "Today the first Caucasian baby was born in Tule Lake, little Margaret Grace Elberson, 7 pounds to Don Elberson and Ruth Siegel Elberson."[1]

I've had a recurring nightmare throughout my life. I try to enter a prison. I am standing outside, reaching in through a high chain-link fence to a beautiful dark-haired woman in a long scarlet dress on the other side. I cry out desperately, wanting to get inside that prison because only there will I find comfort and relief, only there will I belong.

Every time I sat down to write the novel of Tule Lake, I met with resistance within myself. It was an anger of internal conflict, of infantile frustration akin to the sorrow of the dream. I was too small to enter and re-create the story of my parents in the camp, too childish to grasp the complex nuances of the politics and the subtle implications of race and culture.

By the time I got stuck in my attempt to write about Tule Lake, I was in my late thirties, living in New York City where I worked as a consultant to various progressive political action projects and non-profit cultural organizations. My parents had moved yet again, this time to Puerto Rico where my father was organizing young leftist Puerto Ricans into an activist coalition fighting for worker and consumer rights. I decided to interview my father on my next visit. I brought along a typewriter rather than a tape recorder so as not to have to meet his eye while he told his story of what he had done in the camps. There were treacherous questions to be asked. Why, since my mother was Jewish, did he decide to be a conscientious objector? Why was he setting up cooperative stores—operations that were based on non-racist principles and concepts of participatory democracy—behind barbed-wire fences? How could he reconcile the conflict? Was he double-dealing, pretending to do good while really meddling in people's destinies and perhaps spying on them? Didn't he feel that he was helping to perpetrate the crime of the camps by going there and "making an intolerable situation tolerable for people," as he had told me throughout my childhood? Wouldn't it have been better if conditions had become so bad that the prisoners had rebelled?

These questions were informed by my participation in the politics of the 1960s and 1970s, in the antiwar and women's movements and in my five years of working at Pacifica Radio in New York City. I was looking for the co-optation factor, anticipating the lack of purity in his answers. I wanted him to be a hero and yet feared that he was a traitor to the cause. Nothing in between would satisfy me.

We sat out on the patio, my father in a hammock, my mother in a plastic chaise longue, and I at the picnic table with my typewriter. They spoke, and I

clattered away. My mother talked of teaching history and social studies to junior
high children in the earliest days, without blackboards and books, of how there
was no running water during the day and how hard the mineral-filled water was
and how constipated everyone was as a result. She spoke of the endless wind and
the ubiquitous black dust, of how she had to sweep three times a day to keep the
barracks clean. My father told of the divisions between the Issei, Nisei, and
Kibei,* and of his greatest accomplishment in finally getting them to join forces
in the governing of the co-op. He talked with warm nostalgia of the brash
young Fumi Sakamoto, his "right-hand woman" in setting up the co-op; of
Noboru Honda, a Nisei who was the education director of the co-op, and whom
my father held in the highest regard; and of Koso Takemoto, a young Kibei who
was instrumental in bridging the gap between the Issei and Kibei members. At
one point my father said wistfully, "You know the co-op story is one that's never
told and it was such an important aspect of camp history."

As he went on, it sounded like just an ordinary story, much like the work
he had done all his life when he'd organized farmers into rural cooperatives and
later set up cooperative grocery stores in small towns and cities. As a child,
when I wasn't hiding who he was, I was terribly confused by the question,
What does your father do? Other children could answer, "He's a doctor," or
"He sells John Deere equipment," or "He's the president of the bank," or "He
works at the factory." I had to come up with the convoluted explanation, "My
father gets people to sit down together to decide what they want to do." Here I
was again with a complex, undefined explanation of the work my father did in
camp. I still didn't know if he was good or bad, or how Noboru Honda, Fumi
Sakamoto, or Koso Takemoto perceived him.

When I asked my father about his status of conscientious objector and how
it related to the killing of Jews in Europe, I could sense my mother's discomfort; her silence spoke loudly from the chaise longue. My father answered that
at that time they didn't yet know all "the gruesome details" but that in his case
he didn't believe in the use of violence. Then he added, "After a time I became
enraged with the racism of some of the staff members," and how from that
awareness he gradually came to feel that there would be circumstances under
which he would take up arms. He said he went down to San Francisco to
change his draft status and to sign up to fight, but when he was asked at the
draft board what he thought of the relocation of Japanese Americans, he an-

---

*   Kibei: young Japanese Americans sent back to Japan for schooling, usually in the
    primary grades.--Ed.

swered that he believed an egregious injustice had been done to them. "The man doing the interview decided I was unfit to serve," my father said, bitterly twisting out the words.

My mother intruded on the stillness that had fallen. "He called your father a Jap sympathizer to his face and wouldn't take him."

I shifted the conversation, asking what it had been like in the first days of camp. My father became both more animated and relaxed as he described how he had been in the original group of administrators or "pioneers," as they called themselves. He had to meet the trains of evacuees. "It was brutal," he said, his voice becoming somber again. "Some days we had to process five hundred or more people." He described how he would try to spot leadership in the arriving groups. "I'd look for someone other people gravitated toward and also I sought out those who spoke English and Japanese." He needed help in keeping people calm, getting milk for children, taking care of those who were ill. "But nothing mitigated the moment when I had to take them to their new homes." I glanced over at him and saw that his mouth was trembling. "You'd have to take these people into this dingy excuse for a room, twenty by twenty-five feet at best. These were people who'd left everything behind, sometimes fine houses. I learned after the first day not to enter with the family, but to stand outside. It was too terrible to witness the pain in people's faces, too shameful for them to be seen in this degrading situation."

My mother was silent as my father kept speaking. "You know the worst time for me was a year and a half later." He went on to tell what it had been like after "registration," or the forced signing of the loyalty oaths. By then Tule Lake was being turned into a segregation center, in essence a separate prison for the "no-no's." He had gone on business to the Jerome Camp in Arkansas, where nearby the 442nd Regiment was training. It was the Fourth of July, he said. "And I was out on the parade ground. Some of the 442nd soldiers were on leave and had come back to camp to see their parents who were still imprisoned. We stood there in the devilishly hot sun. The parade grounds were packed with Nisei soldiers, their parents, Boy Scout troops. Everyone was pledging allegiance. I looked up, saw Old Glory flapping in the wind and behind it the glint of barbed wire. It sort of all went together for me. Here were these people paying obeisance to the flag of the country that had put them there." My father covered his face. "Oh, my god," he said and began to weep. I had never seen my father cry before.

I sat there helplessly, wondering what else went into my father's long-submerged sorrow. Did it also have to do with his refusal to fight? Here were these brave men, who against all odds were making the sacrifice for the honor of their families and for the country that had imprisoned them, and he had not gone to fight in that same war, even with a Jewish wife whose people had perished. I won't ever know because we got no further in our talk. A scrim of silence descended after that emotional intimacy, and I didn't dare push him or my mother further.

I continued to struggle with writing the novel over the next few years, always vacillating between wanting to write a heroic tribute to my father and a stronger impulse to write the story of a white man who works in the camp and whose ideals are horribly compromised by his own personal frailties.

Then my father died, and with him his story, or so I thought. It took me at least a year to get back to the novel after his death, but when I did, something had been released in me and I wrote at a furious pace, telling the tale of a damaged man who tried to do good for the evacuees imprisoned in Tule Lake Camp, but who, because of his emotional conflicts, made matters worse for people.

I did research, beginning with Michi Weglyn's seminal *Years of Infamy* (1976), continuing on to *The Kikuchi Diary* (1973) by Charles Kikuchi, to Reverend Daisuke Kitagawa's *Issei and Nisei: The Internment Years* (1967), and many other books, often engulfed by emotion at finding the existence of the camps publicly confirmed by writers who had firsthand knowledge of the experience. I wanted to raise the books in my hand and call out to my grade school-teachers, "You see, I wasn't making it up." One day I was reading Thomas James's *Exile Within: The Schooling of Japanese Americans 1942–1945* (1987), when I came upon my father's name in a footnote. It was my father's birthday. He would have been seventy-nine years old. Finding him on that day was like receiving a wondrous gift, as though he'd reached down from the heavens to guide me. And guide me he did.

When I phoned Thomas James, he told me, "Yes, your father, Don Elberson, showed up all the time in my research." James said I would find material in the National Archives in Washington, D.C., and at the Bancroft Library at the University of California, Berkeley.

I traveled to Washington, D.C., filled with excitement and trepidation. What man was I to encounter? My father had given me his view of his place in the camp, but what would the documents reveal?

I waited in the grand main reading room of the National Archives with its twenty-foot-high ceilings and floor-to-ceiling arched windows, surrounded by scholars and researchers. Only the sound of authorized pencils on paper and the soft tapping of computer keys rose faintly above the hush. I thought maybe there would be nothing on my father after all; he was probably too unimportant to be recorded and saved in such an august institution. Minutes later a man came down my aisle pushing a three-tiered library cart filled with cardboard boxes. "You wanted the documents on Don Elberson?" he asked.

The boxes were jammed with my father's letters, memos, meeting minutes, and even everyday notes asking about health insurance and petty cash refunds. I read through letters and memos written in my father's distinctive syntax and signed by him in 1942, 1943, and 1944. He wrote requesting leave clearance for various individual Japanese Americans, and in his passionate letters to the Cooperative League of America and in memos to the camp administration he spoke of racism, of the specific discrimination against Japanese Americans in this country, of the need to undo the harm of their incarceration.

In one letter dated February 10, 1943, he was trying to obtain leave clearance for an Issei man who had worked closely with him in the co-op. He wanted to secure him a job with the Consumers Cooperative Association in Kansas City, but there appeared to be resistance on the other end because of fear of racist reprisals from the local white community. My father wrote:

> It's rather inconceivable to me that employment of one Japanese in an organization the size of the Consumers Co-operative Association could be sufficient to split your organization open on a racial question.
>
> The co-operative movement professes that it puts into practice racial tolerance where other groups merely talk about it. We, who attempt to sell the co-operative movement to the Japanese as an instrument to be used for their general welfare, have made much of this point, and I feel that it is quite obvious that the co-operative movement, as a whole, does not practice these things because it thinks that its existence is more important than the platforms it announces.[2]

When tears blurred my vision, I reprimanded myself: You have work to do, stop crying, you'll have time for that later. It was like having my father back again. The voice in the letters was my father's own—straightforward, pragmatic, idealistic and not averse to biting irony to make a point.

For months after my visit to the archives I was again blocked from working on the novel. I was humbled in the face of my father's accomplishment, saying to myself that the life he lived was far more heroic and profound than anything I could write.

When I went to the Bancroft Library at Berkeley, I found an even greater trove of documentation, daily journals written by Nisei intellectuals and sociologists for the Japanese Evacuation and Relocation Study, a project initiated (in 1942) and conducted by Dorothy Swaine Thomas, a sociologist at Berkeley.

These journals give an intimate day-to-day account of the life and politics within the camp. They proved to be gossipy, erudite, angry, and sanguine and read like the great novels of the nineteenth century. When the loose stack of typed pages was set before me, I plunged in at random. Within a page I found a Nisei saying, "I think there's only one man in the administration who can be trusted, and that's Elberson."[3]

From there I proceeded through two immense journals, third-person narratives in which my father figured prominently. I observed him in the preliminary meetings of the co-op, negotiating among factions of Issei, Nisei, and Kibei, as well as between Japanese American Citizens League members and the people who harbored intense animosity toward them for their stand on internment. In all of these meetings, I learned, he operated democratically:

> While he [Don Elberson] continued to make suggestions to Japanese co-op leaders, he did not protest when they went ahead of their own accord. He insisted on maintaining democratic principles, and preferred to work behind the scene as much as possible. His attitude toward the Japanese, moreover, was that of a liberal who believed in not discriminating because of race.... It made it possible to deal with Japanese without taking a superior attitude that so many of the other Caucasian staff members tended to take.[4]

I came across the name of Fumi Sakamoto, the young woman my father had told me about. He had described her as a gritty young "gal" who "sure knew how to dress." In one journal she was characterized as "*kiryo ga amari yoku nai keredo*," which was translated as "even though she's not so good looking."[5] The writer said she was blunt, impatient, and sometimes aggressive in going after what she wanted. In one vivid image she is said to have a cigarette toughly hanging from her mouth. Here again were details that fit my father; he liked his women smart and aggressive. My mother matched that model, and I'd been groomed to be just as outspoken. The writer continues:

> In the co-op Fumi found the right atmosphere to work in. The fact that she worked for Elberson and not someone else probably helped a great deal in making her adjustment here. Elberson aligned himself with the people, he practiced democratic principles and tried not to force anything on the people; he listened to what others had to say. These were probably good examples which Fumi probably learned to follow to a great extent. Fumi herself, if left without such guides, might become dictatorial and arrogant towards the people because of her greater range and knowledge and her contacts with Caucasians.[6]

This was a man to be lauded, and he was my father. The only problem was that the character I had created in my fiction, Denton Jordan, who was based on my father, was a much darker and more complex human being. Jordan was conflicted, self-righteous, weak and malleable. He betrayed his wife and child, and in the process was tangentially responsible for the death of an evacuee. How could I reconcile the protagonist of my imagination with the real man in these papers? Where had I gotten this unflattering picture? How much of it was true? I felt that in my writing I was betraying my father's legacy. There was also a personal question. Why, if I so desperately wanted my story out there in the world, did I insist on making the main character unsympathetic to the general audience? Wasn't I thwarting my very own desire? But when I tried to re-create the gallant man of the archives and the journals, the character emerged as flat and boring, too good to be true.

As I proceeded through the contemporaneous material, I continued to hear my father's voice in dialogue, sounding astonishingly like the person I knew. In a meeting, apparently at a critical point in setting up the co-op, the board of directors is quibbling over a vote on a resolution. The narrator says, "Elberson is shaking with emotion." My father has been trying to get the floor. Finally he stands to say, "You give Fumi and me the power to make decisions and then you crab. Fumi and I have been working our butts off on this. I've been doing it to the detriment of my family life. Do it for me, do it for Fumi."[7] I looked at the date of the entry, August 11, 1942, less than a week after my birth. I knew from my mother's recollections that she had been furious at him for focusing more on his work than on her and on me, their newborn. Later in the journal, on Christmas Day 1942, the writer is at a party in our barracks and during a discussion of how hard the staff is working, he relates that "Mrs. El-berson smiled sweetly and said, 'Baby plays with rattle while daddy plays with co-op.'"[8] The correspondent finds nothing wrong in this, but I heard my mother's sing-song contempt. My mother's private fury, the rage I knew too well, had crept into her public expression. I remembered the fissures in their marriage and the fact that work always came before family—to be fair, this held true for both of them. I understood then that I had formed my flawed characters out of the crucible of the distressed family I'd come from, the one I'd not wanted the world to know about. But something more was becoming apparent; I returned to the page with my father's plea at the meeting. " . . . Do it for me. Do it for Fumi." What he was saying was, *I've sacrificed myself for you and now you must do what I want.* It was an unusual statement for a man who had always told me, "Listen for the felt needs of people and follow them, even if you disagree with where they're going."

The irony of my father's situation, as well as that of other liberals like him who had gone to work in the camp for humanitarian reasons, could be traced back to the policies of his president. In this instance, Roosevelt, having signed Executive Order 9066, returned to his progressive leanings and determined that he would not put capitalist enterprises such as Sears and Penney's into the camps, where they would merely take money out of the pockets of the internees and out of the camps. Instead, Roosevelt went to the Cooperative League of America, a growing liberal movement in the United States, to find and hire people who could organize consumer-owned and operated, non-profit stores. An expert in cooperatives as a result of his work for the American Friends Service Committee with displaced farmers in the San Joaquin Valley, my father went to work at Tule Lake in order to set up an operation based on non-racist, democratic principles in a racially and ethnically determined prison camp—a stunning paradox.

In a staff report, the Caucasians are described as being divided into three distinct groups. There were the "sociologists," or the "damned sociologists" as they were described by the more conservative members of the staff. My father, of course, belonged to the "damned sociologist" segment, which was known for its close work and social relationships with the internees. The second cluster, the "operators," or pragmatists, was neither against nor supportive of the internees. They simply wanted to get the job done. The third group consisted of outspoken racists who intensely disliked the residents and used racist epithets to describe them both privately and publicly.

> In actual practice a considerable number of people refer to the evacuees, especially among Caucasians, as the "Japs." Often the reference is even more offensive. For example, Mr. B . . . has the habit of calling the evacuees "monkeys," not only . . . when in the presence of Caucasians but even in addressing the evacuees themselves. He has absolutely no regard for their feelings. . . . During the registration crisis . . . references were frequently made to the evacuees or groups of them as "those goddamned yellow sons-of-bitches . . ." "those goddamn yellow bastards . . ." and "those slant-eyed . . ." and other similar terms.[9]

The liberal members of the administration, "the sociologists," became a close-knit circle because, as the staff writer relates, they had trouble with the attitudes of the third group. "On the outside [of camp], an individual can maintain a friendship with another whose ideas on racial problems and social questions are quite different. They [the liberals] have found it not so easy to be tolerant of differences and attitudes at Tule Lake."[10]

My father is cited as a person who had grave difficulty living in "unusually close contact with people who differ from [his] ideas."[11] The report discusses how the liberals disliked the racism not only on moral grounds, but also because it got in the way of their work; the blatant racism angered the internee population and undermined its confidence in the administration. As the staff writer describes the situation, the "sociologists" were more interested in looking beneath the surface of a situation, at the causes underlying the symptoms, and were invested in encouraging the growth of community involvement, community government, and in developing leaders. "They sought to administer the community *with* the evacuees not *against* them,"[12] a difficult organizing task even under the best of circumstances. "Don Elberson has made the assertion that an initial good will towards the colonists [internees] was not enough. It soon wore away unless implemented and bulwarked by a willingness and an ability to look beyond the superficial. Don Elberson found it requires some degree of social processes to preserve the good will that one began with."[13]

One of the racist staff members said, "If people [the evacuees] aren't more grateful for what the government has given them and aren't more obedient to the policies, then force should be applied and the army should step in. These people don't appreciate what you do for them, they are spoiled. They're always belly-aching for something."[14] My father, enraged, responded: "In America we shouldn't expect gratitude from people when they are given things they consider their just possession. That is a characteristic of the American people, that they expect certain things in life they consider human requirements. Some people expect the sort of gratitude a serf would feel when the feudal lord bestowed some good on him."[15]

As I read this exchange, I remembered the day in Puerto Rico when my father told me that it was these very authoritarian and racist attitudes he encountered in the cauldron of the camp that caused him to renounce his conscientious objector status. And I remembered that the army would not take him because of his sympathies for the Japanese and Japanese Americans in our prison camps. It was like being with him again across a dinner table as he prodded me to argue issues, never letting me get away with a simplistic, sentimental or doctrinaire view. Sitting in the Bancroft Library, on the West Coast of our continent where he grew up and came of age, looking out the windows to the sun-warmed Campanile he had sat beneath as a young man, I calculated how old he must have been when he had worked in Tule Lake. To my shock, he was barely thirty. I had thought my father's knowledge had come with time and experience. I saw that he had always had it; it was second nature to him.

Continuing through the Nisei journals and staff reports, I observed the tension building in camp as the loyalty oaths were being administered. The procedure exacted a toll on everyone, my father included. Raymond Best had been assigned as the new project director. Michi Weglyn describes Best as "an unhappy choice for a position requiring infinite tact and understanding."[16] As my father felt increasingly betrayed by the new camp director, he became more adamant in his positions with the co-op members and staff. Even Fumi Sakamoto felt he went too far. "Fumi believes that Don lately has become less tactful than he has been in the past. He is saying things he formerly would not have said."[17] During the early months in Tule Lake there were complaints here and there from internees that co-ops were Marxist, that my father was too far left for their taste. Now his closest allies said that he was ramming co-op principles down their throats. In March 1943, Noboru Honda, the man my father thought so highly of, complained that although Don "won't do anything against the people, he will stretch a point almost to the breaking point."[18] James Sakoda thought that for "Don it was usually co-op first and Japanese second."[19] I remembered my father's letter to the Consumer Cooperative Association in Kansas City and saw that he may have been guilty of an offense similar to the one he complained about, minus the racist component. Even Koso Takemoto, the young Kibei my father had admired for his ability to bring various factions together, began to be suspicious of the War Relocation Authority and in turn of my father. "His [Koso's] suspicion has grown to the extent where he is beginning to look for base motive in all of the WRA policies. The co-op, for instance, he says, was started, even Don admits, for one thing to avoid expenses by letting the people take over. Also, the co-op is trying to take over the community activities, which will again be a burden to the people."[20]

And in one instance it was as if I heard my father erupt in anger. He had been working overtime to get people jobs outside so they could obtain clearances to leave camp. Apparently some of the Issei parents had balked, being understandably terrified of what awaited them in the white world. Without their compliance, their children wouldn't leave. My father, who was by now escorting people to the segregation trains, was worried that once the segregation plan was completed it would be practically impossible to get those who remained in Tule Lake out of there. He exclaimed in frustration to the Nisei journal-writer, "God damn those selfish parents."[21] I thought back to his uncharacteristic outburst in the co-op meeting, "Fumi and I have been working our butts off. . . . Do it for me." When the pressure was on he could be as humanly fallible as anyone. But in all my research, this was the worst I could find out about him.

Paradoxically, as I read on, I grew to suspect that my father's very candor and spontaneous reactions were what caused the people he worked with to trust him most of all the Caucasians, and to like him even when he became rigid and succumbed to his own anger. People had always liked and trusted my father for these traits, so why not in Tule Lake Camp? Telling comments about other liberal staff members made it clear that do-gooder attitudes could be suspect. A Nisei journal-keeper wrote in February 1943, " . . . I find people like E. L. objectionable because of what T. S. calls the 'bleeding heart' gushiness. It's like receiving the abortive consequences of frustrated love. . . . However, I get the feeling behind all her outgoing sympathy are all kinds of demands she is making upon me, not in so many words but in her constant protest of sympathy for our position by which it seems she is seeking sympathy for herself."[22]

Of another staffer, this same correspondent said, "Her pallid features stare out from behind a severe hair line and her earnest eyes have the glint of the reformer in them."[3] Of a male staff member, he wrote, "I felt he wanted to sympathize and 'love' the evacuees too much."[24]

I suppose the most revealing detail for me was that fact that after a certain time, my father was always referred to as Don, whereas when other staff members were written about, they were called by their last names, or by Mr., Mrs. or Miss. It spoke to me of a certain intimacy. When an internee was interviewing my father about his life history, the question of his sensitivity to racial issues was brought up. "Don has had no experience with racial minority groups, but he has worked with minority groups such as trade unions, Okies, and Co-ops. He believes that this understanding of present social structure makes it easy for him to understand problems here. . . . As Don put it: 'You work hard with people and you don't notice the race.'"[25] What wasn't said here was that my father was married to a Jew, and that this may also have had an impact on his attitudes and understanding. Later on in the interview I found another quote that was of personal comfort to me, mostly because it was clear that my mother was present at the interview. "S. is not Jewish, although people think he is. As a matter of fact, he made an anti-Jewish remark in the company of evacuees. Don was going to tell Mr. Shirrell (the Camp Director) about it."[26]

My father died before I found his letters and memos, and he did not know of the voluminous writings about him and the work he did with the co-op. I wonder what he would have felt. Embarrassment? He was a modest man, always turning the discussion back to the work of others. Hadn't one of the reports said that he preferred to work behind the scenes? Would he have felt pride that others thought so well of him? There would have to be some of that. But I believe that he would have felt what I did, enormous relief that his—our—story existed

in the historical archives of our nation for future scholars to find. His greatest
thrill would be that the co-op enterprise was so completely documented and
that it would serve as an example of how intrepid the camp inmates were in
making something good out of such an "intolerable situation." I wish he could
have known this, and I wish it could have eased the complex mixture of shame,
guilt, and sorrow he felt on the day that he told me the story of pledging allegiance on Jerome's parade grounds.

    I finally finished the novel, remaining with the flawed character of Denton
Jordan. If I were to lay bare the in-fighting of Japanese Americans as they were
put under the extreme pressure of the loyalty oath and the subsequent segregation of the no-no's, I did not need to have my main white characters be
paragons of virtue. My father, though a good man, was as fallible as the next. I
look back to those early days, twenty-two years ago, when I began my journey
to understand my unusual past, and I am ashamed that I wanted my father to
rise to some level of purity in his work. His life and the astute observations of
the Japanese American journal-writers have taught me that the people who do
the best socially conscious work are those who are the most candid about their
feelings and flaws. But I don't blame myself completely for wishing this purity
of him. I believe that the silence that kept me and others from knowing what
happened in Tule Lake and the other camps created a vacuum in which a black-
and-white vision of America and its secret crimes was encouraged to grow.

    As I was finishing this essay, I received a phone call. The caller announced,
"I am Noboru Honda, I knew your dad in Tule Lake." He had just finished
reading my novel. He told me he liked it very much and that he understood
why I had chosen to make Denton Jordan such a difficult character. "But your
dad was a great man. He made my life possible in camp. He was a real intellectual. What I remember most about him was that he always said, 'Noby, think,
analyze and then think again.' I was unschooled when I got to camp because I
had to quit grade school to provide for my brothers and sisters. I've used that
advice through these fifty-five years since then. It has held me in good stead."
After a long, wonderful conversation, I hung up, wishing my father could have
heard what had just been said about him, deeply grateful that I'd been able to
tell some version of his story and proud that I was the daughter of such a man

NOTES

1. Edwin Bates, Tule Lake Staff Newsletter, War Relocation Authority Papers, Na-
    tional Archives and Records Service, Washington, D. C., Field Basic Documen-
    tation, August 7, 1942, 2.

2. Don Elberson, Letter to Merlin Miller, WRA Papers, National Archives, Subject Classified General File, February 10, 1943, 2.
3. Frank Shotaro Miyamoto, Diary, Japanese American Evacuation and Resettlement Records 67/14c, The Bancroft Library at the University of California (Berkeley), Part II: Section 5–Tule Lake, R20:18, 2.
4. The Co-operative Movement in Tule Lake, Japanese American Evacuation and Resettlement Records 67/14c, The Bancroft Library, Part II: Section 5-Tule Lake, R20:86, 6.
5. James M. Sakoda, Journal, Japanese American Evacuation and Resettlement Records 67/14c, The Bancroft Library, Part II: Section 5-Tule Lake, R20:81, January 20, 1943, 918.
6. Sakoda, Journal, R20:81, January 20, 1943, 918.
7. Frank Shotaro Miyamoto, Community Council Minutes, R21:06, August 11, 1942.
8. Sakoda, Journal, R20:81, December 25, 1942, 836.
9. Robert Billigmeier, The Caucasian Staff at Tule Lake, Japanese American Evacuation and Resettlement Records 67/14c, The Bancroft Library, R20:01, n.d., 8–9.
10. Ibid., 3–4.
11. Ibid., 4.
12. Ibid., 12.
13. Ibid., 13.
14. Ibid., 12.
15. Ibid.
16. Michi Weglyn, *Years of Infamy: The Untold Story of America's Concentration Camps* (New York: William Morrow, 1976), 159.
17. James M. Sakoda, Diary, R20:83, January 29, 1943, 974.
18. Ibid., March 24, 1943, 1224.
19. Ibid.
20. Ibid., 1213.
21. Sakoda, Journal, R20:81, September 13, 1943.
22. Miyamoto, Diary, R20:18, February 17, 1943. I have replaced names with initials.
23. Ibid., October 27, 1942, 1.
24. Ibid., October 31, 1942, 2.
25. Sakoda, Journal, January 28, 1943, 964.
26. Ibid.

GEORGE F. BROWN

RETURN TO GILA RIVER

I FELL IN LOVE WITH THE DESERT THE FIRST NIGHT we arrived in Gila River. It was pitch dark, oven-hot but dry, as we were driven to the camp in an army truck. The sense of vast open space was overwhelming. For a seven-year-old boy from Philadelphia, it was unbearably exciting and mysterious.

The excitement remained with me for the two years that my family and I lived, worked, went to school, and played in the midst of the dusty barracks of the Gila River War Relocation Project, the euphemistically named concentration camp for over 13,000 Japanese Americans constructed in 1942 in the middle of a Pima Indian reservation forty-five miles southeast of Phoenix, Arizona. My parents, my brother and I lived at the edge of the camp in an army-style barracks externally identical to dozens of others, each housing four Japanese American families in tiny spaces. Our apartment had amenities: air cooler, bathroom, kitchen, decent furniture. In contrast, the Japanese Americans had public latrines, public mess halls, homemade furniture, no air cooling, and very little privacy. Temperatures were frequently over 120 degrees in summer, and powerful winds blew sand and dust through the poorly constructed barracks walls.

I vividly recall the beauty and mystery of the desert. The giant saguaro cactus grew all around us, with sage, jumping cactus, and mesquite everywhere. We played in the dry creeks that sprang to watery life only two or three times with brief, heavy rains. The camp was ringed with small rocky hills, called buttes. Many times I made the long, arduous climb up the butte immediately behind my barracks, ever watchful of scorpions and rattlesnakes, to see the spectacular desert sunset.

I was the only Caucasian in my classes, grades three and four. My memories of school were happy and uneventful: good teachers, serious classmates, and seemingly no problems. Every day I walked across the camp to school, also in identical

The author at the site of his family's barracks, Gila River, 1999.

barracks, studied happily and returned to play on "our" side of the camp, in the vast expanse of desert around us. Only once was I confronted with racial tension. On my first day at school I was chased by a group of boys my age who called me a "dirty Jap." I ran home in tears, but my parents laughed off the incident, amused that both the Caucasian and Japanese American children took the same racist epithet so seriously. In fact it became a family fable about the insidious nature of racial discrimination.

My older brother Jeremy had a completely different experience. On his first day at school, he was elected class president, to his great embarrassment, since he knew none of his classmates. He immediately realized that he was elected simply because he was Caucasian, and he stepped down after the first semester.

In the summer we played in the sand and swam in the irrigation canal. I developed such callused feet that I was able to walk barefoot on the burning sand. But I also remember the trips outside to Phoenix and Tucson, and once to a YMCA summer camp in northern Arizona. Only much later did I consciously realize that my Japanese American classmates had very few similar opportunities to escape the confines of the camp.

In fact, I played almost exclusively with Jeremy and a few other Caucasian kids in camp, most of them older than I. My only positive memory with a Japanese American classmate was happily playing baseball one day after school, the two of us alone on a baseball diamond. He was friendly and strong, and I felt a bond between us. We never played together again, and the day sticks in my mind with a pang of regret. Was he told by his parents never to play with Caucasians? Did we both instinctively know that this behavior was out of bounds? I don't know.

In my last year at Gila River, 1945, I remember the news of President Roosevelt's death, many Japanese American families relocating to the outside world, and then the momentous announcement of the end of the war. We returned to Philadelphia, and then to Toronto, but I kept my happy memories with me. At first I liked to tell friends that I had been in the Arizona desert during the war, and would proudly say that I was the only Caucasian in my class. Proud because of the fact that I survived the event? Or perhaps because, as a son of anthropologists, I had demonstrated that I was able to function successfully in a different cultural setting? But I was then always asked why I had been there. The simple answer, repeated by my family on the infrequent occasions that we discussed the experience, was that my parents were there to help make a terrible situation better.

This response became more and more simplistic and uncomfortable as I began to learn in my teens of the enormity of the government's unjust and racist act in forcibly uprooting 110,000 Japanese Americans, and of their suffering, their loss of homes, jobs, property, and of their incarceration in ten isolated concentration camps, including Gila River. So I stopped talking about it. But I didn't forget. Years later, when I met several Japanese Americans and Canadians who had lived through the camp experience, I always felt reticent and uncomfortable, intuitively fearing that I would be perceived as part of the camp administration, and ultimately allied with the oppressors.

While I rejoiced at the success of the movement for redress, which culminated in the presidential apology of 1988, I still kept quiet. Then in 1998 the touring exhibit "America's Concentration Camps" came to Ellis Island. I had moved to New York some years earlier, and felt a strong urge to attend the opening ceremony. Among the events was a camp reunion. I was welcomed so warmly and was so deeply moved by the powerful and poignant exhibit that I felt compelled to break out of my shell, to confront the truth and try to understand what my parents were doing in Gila River. Since they had died many years earlier, I had only my brother to turn to for direct information. His memories, like mine, were hazy but generally happy, and he had little more to add to my understanding of what our parents were doing in the camp. But I soon found a vast literature, thousands of documents in the National Archives, and many Japanese American and Caucasian friends who were eager to help me in my search.

My search began with my father's research publications, then extended to the National Archives in Washington, D.C., and to the wide body of published information on the camp experience. Over time I began to learn what my parents were doing in Gila River. My father, G. Gordon Brown, had been hired by the government's War Relocation Authority (WRA) as a "community analyst," one of a group of anthropologists who were assigned to each of the ten concentration camps. Their function, as described by my father, was "to present such facts of social organization, attitudes and reactions of the resident community as will assist in efficient administration, and to be of use in the formulation, modification and execution of both national and project policies."[1]

The intentions of the government in assigning community analysts to understand the social and cultural reactions of the Japanese Americans to the imprisonment and relocation were varied. The notion of having administrative officials in each camp and in Washington receive regular objective information on the reactions of the evacuees—much of it collected by Japanese American "assistant community analysts"—seemed laudable. But another major motivation was to identify tensions and incipient crises and to advise camp authorities in order to prevent unrest and rioting, which had taken place initially in several camps. A third motivation was to gain experience in managing large populations of different cultures in postwar situations.

My parents were applied anthropologists who had worked for eight years in East Africa and Samoa, where I was born, before returning to teach in North America. My father's training and experience in working with different cultures, and then applying this knowledge to specific problems confronting administrators in the societies under management, appeared to be relevant in many respects to the concentration camp experience. But were they really? Could a Caucasian social scientist who had had no previous experience with Japanese culture truly practice his profession in an objective fashion under such oppressive conditions? Could he make a difference? Was the situation so fraught with the psychology of jailors and jailed that any serious research would be doomed? And would he be so suspect by the Japanese Americans that his work would be hopelessly compromised?

My father confronted these issues and described them in his Final Report, published immediately after the war. He states that all his surveys and reports of Gila River are open to the community. He emphasizes that "the residents are suspicious of the administration. Some will brand as 'inu' [spies; literally 'dogs'] all the fellows who have more than the necessary contacts with administrative personnel. And they are quick to resent the appearance of condescension or pa-tronage." The community analyst from the outset, he notes, is identified with the administration: "If he adopts the subterfuge that he is really not a member of the administrative staff he is apt to be discredited as a fool for thinking he can get away with it, or a liar, or both."[2] He praises the work of the six Japanese American assistants on whom he relied heavily over the two years for their ac-cess to fellow internees and their perceptive observations.

The bulk of my father's reports addressed practical problems in the admin-istration of Gila River. His report, "Evacuee Attitudes Toward the WRA,"[3] written in October 1943, four months after he arrived, describes in detail the views of the Japanese Americans on the evacuation, the oppressive policies of the WRA, and the insensitive and sometimes racist attitudes and behavior of many of the Caucasian administrative personnel. The report highlights the in-ternees' fear of the use of force against any public dissent, their fear of the camp's closing and another forced relocation, and a belief that any policy could be changed overnight without warning or consultation. Evacuees, according to the report, "have been deprived of their constitutional rights, been uprooted from their communities, and in some cases separated from their families. Some have lost property, good positions, and their education disrupted. The total sit-uation is one to cause insecurity, fear, suspicion, and resentment. This situa-tion, while obvious, is yet of the utmost significance."[4]

My father's report also describes the loyalty registration, which was im-posed by the WRA in early 1943, as the evacuees' worst experience following the evacuation itself. The decision to answer yes or no to the two poorly worded loyalty questions caused profound divisions within families, anger, and mistrust of the government's actions. Following public protests, twenty-five Ja-panese Americans were summarily removed from Gila River by the FBI and sent to isolation camps. While these events happened six months before our ar-rival, the anger and fear of reprisal against any complaints about the govern-ment's policies continued to be strongly felt. My father noted the "belief that any evacuee's protest against the WRA policies will be answered by investiga-tions and arrests."[5]

His report also describes evacuee attitudes toward the physical hardships of the camp, racial discrimination, and the subordinate position of the evacuees in all internee-staff relationships. My father's general estimation was that the level of unrest in Gila River was similar to that at Poston, the other Arizona concen-tration camp, prior to the general strike of 1942, which caused great turmoil.[6]

The reaction by the WRA senior staff to this report was one of consterna-tion.[7] The camp director attempted to reduce levels of discrimination by holding meetings with Caucasian staff, by sensitizing them to authoritarian and discriminatory practices, and even by organizing a picnic. Whether or not these efforts accomplished anything to improve the conditions of the internees, my father was at least fulfilling his duty to provide objective information on evacuee attitudes to the WRA administrators—even if it was information that they didn't want to hear.

Reading subsequent reports on various aspects of camp life by my father and his assistants strengthened my belief that my parents were performing a significant corrective function in attempting to counter insensitive and sometimes abusive behavior by the WRA administrators, hospital staff, and other employees. As most of the overall policy actions were dictated by the Washington headquarters of the WRA, only modest changes could be made at the local level. For example, my father supported the effort to introduce Japanese language teaching in Gila River, but the proposal was rejected by the WRA in Washington, presumably because of the desire to "Americanize" the younger generation of Japanese Americans. He also reported extensively on the problems and fears of families faced with the daunting problems of relocation, but WRA policies remained inflexible and mostly unsupportive.

Apart from a brief study of family structure,[8] my father undertook no systematic anthropological studies of the Japanese Americans. In general, the group of community analysts as a whole refrained from performing such studies. Perhaps their functions were circumscribed by the situation of the concentration camp, or by their limitations as Caucasians; or perhaps they saw their obligations as limited to reporting on the implications of WRA policies, and the internees' attitudes toward evacuation, incarceration, and relocation. The fact remains that they contributed little to a deeper understanding of the Japanese Americans' complex reactions to their forced uprooting and incarceration, or to the deeper process of social change in this ethnic group.

Another task given to my father was less benign. On his arrival in Gila River in July 1943, he was assigned for several months to help screen those who had answered no to the notorious loyalty questionnaire, and who were to be sent to the Tule Lake camp, the designated "segregation center" for supposed disloyals, the "no-no's." Some of those who had originally responded negatively to the loyalty questions in Gila River wanted to change their position to yes. But that desire entailed painful family debate, intrusive bureaucratic procedures, and interviews. My father was one of the interviewers.[9] In his Final Report, he stated that it was a mistake for him to have been assigned this task, as it detracted from his anthropological work and compromised his scientific role. "These administrative tasks put the Analyst in the position of making decisions which may be considered oppressive."[10] While a few hundred Japanese Americans did have their status changed and stayed in Gila River, 2,000 were transferred to Tule Lake in the fall of 1943.

During our final year at Gila River the internees were occupied with anguished decisions over resettlement, as the WRA strongly urged them to leave camp despite their deep fears of racist attacks on "the outside," uncertain job and housing opportunities, and concerns about moving to unfamiliar parts of the United States. Frequently there were deep and painful intergenerational differences within families. Both of my parents were profoundly involved in this process: my father did repeated surveys of evacuee attitudes toward resettlement, and my mother was hired at this time by the WRA to help individual families make their decisions and plan their moves. Her anthropological training helped her understand some of the social and cultural issues involved in this difficult process, although her position was essentially that of a social worker.[11]

Many years later, the use of social scientists in the camps came under strong criticism. The anthropologist Peter Suzuki assessed the work of the community analysts and concluded that their anthropological contributions were minimal, ethically compromised, and sometimes racially stereotyped.[12] Suzuki cited instances in which community analysts aided the oppressive actions of camp authorities.[13] He showed that a few community analysts provided names of potentially dissident individuals to security personnel or provided other information useful in maintaining authoritarian control. He cited my father's role in interviewing individuals in Gila River who wanted to change their "loyalty" status as an example of an action inappropriate for an anthropologist. (You will recall that my father regretted this involvement himself.) Suzuki bitterly concluded that "the methods, assumptions and pretensions of conventional American anthropology were tested in the Japanese internment camps during World War II, and were found wanting."[14]

A different criticism was offered by Orin Starn, who analyzed the assumptions of the field of applied anthropology that had come into prominence in the 1930s.[15] Applied anthropology aimed to contribute to the "social engineering" of societies, especially those that were managed by colonial powers or other external forces. Starn argued that the use of applied anthropology in the setting of the wartime camps may have been well-intentioned, but was paternalistic and misguided. He asserted that the anthropologists aided the government in conveying to the public the false impression of a humane handling of what was frequently described as a "wartime necessity."

Did my father, along with other community analysts, help to improve the lives of the internees? His reports alerted local and national administrators to specific problems and tensions within the camp and recommended specific actions that were intended to improve camp conditions. The camp director stated that he valued these objective reports highly and recognized the utility of having an experienced social scientist's help in understanding the attitudes of the evacuees as they reacted to the often arbitrary policies of the WRA.[16] In reading my father's reports, it is easy for me to imagine that he provided a useful service to the local authorities and that he helped them to understand tensions in the camp. Certainly there was less overt expression of unrest in Gila River in its last two years. But it is impossible for me to ascertain whether his work really made much difference in the larger circumstance of the authoritarian conditions that prevailed at the Gila River concentration camp.

The more painful thought is that the community analysts collectively may have been a tool of the WRA in providing a scientific patina to the image of a thoughtful and caring administration. A number of anthropological articles written during and immediately after the war give strength to this argument by portraying anthropology as a positive force in the application of concepts of "social engineering" to the management of the camps.[17] Although I see no evidence of this tendency in my father's writing, I think that the argument may have some validity.

Coincidentally, shortly after the war my father collaborated with the prominent anthropologists Margaret Mead and Elliot Chapple in writing a code of ethics for applied anthropologists. Although the code did not include mention of the Japanese American evacuation and internment, it did refer explicitly to the conduct of anthropologists in both peace and war. It underlined the need for applied anthropologists to take responsibility for the effects of their recommendations. They "must strive to achieve a greater degree of well-being for the constituent individuals within a social system."[18] The underlying message of the code to applied anthropologists was to advance forms of human relationships that contribute to the integrity of the individual. This code of ethics would have been a valuable guide for the WRA and the community analysts, had it existed before the war.

The camp administration was obliged to carry out the policies of the WRA leadership in Washington. Any attempts to improve camp conditions were greatly constrained by policy decisions taken at headquarters, which frequently appeared arbitrary to local administrators and evacuees alike. Especially difficult was the WRA policy of resettlement, according to which evacuees were strongly encouraged to move to hostile and unfamiliar cities in the East and Midwest. But the "resistance to freedom," as one anthropologist described it,[19] was profound, and could not easily be overcome by WRA actions. Conflicting policies on loyalty status, poor information on job opportunities and housing, ridiculously small amounts of financial support for those willing to relocate, and internees' profound fear of discrimination were major obstacles. Both of my parents worked with individual families to help surmount these problems. Four months after the war's end, the last evacuees left, and the Gila River concentration camp was closed forever.

I returned to Gila River in 1999 for the first time since my departure fifty-four years earlier. The Pima Indian official in charge of escorting visitors to the site drove my wife and me through lush fields of wheat and alfalfa and rich orchards of oranges and olives, miraculously created out of the dry desert by irrigation. Abruptly the car turned into a narrow dirt road and we were back in the desert. The remains of the Gila River camp appeared before us, ringed by small cactus-covered buttes. We drove to the top of a butte and the remnants of a war memorial erected during the war by camp officials to honor all the young men from Gila River who had served in the armed forces. The names were no longer there.

In front of us stretched a barren, flat plain, overgrown with mesquite and sagebrush, where so many people had lived for three years. This community of 13,000 was then the fourth largest city in Arizona. (The other concentration camp, at Poston, was the third largest.)

A deep feeling of sadness came over me as I viewed this desolate scene. Through the sand and overgrowth of dry vegetation a grid of roads and firebreaks could barely be seen, with small blocks of cement footings scattered about, marking the spots where dozens of wooden barracks had stood. Larger cement floors marked the site of the fire hall and the high school auditorium. As I walked through this empty shell of a city, I saw the remains of small Japanese stone gardens in the sand, with cement-lined pools, now dry, where carp had swum. Bits of wood, wire, and asphalt roofing lay scattered in the sand and mesquite.

At the far end of the camp a small butte marked the section where the administrative staff had lived. I climbed the butte as I had many times as a child. This time it took only three minutes, so quick compared to my childhood memories. Looking down, I saw the solid cement base of my family's barracks, much more substantial than the tiny footings of the barracks housing the Japanese American families. I descended and stood, then sat, then lay down in the place that had been our living room. I was in the spot where I had such happy childhood memories, but now I felt insignificant and profoundly sad.

A thriving community, forced here by an unjust and racist act of the government, was forged in this inhospitable desert. The site stands for so much:

for abrogation of civil liberties; for the strength and perseverance of many Japanese American families; for courageous opposition to the government by some and for brave military service by others; and for overcoming terrible hardship to build new lives after the war.

Gila River and the other concentration camps must be preserved and visited so that Americans will never forget that, in the words of former United States Senator Alan Cranston, "with the exception of the sanctioning of human slavery, the removal and detention of 120,000 Japanese Americans by our Government in 1942 merely because of their ancestry remains the single worst mass violation of civil rights and liberties in our nation's history."[20]

As to my father's role, I now see that through his research and reports he sought to make a positive effort to improve the daily lives of the people incarcerated in the Gila River camp. What comes through is his sensitivity to cultural issues, his opposition to racism, his ability to be a mediator between the evacuees and the administration, and his efforts to reduce racial tensions. My mother also contributed to the difficult decisions that individual families had to confront in the process of resettlement. I do not think that the WRA was above reproach in employing anthropologists in the camps. No doubt there was paternalism in the idea of viewing the concentration camps as communities suitable for "social engineering" and objective social research. The community analysts may well have added to the WRA's image of itself as a thoughtful, humane agency for handling the relocation of people from one part of the country to another, an image that masked the reality of unjust incarceration in harsh, isolated concentration camps.

For the first time since I left Gila River in 1945, I have achieved a measure of understanding of my parents' roles. As employees of the WRA, they tried to support the incarcerated Japanese Americans and to ameliorate their condition. Yet they worked within an oppressive system in which only limited opportunities existed for positive change, and in which the racist behavior of some WRA staff created still more barriers. In the process of uncovering my parents' roles, I have become reconciled to my own unease and guilt. I now feel great satisfaction in the friendships that I have established with those Japanese Americans who have helped me along the way. And I can now speak out in full support of the continuing efforts to strive for reconciliation and to educate the larger public about this terrible injustice.[21]

NOTES

1. G. Gordon Brown, "Final Report, War Relocation Authority, Gila River Project," *Applied Anthropology* 4:4 (1945): 7.

2. Ibid., 6.
3. G. Gordon Brown, "Evacuee Attitudes Toward the WRA" (October 30, 1943), National Archives, Washington D.C., "Community Analysis Reports to the WRA," Microfilm Roll No. 12.
4. Ibid., 1–2.
5. Ibid., 5.
6. Ibid., 8.
7. Rosalie Hankey Wax, "Report to Dorothy S. Thomas," University of California, Berkeley, Japanese American Evacuation and Relocation Study, Bancroft Library, Microfilm Roll No. 280.
8. G. Gordon Brown, "Notes on the Family and Social Stratification" (December 1943), National Archives, "Community Analysis Reports to the WRA," Microfilm Roll No. 13.
9. G. Gordon Brown, "Notes on Changes of Answers to Question 28 of the Army Questionnaire" (October 1943), National Archives, "Community Analysis Reports to the WRA," Microfilm No. 12.
10. G. Gordon Brown, "Final Report," 6.
11. Elizabeth F. Brown, "Family Planning Reports" (1944–45), National Archives, "Community Analysis Reports to the WRA," Microfilm No. 14.
12. Peter T. Suzuki, "Anthropologists in Wartime Camps for Japanese Americans: A Documentary Study," *Dialectical Anthropology* 6:1 (1981): 23–60. See also Peter T. Suzuki, "A Retrospective Analysis of a Wartime 'National Character' Study," *Dialectical Anthropology* 5 (1980): 33–46.
13. Ibid., 31.
14. Ibid., 45–46.
15. Orin Starn, "Engineering Internment: Anthropologists and the War Relocation Authority," *American Ethnologist* 13:4 (1986):700–20.
16. G. Gordon Brown, "Final Report," 8.
17. See, for example, John Embree, "Community Analysis: An Example of Anthropology in Government," *American Anthropologist* 46 (1944); Elliot Chapple, "Anthropological Engineering: Its Use to Administrators," *Applied Anthropology* 2: 2 (1943): 23–32; John Provinse and Solon Kimball, "Building New Communities During Wartime," *American Sociological Review* 11:4 (1946): 396–410.
18. Margaret Mead, Elliot Chapple, and G. Gordon Brown, "Report of the Committee on Ethics," *Human Organization* (1949): 20–21.
19. John Embree, "Resistance to Freedom: An Administrative Problem," *Applied Anthropology* 2:1 (1943): 2–14.
20. *Rafu Shimpo* (August 30, 1984), 1.
21. Many individuals have helped me in my search for a measure of understanding of my experience, but I can thank only a few: my brother Jeremy, who recalled the Gila River years with me; Yuzuru Takeshita, who deepened my understanding of the terrible events of the evacuation and the camps; Lane Ryo Hirabayashi and Arthur Hansen, who gave me greater insight into the role of the social scientists in the camps; Erica Harth, who was the driving force behind this endeavor and who is a wonderful and sympathetic editor; and my wife Nora, who joyfully joined and supported me in my journey of discovery.

PART III

WHAT WE TOOK
FROM THE CAMPS

JOHN Y. TATEISHI

MEMORIES FROM
BEHIND BARBED WIRE

THE SUMMER OF '42 WAS NOT FOR US WHAT IT was for the rest of America's children. The innocent laughter of kids at play on America's tree-lined streets was not the image of our youthful years. While the rest of America remembers those years of World War II with a sense of pride and nostalgia for a glorious past, for us, the kids of the camps, the experience was very, very different.

For us, the summer of '42 was a time of confusion and fear, and a time of lost innocence. There were no tree-lined streets in our world as we suddenly found ourselves in prisons in the middle of deserts, displaced and bewildered outcasts in our own country. We clung to our parents, trusting that they would protect us from what we could not possibly understand. We looked up at guard towers and felt a deep fear of armed soldiers who stood guard over us, and felt within our hearts the meaning of barbed-wire fences which, for us, was a symbol of a new America.

We were the children of the camps, prisoners in our own country. My personal story begins at a place called Manzanar, located in the Owens Valley, a couple of hundred miles east of Los Angeles. Manzanar and the Owens Valley sit at the edge of the Mojave desert along Route 395, where you drive past places with names like Red Rock Canyon, Black Mountain, Homestead, Lone Pine, and Independence, names that were part of the romantic West, names that echo a forgotten past. These places are open to the elements—the heat, the wind, the rain, and snow—and they are names that speak of a hard life in a harsh land.

At the heart of the Owens Valley is Mount Whitney, the second highest point in the continental United States. Whitney is a magnificent mountain, reaching above its neighboring peaks in the southern Sierras, a mountain alive at every hour of the day, its snow-covered peaks reflecting the earliest morning light, the valley sequestered in its shadows in the evening. At the foot of Mount Whitney, a couple of miles from its base, halfway between Lone Pine and Independence, there stands a small stone building, once a guard house, today the only remaining memory in the valley of an American tragedy. This is Manzanar.

If you talk to anyone who spent the years of World War II at Manzanar or in any of the ten camps, the one common denominator of the experience they will cite is the wind. At Manzanar, the wind comes sweeping through the Owens Valley, creating great dust storms that come tumbling across the land. However quiet the air may be during the day, at dusk, as if at an appointed hour, the wind begins to blow. One can often watch it approaching, a great cloud of dust like a tidal wave wreaking havoc over the land. It brings dust to everything: the eyes, the mouth, the nose; it even gets under your clothes, through every crack and tear of every building. At its angriest, it howls through the night, carrying the sounds of the night into the distance. In that remote land, it's a force that one learns to reckon with, to live with, I suppose, as men at sea learn to live with the angry thrashing of stormy waters.

For me, Manzanar is as much a memory of senses as it is a memory of events. Even after all these years, I can still recall the smell of summer heat, the sounds of the desert valley at night, the ever-constant wind that brought afternoon dust storms that came like giant waves off in the distance, the image of Mount Whitney in the distance, snow-capped even as the summer heat approached. For me, a child of the camps, the memories flood back when I get lost in the senses of the experience, when that part of memory that still clings to the sounds, the smells, and the images brings back the years at Manzanar.

It is the images that still occasionally haunt my thoughts of those years: the guard towers, the fence, the soldiers with their rifles, the searchlight sweeping the camp at night, lonely Issei men staring blankly into an unknown distance more distant than the mountains or the desert floor.

Even after all these decades, in moments when I lose myself in memories of those years in Manzanar, I can still recall the feeling of isolation and abandonment I felt so very long ago. I can recall the sense of loneliness I felt as I looked out at the land beyond the barbed-wire fences. It is a memory that came back to me many times as a young boy, a sense of loneliness that sometimes reached into my soul.

In many ways, Manzanar is where memory begins for me and is what my life is all about: it is what has shaped my life, who and what I have become. The memory of Manzanar—its images, the visceral, gut-level memory of what

Manzanar was for me—has always been at the core of me, so strong at times in the years following the war that it would sometimes draw me back to those days behind barbed wire.

Even as a young child in the camp, I understood the physical realities around me and something of the consequence of what Manzanar stood for. Even a child understands such things, knows the fear that others cannot hide, knows that there is some great consequence to barbed-wire fences closing you in and guard towers and men with rifles pointing at you. I am part of that generation of Japanese Americans, now approaching or in their sixties, who grew up with barbed wire and guard towers around us, while other children in America were growing up with maples and sycamores and picket fences around them. Ours was the "other" America, the one this nation left behind in the past to be forgotten.

And yet, ours is an American story, so real and so profound that it could not be forgotten because we could not forget what the camp experience had done to our lives and the collective shambles the experience had created out of our psyches. For forty years, our parents' generation could not talk about the war years, about the camps, about the terrible guilt and shame they felt for the violation of their spirit. They became silent and healed the exterior of their lives—and ours—but could not heal the pain within because they could never fully come to terms with what had happened to them. They were the victims, but in their minds they carried the collective guilt of the nation.

For us, the children of the camps, silence was never a choice. In the way that most children identify each other by the schools they attend and the towns they come from, we identified ourselves by our camps so that "camp," as we called the experience, remained always a psychic and emotional reality for us. Talking about camp for us was not a way to prolong the agonies of that experience so much as it was a means for us to grasp the realities of it for ourselves. It was a way for us to cope with our own guilt and shame for having been prisoners in our own land.

We told each other our stories about camp or shared the lighter moments of the things we remembered. It was a way for us to keep the memory alive and at the same time to work out the confusion and hurt the experience brought us. So we boasted, we joked, we bragged, we laughed. And we remembered. And always, always at some moment in those conversations, we grew silent, crept into those private thoughts that we each kept hidden deep within ourselves. We protected ourselves by our silence, kept those private moments to ourselves. Even to this day, there are memories of camp I share with no one, not because they were awful things I did or that had happened to me, but because they were the moments that went beyond words to the awful truth of what had happened to *us*. We knew even then as kids that we carried the same guilt and shame that our parents felt. They could not protect themselves, and worse, they could not protect us or hide the humiliation they were forced to endure. I suppose that in many ways we understood our parents' guilt in not being able to protect us children from what was happening to us. It was the pain of that knowledge that we found so hard to face. And so we buried it deep within ourselves, hid it even from ourselves, tried in our own ways to protect our parents. And so we laughed and talked about camp. And we remembered, for us and for our parents.

I don't remember the day we were forced from our home along with the rest of our community to the isolation of Manzanar. I was just turning three, the youngest of four boys, and too young to remember. On that day, when my family boarded the buses that would take us from Los Angeles to Manzanar, I broke out with German measles and was taken from my mother and placed into quarantine at Los Angeles General Hospital, placed under armed guard because I was, after all, someone the United States government deemed "dangerous" to the security of the country. It would be two or three weeks before I would be reunited with my family at Manzanar, sent by train with one of the last groups to be shipped off to the camp.

On the day I arrived at Manzanar, I can remember lying on the floor of our barracks dropping my mother's bobby pins through a crack between the boards, watching the pins fall in patterns on the ground under the floor like some homemade kaleidoscope. What I remember of that scene was wanting to go home and crying silently to myself because I somehow understood that this was where we had to be and that my parents could not make it otherwise. And I can remember later that day my mother taking me to the barbed-wire fence and telling me always to stay with my brothers and warning me never to attempt to go outside the confines of the fence, all the while looking up anxiously at the guard tower. Barely five feet tall, petite and pretty with soft, gentle eyes, my mother is a loving, very gentle person who has always tried to keep her fears and disappointments in life hidden within her. But I can remember clearly that day at Manzanar the fear in her voice and the anxious, worried look in her eyes as she clutched my hand by the fence, and I never forgot the meaning of barbed wire and guard towers.

If there has been one image that has symbolized for me the sum total of the concentration camp experience, it is the image implanted in my mind that day with my mother, the image of barbed wire and the guard tower against the backdrop of the desert valley. I know that I understood—if not on that particular day, at least sometime early in my experience in Manzanar—that even though I had come from some distant place to this desolate prison camp, my life would never again be the same out there. I learned that life is not parceled out equally, sometimes despite what you are but too often because of the way you look or the way you think. I knew (and I can distinctly remember being aware of this) that my confinement was because I was Japanese. I knew, even at the early age of three or four, that I was different from the men who stood in the towers, different from the white faces that stared curiously at the camp and at us from the cars that passed by on the distant highway. I understood this as I stood near the fence, watching an occasional car pass the camp along the highway, its wheels humming on the pavement until it disappeared, solitary, into the vast distance. And somehow for me, in the strange logic of a child's mind, that represented America, riding off into the solitary distance away from this wasteland and this prison. And for years after the war, when I was years and miles away from Manzanar, the image would come stealing back unsuspected into my memory at night or in solitary moments.

There was no ignoring what had happened to us, no way to cast aside the dismay and disbelief once we saw what we had become, prisoners in our own land. But we could not return now, nor could we awaken from this most awful of nightmares. By day, the adults put their minds and backs to the business of life and found ways to pass the days and to fashion some semblance of a normal life for all of us, as if there could be anything normal about it. But at night, when the wind howled and Mount Whitney rose up against the darkness, what staggering thoughts must have echoed through the conscious minds of all those who lay awake listening to the wind, thinking about some distant place of the heart. However much you are able to sidestep certain truths and pains and considerations during the day, at night they come creeping home to you and bring you back to yourself, bring you back to the realization of what you've allowed to have happened and what you've become.

I was too young, of course, to understand the real meaning of our imprisonment, and too young to feel the full impact of our situation. I understood well enough the significance of the barbed wire, but I was protected from other terrible truths: America's racism against us, white America's hatred of me because of my ancestry, the fact that even as a child I was viewed with diminished humanity. As a child of the camps, I was protected from these truths, and in some ways, I suppose, my life was not too different from a lot of kids' lives in America between the years 1942 and 1945. I spent a good part of my time playing with my brothers and friends, learned from my brothers to shoot marbles and catch rattlesnakes, envied the older kids who wore Boy Scout uniforms. We shared with the rest of America the same heart-breaking songs of the forties. We imported much of America into the camps because, after all, we were Americans. Through imitation of my brothers, I learned the salute to the flag, and I was learning, as well as one could in Manzanar, what it meant to live in America. But I was also learning the sometimes bitter price one has to pay for it.

My lessons in life came early. I'm talking here not about the rules that help you to survive and get you through the day, but about the *real* lessons, the ones that really count, that shape our lives and account for what we become. Survival, yes, but only in its most profound sense. For me, it was the winter of 1942, the December of that year when the cold and cutting winds swept across the valley, just eight months after our imprisonment and one year after Pearl Harbor. I was about three and a half years old then, when my father, who refused to accept our imprisonment quietly, was arrested by the soldiers and taken from the camp. Early in December of that year, a friend of my father's, Harry Ueno, had discovered a shortage of sugar, flour, and meats on shipments to the camp mess halls. He discussed it with my father, and the two realized that the guards or administrators were stealing provisions intended for us and selling them on the black market. Mr. Ueno confronted the camp authorities about the thefts and was arrested and accused of being a troublemaker. My father went to the authorities later that day to demand Mr. Ueno's release, and as he was negotiating, a riot broke out in the camp. Accused as the instigators of the Manzanar riot, my father and Mr. Ueno were taken to the jail at Independence. I watched as they took them away, handcuffed and shackled.

That night was terrifying. All night long, the searchlights swept the camp, and bands of men could be heard running past our barracks, shouting angrily. We had no idea what had happened to my father, and at one point in the night I sneaked out to try to find him. I can recall running from building to building, avoiding the searchlights and the bands of men and, most fearfully, hiding from the soldiers as they swept through the camp. At one point during the night, while the riot was still raging throughout the camp, a group of men brandishing sticks stood near the front gate, angrily shouting at the guards. At some point, the guards opened fire on the crowd. I didn't know I had heard gunfire but recall seeing the crowd of men running and shouting in all directions in what seemed a mass of confusion. I was terrified. I turned and ran all the way back to our barracks and, once inside, said nothing to my mother or my grandfather or my brothers. I was sure the guards were going to come and get us. I don't recall when I eventually fell asleep, but I remember being awakened throughout the night by the angry shouts of men stampeding past our barracks.

As it turned out, it was a night of violence that ended up not only with the guards firing at the crowd of rioters, but with attacks against men accused of being snitches who cooperated with the administrators to single out the men they wanted arrested and taken from the camp. Many of the rioters that night were the Kibei, Japanese Americans born in this country and educated or raised through part of their youth in Japan. Mr. Ueno was a Kibei, as was my father. The Kibei felt doubly victimized by the camp experience because their outspoken criticism of the government's action in imprisoning us resulted in their being blacklisted by both the camp administrators and some of the leaders within the camps. They were considered troublemakers and were treated accordingly. The Kibei were unrelenting in their criticism of the government for its racist imprisonment of us and unforgiving of those who they believed betrayed other Japanese Americans at Manzanar by cooperating with the authorities.

After my father had been taken away, I remember telling my mother that they were going to shoot him, because it seemed to me that was what they did with those guns when they took you away from the camp, forced you away from the safety of your family and your friends, took you beyond the barbed wire into that fearsome distance. Nothing my mother told me could convince me otherwise, especially as the days and weeks passed without his return. I never mentioned my fear again to anyone, not even to my brothers. I kept my fear buried within me, lived with it day and night because it was too frightening to mention or even to think about. It was our first Christmas in camp, the first Christmas my brothers and I had spent without my father. We wouldn't see him again for over a year.

I don't remember now, but I suppose that in time I learned to live with the thought of what had happened to my father, forgot as children sometimes mercifully do, about the fear and pain of the experience—in essence, began to forget my father. And yet, this single episode would in many ways prove to affect my life more than any other incident of my three years at Manzanar, perhaps, in its own way, as much as the entire camp experience itself. In the long run, it was not only the soldiers leading my father away that had such an impact on me, nor was it the fear I experienced for my father. In the long run, it was that I never understood what happened or what it meant, why my father had been singled out. For years afterwards as I was growing up, I suffered the contempt of adults who accused my father of starting the riot. My father and Mr. Ueno had been leaders of the Manzanar riot, I was reminded, and he had not played by the rules, and for this he had had to pay the price. I had been made to feel guilty for his part in the trouble, had too often seen the look in the eyes of the adults. In many ways, it was the discomfort forced upon me by the sneering looks of adults at my being my father's son that had its lasting impact on me. As a young boy growing up in the aftermath of the camp experience, I never understood the reason for those looks. As a young boy, I was completely defenseless against such looks, and as I look back on those postwar years now, I realize that the ostracism I faced and the demeaning treatment of my father had as much a lasting affect on me in some ways as the camp experience itself.

What I did not understand for some years was that my father refused to accept that there could be any justification at all for our imprisonment and suffering. And what I did not know then was that my father believed so strongly in the integrity of being Japanese American that he could not forgive anyone among us for betraying another in such dire times. Be proud of who you are, he would always say. Live by your principles, he always told me: if you believe in them, always stand by them, even die for them if you'must. It was the price he paid for what he believed in. And so he was taken away by the soldiers.

The days passed, the weeks, the months, the years, and all of our lives fell into the rhythm of the valley: to the changing light from morning to evening and from season to season. I spent most of my days with my grandfather, who had come to Manzanar with us. He was given the job of watching over a dam at a place named George's Creek. I've never understood exactly what his job was (how does one watch over a dam?), except that every morning he passed through the back gate of Manzanar (he had a special pass for this) and walked two or three miles to the creek. After a time, he built himself a hut out of branches, and there he would spend much of his time. It was an adventure for me to be with him, for he was a man for whom life, even at it its lowest common denominator, was always an adventure, a man I've always felt was full of wisdom and an understanding of life, a gentle and compassionate man whom I loved dearly. We would take our time walking to the creek in the early mornings, I and this man whose body stood straight and proud, whose eyes were kind and tender; and holding his hand, I felt warm and safe in the world.

It was an idyllic life with my grandfather out there at the creek, almost as if the war and the barbed wire never existed. I learned a great deal about life from him on those days by the creek, listened to him talk about his youth, about the wind and the water, learned that there was more in the majestic flight of the hawks above than in the words of men. And I laughed with delight as I watched him stride naked into the creek, sit unflinching for what seemed hours in the icy water, and finally emerge with a struggling trout in his bare hands. And he would sit by the creek for hours and sing his *utai*, an ancient form of Japanese song that told of forgotten legends and glories. And all the while he talked to me about life, and I would hear his song mingle with the rushing water, with the trees and clouds. And I would fall asleep curled in his lap, listening to his quiet singing, and I knew everything was all right. And in the late afternoon he carried me on his back, sometimes the entire distance to the camp.

My days with my grandfather remain even today some of my best memories of my youth, despite those days having been at Manzanar. Our days and years at Manzanar and at all the camps forever changed our lives and are the benchmark of who and what we are and whatever we might become in the future. Looking back now, I know that our lives were destroyed simply because of who we were. And even worse, we destroyed ourselves in the process in so many ways. We were torn apart by untenable confrontations that were forced upon us, and instead of directing our anger and hurt at the government, we directed it against ourselves and in some cases caused emotional chasms that can never be bridged. I don't know if any of us children of the camps understood how profoundly the wound cut into the psyches of the Issei and Nisei generations or how unforgiving brother would be to brother when it was all over.

But "camp" has never been "all over." We children of the camps continue to measure our lives against where we've come from. That moment in history when we looked around our desert isolation and saw what we had become as Americans was where our lives began. It's where memory is, where we defined ourselves. But I sometimes wonder whether we have looked honestly at the bitter truths about our lives during those years and truly reckoned with ourselves. I read somewhere that psychological wounds cut so deep sometimes that you really never get to the core of them. I know that's true in our case. I'm sure there are words for the anger, but are there words for the pain, and is there a way to reach that deep and that far? Perhaps it's simply a matter for the heart. Perhaps others can express the anger for you, but in the end, that becomes little more than words. In the end, it is you alone who knows the real pain. And it is you alone who sheds the real tears. No one else can walk those lonely miles on the wastelands of America and hear what you hear in the wind.

I returned to Manzanar in the early summer of 1975. It was a private journey, a personal sojourn past thirty years to the images that had remained in my memory. Very little remains there: the guardhouse, the old auditorium (now a maintenance building for the local utility company), the foundations of the latrines and of some barracks. I walked around Manzanar aimlessly for hours, perhaps looking for my past but never quite finding it. I hiked out to George's Creek and walked up and down the dry creek bank. I'm not sure what I was looking for or what I hoped to find. Perhaps my grandfather's hut, perhaps the image of a young boy listening quietly to an old man singing. For a time, I stood at the edge of the camp, where the barbed wire had been, and looked to the distance, looked at Mount Whitney, still magnificent as it has always been in my memory. And standing there, I realized that I have never been free of this place, realized just how much Manzanar has been a part of my existence all those years.

Over the years, I have come to understand the effect of the camp experience on myself and maybe even on all of us who were there. In walking around Manzanar, in seeing just what little hope was offered there, I was convinced that something in each of us died a little, gave way a little to the barrenness of the land. There is no mercy to that land there nor to any of the camp sites, and certainly we had not been prepared for what our lives would become in those desolate places. The experience of America's concentration camps shaped my generation of Japanese Americans, left its indelible mark on all of us, and kept us bound forever to the image of barbed wire and guard towers. No, I thought to myself as I sat there looking at the fading light of Manzanar, no one really ever leaves this place. I left Manzanar more than fifty years ago, but out there, somewhere on the deserts of America, I'm still a young boy running in the wind.

PATRICK S. HAYASHI

PICTURES FROM CAMP

MY MOTHER USED TO TELL ME A STORY ABOUT TOPAZ. An old, deaf man had adopted a stray dog. When his dog got caught in the barbed wire, the man went to free him. The guard in the tower commanded him to move away from the fence, but of course the old man did not respond. The guard shot and killed him. She said that the old man just wanted to help his dog, and that the guard was "just a boy." The more I heard the story, the more I thought that she was telling me to be careful, not to trust white people. That's why I hated the story—because all her other messages were so different. She taught me to be open to people, to judge people just as people. And that's how I tried to live my life until I got involved in freshmen admissions at Berkeley.

In the 1980s Berkeley was embroiled in a controversy over Asian American admissions. The controversy got so heated that in 1988 Chancellor Ira M. Heyman went to the state legislature and said that Berkeley should have been more sensitive to Asian American concerns, and he formally apologized to the Asian American community.

Asian community leaders said, "Thank you very much. We accept your apology but we can't help but notice that there are zero Asian Americans in top-level positions." They said, "If you really mean what you say, you will appoint at least one."

At the time, I was Chancellor Heyman's assistant. I would meet with him every morning. He was having a hard time with the Asian controversy. He'd walk around the room holding his head.

He said, "You know, Pat, they're right. I should appoint an Asian American, but where can I find one?"

He looked at me as if he were seeing me for the first time. "How would you like to be in charge of admissions?"

Hatsuki Wakasa, Shot by M.P.
April 11, 1943
Sumi on paper, 11 x 15¼ in.

"April 11, 1943, Hatsuki Wakasa, Shot by M. P." Watercolor by Chiura Obata. By permission of the Obata family.

I replied, "Sure, I'd be glad to!"

That's when I began to feel the pain of affirmative action. The critics are right. Affirmative action can make you doubt yourself. Remember reading *The Scarlet Letter* in high school? I felt just like Hester Prynne. Instead of a scarlet A, I had AA branded on my chest. Wherever I went people asked, "Just how did you get your job?"

I would try to keep things light. I would smile and say, "Berkeley had this controversy over Asian American admissions and Chancellor Heyman had to do something. For me, it was just a matter of being in the right race at the right time." Portraying myself as the Asian for the occasion always released the tension.

But the trouble was when I told jokes, I felt awful. And when I looked at older Asian American staff who were proud of me and happy that I was getting the chance they had never gotten, they just looked sad.

Then I went through a second phase. I started hearing criticisms of me. I heard that some people were going around saying that I didn't deserve the appointment, that I was just a token. Now those words hurt. Because sometimes they came from people I had worked with for years and thought were my friends.

So I then started my third phase: I got angry. I thought about what happened to my family during World War II. Before the war, my family had had a huge nursery in East Oakland. During the war, my parents and grandparents lost everything.

They were stripped of their civil rights, rounded up like animals, penned up for months in horse stables, and then shipped off to Topaz, a concentration camp in a desert in the middle of Utah. And as soon as we were taken away, our family nursery was pillaged. People, *neighbors*, came and stole pipes, hoses, windows, light fixtures, floorboards—everything.

I thought about how it took my grandfather a lifetime to build our nursery. In twenty-four hours it was stripped bare. I thought about my cousin who was picked up by the FBI for questioning and, during the interrogation, mysteriously died of a heart attack. I thought about my father. After we were released from prison, the only job he could get was as a gardener. I thought about how I was born in that concentration camp. I thought about my education. All through elementary school, high school, and college, in all my textbooks, I found only one paragraph on Japanese Americans. And that paragraph was wrong! I thought, "Racism is real. Asian Americans have suffered. I've suffered. I deserve this job."

The trouble was that getting angry didn't feel good either. I felt diminished. I knew that I was the product of social forces. But I also hoped that I was more. Much, much more.

So I was stuck. Jokes made me feel awful. Feeling sorry for myself didn't help. Anger just left me feeling empty. So I asked myself, "Why did Chancellor Heyman choose me?" And I made up an answer. Maybe he saw that California was changing. Our population was changing. Berkeley was changing. The job of admissions was changing.

Before, the job had required the ability to process thousands of forms. Now the job required new skills, the ability to make policy for a multiracial society. Maybe he looked at what I had done so far and thought that I was qualified, that I had the combination of education, skills, and experience to do this entirely new job.

Did it make a difference that I am Asian? Of course, it did. My race was an important factor. But there were other important factors. Chancellor Heyman balanced them all and decided to give me a chance to prove myself. It didn't matter where I came from. What mattered was what I could do.

I like this explanation. I don't know if it's true. And it doesn't matter. What matters is this explanation allowed me to stop putting myself down, to stop feeling sorry for myself, and to stop blaming others, and to get on with my job.

GETTING ON WITH MY JOB

Getting on with my job was hard. I'm very shy. Whenever I spoke in public I felt as if I were watching myself on a TV monitor. I always paid more attention to the monitor than to what I was saying. Naturally, I would get confused and lose my train of thought. Sometimes I literally did not know what I had just said. When that happened, I'd panic. I'd try to talk myself out of the mess but things would always just get worse. Needless to say, I tried my best to avoid speaking in public. But in this job I couldn't.

I was invited to speak at the annual banquet of a local Japanese American service club. The members were mainly well-established, second-generation Japanese Americans—my family doctor, for example. I was the guest of honor and during dinner I was treated very, very well. Many of the old-timers knew my father and my grandfather, and they were proud that Henry's boy had done well. I was really happy to be there. I was able to relax in a way that was unusual. Usually, I felt as if I had to be on my guard, that people were just waiting for me to stumble. But here, with my own people, I felt that I was able to speak honestly and openly. I explained that the hardest part of my job, and the part that also gave me the most satisfaction, was the work I was doing for racial integration at Berkeley. All of them had been imprisoned in the camps, most in Topaz, and so I trusted that they would understand the importance of giving all people a chance to better themselves and live their lives fully.

As I spoke, people stared to murmur, and then, perhaps because they had been drinking heavily, some started to talk loudly to themselves. I could hear them say things like, "They should get off welfare and go to work!" I started to get flustered but I went on. I tried to ignore what they were saying but they became louder and louder and even more explicitly racist.

Then someone yelled out, "Why should we let blacks into Berkeley? After all, they have professional basketball all to themselves!" Before I could think, I looked at him and said, "Fuck you." When I realized what I had said, I pulled back and looked at the entire room. Then I collected my thoughts before I spoke. And I said, "Fuck all of you. You should be ashamed of yourselves."

What followed is still hazy. Someone put his hand on my shoulder and told me to calm down. I said, "Touch me again and I'll rip your arm off." This brought an end to the festivities. They decided to end the program early. They gave me a sake set as a present.

When I was driving home I was very angry. I replayed what had happened over and over again. I went over all the things I should have said to them. But beneath my anger there was a deeper feeling. I was ashamed of myself. I was ashamed that I had cursed someone, that I had threatened someone, that I had lost control. And one thing became crystal clear. I needed help. I needed training. I needed more in my rhetorical repertoire than "Fuck you." So the next week I organized a speech class. I worked and worked on my public speaking. I learned to type out my notes in bold 18-point font, to leave a margin of four inches at the bottom so that my head wouldn't droop over the page, to move my notes side to side rather than turn them over, to record presentations so that I could critique them later. I've learned a lot. I still get anxious, but now at least I have a system, and sometimes I can even use my anxiety creatively.

And something else happened, something really unexpected. As I worked on public speaking and started to gain confidence, I found out that I wanted to speak to people, to talk about what goes through my mind as I deal with deciding whom to let into Berkeley and whom to turn away.

I have trouble with the public debate over affirmative action. Most of the public discussion has been based on slogans: level playing fields, color-blind society, reverse racism. We've heard them all. But the discussion shouldn't be about slogans, it should be about people. We're talking about kids, about giving seventeen- and eighteen-year-olds who have not had many chances a chance to work hard and improve themselves. And perhaps because I myself know how empty slogans can hurt, I've tried to find out more about these young people. And the more I've learned about them, the more I've wanted to tell their stories. Let me describe three students I got to know.

MY THREE STUDENTS

I'll begin with Yvette. Yvette suffered her first stroke when she was three. She had another stroke when she was twelve. As a result, her right leg, arm, and side of her face were paralyzed. She also had some brain damage; she had a very hard time learning languages. I met her at a conference, where we sat together at dinner. Hoping that we could have a nice light conversation, I said, "Hi. How are you?" She said, "Really angry." I gulped and asked why. She said that she was upset by the *Daily Cal*, Berkeley's student newspaper. A student had just killed herself by jumping off of Eshleman Hall. The *Daily Cal* explained the suicide by saying that the student had multiple sclerosis. To me, that seemed like a perfectly logical explanation, but I didn't say anything. Yvette said, "The *Daily Cal* was saying that the disabled somehow aren't fully alive, don't have as much to live for as able-bodied people."

I asked her what she was going to do with her anger.

She said, "I'm going on a one-woman crusade to make people stop locking their bikes on disabled access ramps."

She said that the bikes really make it hard to get into buildings. To her, it was just a matter of teaching people to be civil, to think about others when they act and speak.

I learned a lot from Yvette that night. A few months later, I saw her at a ten-kilometer road race held to raise funds for a science program for children. We didn't have a chance to speak to each other. She was too busy helping register runners and pinning on their numbers. As I watched her, I thought of my mother who, because of a rheumatic heart, also had trouble walking. She tried not to let this bother her. In order to make ends meet, she would take on seasonal work at Hunt's Cannery pitting fruit or sorting stewed tomatoes. Because her heart couldn't pump enough blood, her legs would ache and she'd have trouble walking home after her shift ended. She never complained because that would have made my father, who was already feeling helpless, feel even worse. Each season he would say that she didn't have to work. But each season she insisted on working for a few weeks so that she could buy all us kids new clothes for school, and my father would stop objecting. He didn't even say anything about the work or about her lending money to other women on her shift so they could make it to payday, although she knew that the chances of getting it back were small. He would just try to get up in the middle of the night and drive the six blocks to the cannery and meet her after her shift ended. I'm not sure why Yvette reminded me of my mom—maybe because of her legs, or maybe because she didn't seem to think about herself at all.

Later, I saw Yvette again. In 1990, there was a big demonstration on admissions. I had heard that students were planning to take over my office. I work in Sproul Hall, a favorite target for protesters.

This didn't make me happy. Frankly, I panicked. So I called my boss, Russ Ellis. He worked in California Hall. I said, "Russ, what should I do? The students are planning to stage a sit-in right in my office!"

After listening to my fears he told me, "Look, Pat, this is Berkeley. You gotta go with the flow. And find a way to honor and celebrate their passion."

The next morning about two hundred students took over California Hall. And I got a call from Russ. He said, "Pat, the students have taken over the building!"

I chortled, "Russ, this is Berkeley. You gotta go with the flow!"

He said, "I'm glad you feel that way because they're chanting your name and the police want you here *now* to negotiate with them." The chief of police came by to pick me up.

As we were walking over, he said, "Pat, the men want you to know that if you're taken hostage, they'll do everything it takes to get you out even if it takes a week!"

I didn't think he was funny. I asked, "Where in the hell were you guys? How did they get in the building?"

He said, "Oh they were really clever. They used this disabled student. She was friends with the student aide named Tyrone who was guarding the door. And she asked him to let her in the door for the disabled. She was just a decoy. When he opened the door, all the protesters rushed in." Yes, it was my friend Yvette.

A couple of weeks later I took Yvette out for coffee. I was really angry both with Yvette for using Tyrone and with the rest of the protesters for using Yvette. I asked her if it was true that she had acted as a decoy. When I asked, she sat up straighter, she started smiling, and her eyes glistened.

She said, "It was really exciting. I felt just like a spy. I've never been able to do anything like that. I've never been able to do anything daring, to do anything that took physical courage. It was the best day of my life!"

I had planned to shake my finger at her. But I just mumbled, "Well, you should maybe apologize to Tyrone."

She said, "Oh, I did that right away. He understood."

Now let me tell you about another student, Robert. I hired Robert to help me clean up our office files. We worked together over the winter break, so I had a chance to get to know him. We hit it off because he was an English major, just as I had been. I found out that he had a complicated life. His father was in prison. His stepbrother had just been arrested for manslaughter. His mother was on welfare. As the oldest son, Robert had the responsibility to keep everything together. He was on the verge of flunking out. He was very bright, but he had a lot on his mind.

The thing that was bothering him at the moment was that his aunt was a crack addict living with another crack addict. And they would punish their three-year-old baby boy, Santos, by locking him in a closet. Robert's mother called a social worker who took Santos into protective custody.

This infuriated Robert's aunt. Her boyfriend went over to Robert's mother (they lived in the same complex), tore her apartment apart, and threatened to beat her up. Robert felt it was his responsibility to go home, to confront this guy, "call him out," and protect his mother.

He asked me what he should do. He was scared, but he made it clear that he could not—he would not—back down. I recognized this stubbornness, really anger. It's what had gotten me into trouble at the banquet. It's what my mother and father passed on to me through stories. I thought about a story my mother used to tell me. It was about a private in the Japanese American 442nd Regimental Combat Team whose platoon was pinned down by German machine-gun fire. My mom and dad described how he had rushed the machine-gun nest and managed to save his friends by blowing it up with a grenade. She said that his friends counted twenty-two bullets in his body. They never told me the moral of this story. They never had to.

My parents taught my brothers and me by example. Mostly, they taught us to endure abuse, not to endanger ourselves or embarrass our families by fighting back. But we were also taught that there were some lines that we could never let people cross. What those were, we were never told. We were just expected to know. Japanese Americans understand this. I understood it in Robert.

So I understood that there was nothing I could say that would change what he was planning to do. In the end, I suggested that he write down what he was thinking and feeling and what happened. He did, and he ended up writing a short story.

Robert stayed in school and enrolled in Maxine Hong Kingston's creative writing class. He got an A+. Later he won second place in a campus short-story competition. He managed to work himself off probation, and once he felt part of Berkeley he became a social activist and started Berkeley's first Chicano fraternity.

Finally, let me tell you about Jenny. She was born in Cambodia. When she was seven her mother took two family photos, punched holes in the tops, and hung them by string around the necks of Jenny and her little sister. And said goodbye to them. Their two older brothers, who were guerrillas fighting against the Vietnamese, took them into the jungle so that they could work their way out of the killing fields of Cambodia into Thailand and to safety at a refugee camp. As they left the village, they walked over the body of their neighbor who was lying dead in a creek bed, being eaten by small fish.

They stayed in the jungle for two weeks. They were scared the whole time. They had to hide from the Vietnamese, and also their own countrymen, the Khmer Rouge. They had some rice, but mostly they had to scavenge for food in order to eat. Jenny told me that the most horrible thing of all was when she and her little sister saw their brothers torture and then kill a Vietnamese soldier.

Jenny at age eleven somehow made her way to Oakland where she lived on welfare and attended her first American school. She and her sister started school right before Christmas. That was hard because they knew nobody, but they got lucky—they found some wonderful teachers.

Jenny's first teacher made a change in the school's Christmas program. She had Jenny and her sister sing "Twinkle, Twinkle, Little Star" because those were the only English words they knew. It didn't quite fit into the Christmas pageant but this teacher, who was black, was determined that they not be left out in their new country.

She had even more problems, ones I could not discuss with her. I knew from a friend, who had worked with her little sister, that when Jenny lived with her brothers, she was the victim of abuse. One evening I went over to her family's house for dinner. The whole family was there, even her brothers, and we all ate an incredible twelve-course Cambodian meal. I wondered about how the family managed to stay intact. As I watched the family, it became clear that it was Jenny who was keeping everyone together. I couldn't understand how she could still live with, let alone forgive, her brothers. And then, for some reason, I thought of a scene drawn by Estelle Ishigo, an artist who was incarcerated at Heart Mountain, of a young woman walking in the snow, cradling her newborn, "illegitimate" baby in her arms, to the camp incinerator. I thought about how that woman—girl, really—must have tried to hide her pregnancy, how she must have had her baby in a far stall in the bathroom, how her family must have known all and ignored all—to keep life going, because there was nothing else to be done other than whatever it took to keep her family's dignity intact.

Jenny went on to high school, fulfilled her University of California requirements, and applied to Berkeley. There was absolutely no doubt that she would succeed at Berkeley. She had come too far to stumble now. She had very good grades—straight A's. She did have the lowest SAT verbal score that I've ever seen. But she had as much to say as any student I had ever met.

THE MORAL OF THE STORIES

What's the moral of these three stories? For me, the moral is that policy-makers should always consider the human dimension. The stories tell us a great deal about what a fair admissions process would look like. The stories make clear that it would be foolish to take the students' measure or to judge them by using only grade-point average. They had very, very high grades, but they didn't attend wealthy schools with a lot of honors and advanced placement courses for which the University of California awards bonus points. So they didn't have the opportunity to earn astronomical grade-point averages. Their stories also show that it would be unfair and foolish to evaluate them only by their SAT scores.

Not one of them had the opportunity to take SAT prep courses and boost their scores. At most, the SATs indicated to us how hard the students would have to work in order to do well at Berkeley. But the students knew all that already. Most important, the SATs said nothing about how well they would do at the University of California. Or what they might contribute later.

The stories also tell us something more subtle—that preferences for disadvantaged students might not help much either. The notion of "personal disadvantage" was completely foreign to Yvette, Robert, and Jenny. They did not see themselves as "disadvantaged" in any way. They saw themselves as blessed by good fortune. And why not? It was also absolutely clear that given their opportunities, they had excelled beyond belief. I doubt that any one of us could honestly say that we know we would have done as well. I know I wouldn't have.

By listening to these stories we learn that rather than create admissions criteria to judge people, we should think about Jenny, Robert and Yvette, and students like them and use them to judge ourselves, to take our own measure. If our universities cannot find a place for them, then we must find our universities wanting.

When we look at their lives, we realize that any university in the United States, but especially a public university, should be eager and proud to admit Jenny, Robert, and Yvette. They are hardworking and smart. They are brave and good.

But deciding that these three students deserve to be admitted is easy. What's hard is deciding whom to deny. In order to admit these three students, we have to deny six others. They have their stories too, many of which are equally compelling. That's how we learn another lesson. There are no easy answers. The best we can do is continue to talk to each other about this essentially unsolvable problem. We also learn that when we do talk, we must avoid slogans and instead speak in a way that respects the complexity of the issues.

Perhaps we can start by reminding ourselves that not everyone who supports affirmative action is asking for a handout. Racism is unfair, ugly, and real. If we are to survive as a nation, we must find ways to give all people the opportunity to succeed.

We can also teach ourselves that not everyone who questions affirmative action is a Nazi. In our lifetime, we have seen governmental policies that focus on race, here and elsewhere, put to unspeakably evil ends. We must constantly examine policies that give preference because of race. We should never feel comfortable about them or take them for granted. People who raise questions should not be branded as racists. If we can get ourselves to see that there are good, thoughtful people both for and against affirmative action, then we can begin the discussion with respect and tolerance, and, who knows, maybe we'll be able to see each other as human beings.

WHO WE MIGHT BECOME

I like my job. Actually, I love my work for a lot of reasons. I get to work on great issues—questions with no clear answers. I believe that I can make a difference—not much, perhaps, but some. What I do might change some lives. But most importantly and most selfishly, my work has changed my life. I work primarily on racial issues. This can get very oppressive. It's hard to think about race all the time.

When I get worn down, I think about a poem by Muriel Rukeyser, called "The Gift." The poem is about what it feels like to be a Jew. It's about how, for her, Jewishness and the persecution that comes with it have strengthened her intellectually, emotionally, and morally.

Perhaps because of all the unspoken lessons given to me by my parents, her poem resonates with me and I feel the same way about my work. I've gotten smarter because I've had to study issues as I've never studied anything before. I've had to study history, philosophy, and law to understand how people think about affirmative action. I've had to read novels and poetry so that I could understand how people feel about race. I've had to find ways to keep my mind fresh and creative. Much of what I do involves words, so many words that they dull my mind.

And I've turned to art. Like most third-generation Japanese Americans, I was not exposed to much art when I was growing up. I don't know if my father and mother liked art. I imagine that they didn't have much time for it. My own introduction to art came in a roundabout way. A local museum had an exhibit of art of the Japanese American concentration camps. The exhibit began with some landscapes painted in the Sacramento Delta region right before the war. They were simple landscapes, but for some reason as soon as I saw them, I choked up. Then came pictures that were painted in the camps themselves. The seventh painting on the wall was a watercolor by Chiura Obata, a Berkeley art professor who had been sent to Topaz. The watercolor, titled "April 11th, 1943, Hatsuki Wakasa shot by MP," shows the old, deaf man crumpling over by the barbed-wire fence as his dog looks on. I looked at it and started to cry for reasons I did not understand, maybe for Wakasa, maybe for Obata, maybe for my mother and me.

What I have learned from art deeply affects how I approach policy questions. When I create policies and programs, I pay attention to composition, to balance, to tone, to the weight of different lines of development. I try to see if the shape of the policy and program expresses their emotional and moral dimensions.

And in a mysterious way, this attention to the art of what I do has made me more spiritual. I am not a religious person, not at all. But at the heart of the debate over affirmative action lies a set of moral questions. We cannot answer these questions through analysis and logic alone. Instead, I now understand what my mother was trying to tell me. She was saying that we must also approach these questions with generosity, empathy and compassion, that we must see people as human beings.

When I think about all these issues, I find myself thinking about what I share with others—other Japanese Americans, other Asian Pacific Americans, other minorities. Then I find myself asking, "What do I share with all other people?" In other words, I find myself wondering about my humanity. This sense of wonder is allowing me to become someone I would not otherwise have become. Perhaps someone better.

WHO THEY HAVE BECOME

Let me finish this story by telling you who Yvette, Robert, and Jenny have become.

Robert got married and dropped out of school, but he came back and graduated. He ended up going to my school, the Graduate School of Public Policy. He did very well and is now working for the City of San Jose. He's still having a hard time, but I realize that Robert will always have a hard time because he likes having hard times. They give him more to write about. And write he does. He's published several poems and short stories. Most are good. Some are wonderful. All are honest.

Jenny sailed right through Berkeley, as we knew she would. While at Berkeley, she helped some of our faculty gain entree to the Southeast Asian community. After she graduated, she worked in a community agency that worked with at-risk Asian youth, which is a euphemism for Asian gangs. Now she's at graduate school studying education.

Yvette had a tough time. She did very well at Berkeley and was admitted to Harvard Law School, but there was one really cold winter here, the coldest we had in fifty years. She told me that she found that her body just shut down in the cold. She had to take 800 milligrams of painkiller just to be able to walk from class to class. The painkillers had awful side effects. Worst of all, she knew that she could never last a winter in Boston. So she knew she had to make other plans. But before she could make those plans she got cancer. This really upset her, because she got it in what she called her "good leg." Yvette has more courage than anyone I know. She went into the hospital and went through radiation and chemotherapy.

While she was in the hospital at the ripe old age of twenty-two, she became a grandmother. The hospital had a program where people "adopt" terminally ill children who have nobody else and love them as only a grandmother can. In addition to adopting two small children, she also became the hospital ombudsman and promptly began suing the place. I like to think she got her training at Berkeley.

As for my family? When my family was rounded up and shipped to Utah, we had a neighbor. He was just like my grandfather. They were the same age. He was an immigrant, too. He also had a nursery. He was just like my grandfather except he was Italian. The day my family was taken away, he came to our nursery and took some cuttings from some of our azaleas. During the war he raised them in bedding boxes. He transplanted them into terra-cotta pots. And the day my family returned, he brought them over and said to my grandfather, "Here are your flowers. I've kept them for you so you can start your life again."

ROBERT J. MAEDA

"ISAMU NOGUCHI: 5-7-A, POSTON, ARIZONA"

FOR MY GENERATION OF NISEI WHO WERE INTERNED during World War II as children, the camp experience was a disruption of childhood, a fraying of those family intimacies that so often make childhood memories pleasurable. I carry few remembrances of everyday events or even special occasions like birthdays from Poston. What images I retain are random and isolated, vivid enough to be remembered but in a context wholly divorced from Poston's communal, regimented life, almost as if I had rejected the reality of that existence. One image that has stayed with me, however, is that of Isamu Noguchi, the sculptor, working on sculptures outside his barracks a block away from ours. I cannot say why at age nine I found this man so memorable. Was it because of his appearance, or was it his single-minded concentration on his work, which seemed to make irrelevant the world around him? It was certainly my first encounter with a real artist. Later, when I chose a career in art history, I would sometimes think back to that image of Noguchi in Poston as a defining moment in my life.

Not too long ago Noguchi reentered my life when I decided to examine his career as one of the great figures in the modernist movement. To do this I had to start from scratch, since I had never learned much about Noguchi beyond my childhood impression of him. The single factor that drew me to study him was my involvement in the redress movement, which brought with it the release of dormant memories of internment, including that of Noguchi. My life as an Asian art scholar and a Japanese American began to converge. Inevitably, perhaps, my research on Noguchi began with my child's eye memory of him.

To write the following essay I had to relive those days and years of infamy with Noguchi as my guide, and, ultimately, I had to confront and reconstruct my own interrupted childhood.[1]

This is the wierdest [sic], most unreal situation—like in a dream—I wish I were out. Outside, it seems from the inside, history is taking flight and passes forever. Here, time has stoped [sic] and nothing is of any consequence, nothing of any value, neither our time or our skill.

Isamu Noguchi
5–7–A, Poston, Arizona[2]

What seemed unreal to sculptor Isamu Noguchi (1904–1988) was in fact a bitter reality to him and 120,000 other Japanese aliens and Japanese Americans living on the West Coast. Their lives irrevocably changed after Pearl Harbor and the signing of Executive Order 9066 by President Franklin D. Roosevelt on February 19, 1942. Within a matter of months, time did stop for those thousands who were forced from their homes to face uncertain futures in bleak internment camps such as Poston. For Noguchi, confinement was voluntary, since he lived in New York City, far beyond the Western Defense Command area that people were ordered to evacuate.

The circumstances that led to Noguchi's decision to enter Poston, and his efforts to ameliorate what seemed a hopeless situation both within and outside the camps, provide powerful evidence of Noguchi's social conscience and identification with his Japanese heritage. It is an aspect of his life that he briefly discussed in his 1968 autobiography, *Isamu Noguchi, A Sculptor's World*.[3] Fortunately, unpublished documents preserved in the Isamu Noguchi Foundation, Inc., give us a fuller picture of Noguchi's determined efforts to help his fellow Japanese during that turbulent period.[4]

Much has been written about Isamu Noguchi as a major artist of the modernist movement. However, it is clear that critics were not always comfortable in discussing him solely in terms of Western art, preferring to see him as a hybrid artist whose work bridged many aesthetic and cultural styles. Noguchi's biracial background contributed to the unease and lack of understanding on the part of his critics. Even Noguchi was equivocal about whether he belonged to the East or West. His father, Yone Noguchi (1875–1947), was a well-known Japanese poet who achieved international recognition as a writer of English poetry. Noguchi's mother, Leonie Gilmour (1873–1933), was a cultivated and well-educated Caucasian American woman who also was a writer. Their devotion to the arts and the unconventionality of their relationship from the time of their meeting in America to their later life in Japan greatly influenced Isamu's own artistic sensibility and, tangentially, his psychological tensions.[5]

There were a number of important factors that distinguished Noguchi from prewar Nisei, the majority of whom were living on the West Coast and Hawaii: his Eurasian origins, his formative childhood years from two to thirteen spent in Japan, his life as a lonely teenager in Indiana, and, finally, his adulthood as a prominent artist in New York. With the coming of war, he suddenly realized, "I was not just American but Nisei." And with that recognition he felt that he had to do something.[6]

That "something" was made more urgent by the fact that Noguchi was in California in 1941 through early 1942. He had gone there from New York, according to Dore Ashton,[7] seeking artistic renewal after a fallow period in his career. But the Japanese attack on Pearl Harbor put a halt to all of his artistic activities. Suddenly, in the face of war hysteria fueled by racism against West Coast Japanese, he and other Nisei felt compelled to demonstrate their loyalty to American democratic ideals and the war effort. Noguchi's response to these perils was to change him abruptly from a guarded, private person into a very public persona.

Throwing in his lot with the embattled Nisei whom he scarcely knew, Noguchi formed an organization in San Francisco, probably late in January 1942, which he called Nisei Writers and Artists Mobilization for Democracy (NWAMD), and which he modeled on a similar group formed in Los Angeles.[8]

Later statements by Noguchi indicate that his organization was hastily conceived without benefit of discussion among its board members, one of whom at least may not even have been informed of his role on the board. Noguchi's sense of desperation was reflected in his opening statement of NWAMD policy goals: "The extraordinary conditions of evacuation call for extreme measures." Because of the steady drumbeat of propaganda for evacuation by the media beginning in early January 1942 and the designation by Attorney General Francis Biddle on January 29 of strategic areas on the Pacific Coast from which all enemy aliens were to be removed, Noguchi and his group were voicing their concerns about evacuation even before the proclamation of Executive Order 9066. On the following day, Colonel Karl Bendetsen reportedly told a West Coast congressional delegation that "military judgment on the West Coast on whether or not this evacuation of citizens and aliens should take place was positively in the affirmative."[9] To counteract the "propaganda purposes to which evacuation and resettlement" might be put, Noguchi set forth the group's twofold function in his policy statement:

First to present to the public at large a clear and accurate picture of the American citizen of Japanese extraction—his background, his present status, his aspirations. Second, to perform an educational service to the Nisei themselves by dispelling whatever confusions may exist among them as to democratic principles, the issues involved in the war, and their duties as American citizens, thereby promoting their morale and consolidating their trust in American institutions.

The statement asserts that these goals can best be realized by the "experienced writers and artists" comprising the group because they are "the most articulate element in our community and who, through their background of liberal thought and action, have been consciously and consistently opposed to the programs and politics of Japanese militarism."[10]

In its tacit faith in the rectitude of American institutions, Noguchi's statement reflects ideals similar to those then held by the Japanese American Citizens League (JACL), the largest organization then representing Japanese Americans and the major conduit through which the government communicated with the larger Japanese community. Instead of protesting the evacuation as a violation of constitutional rights, as they might have done had there been more outcry from liberals, Noguchi and the members of his group were put on the defensive. They were concerned that their fellow Nisei might be swayed by Japan's militarist view that it was waging a race war and that their internment would be corroboration of America's racist treatment of Japanese, thus strengthening Japan's propaganda efforts. Had Noguchi and other influential Nisei voiced opposition instead of compliance with the idea of internment, the final results would undoubtedly have been the same, but the bitter recriminations and violent eruptions that followed among the Nisei in the camps over matters of national loyalty might have been considerably softened.

Noguchi intended his group's mission to be accomplished through a "government sponsored vernacular press," since the "existing Japanese press [which included English language sections] can no longer economically survive." Other communications media such as radio and film were to be included. The making of a documentary film recording the mass evacuation was begun, chronicling the arrival of the first thousand evacuees at Manzanar (the first "volunteers" arrived at Manzanar on March 21, 1942).[11]

In a memorandum on the making of the film, Noguchi leaves its purpose ambiguous. Should it be used for "propaganda, a legal document, a sociological study, a demonstration of democracy under trying circumstances, or a moving human story"? The incompatibility of these various goals suggests that Noguchi and his cohorts did not have the luxury of time to think through what they were trying to accomplish. To record on film their own entry into the camps must have been demoralizing no matter how laudatory their goal of preserving history. In asking the government to take over the task of filming "the work which we have already started in our small way," Noguchi reinforces the sense of tragic inevitability hanging over the project.[12]

Other than the Manzanar documentary, there seems to have been little visible impact of Noguchi's group on its intended audience. Noguchi's involvement with the film project was probably a close one, since he was friends with Herbert Kline, a documentary filmmaker who recommended hiring as cinematographer Frank Judson, an instructor at the Art Center School in Los Angeles. Carey McWilliams served as adviser.[13] In 1935, Noguchi had been in Hollywood where he did portrait sculptures of famous people in the entertainment world in order to raise funds for a trip to Mexico, so he was not unfamiliar with that milieu. His contacts on both coasts included a wide range of important people and gave him considerable access to a society outside the reach of his West Coast Nisei contemporaries. His good friend and fellow NWAMD member, Shuji Fujii, wrote him a letter on March 30, 1942, warning him to stay out of Zone Number One: "We need a good man like you to contact people and *stay outside* of the Zone until you accomplish something."

At the end of March, Noguchi traveled back to the East Coast preparing to go to Washington, D.C. His work in organizing the Nisei writers and artists group was "all to no avail," he said.[14] He hoped that he could make himself more useful by going to Washington. Noguchi describes his return from the West Coast to his residence in New York as an "escape" from possible internment.[15] Ironically, his Washington mission would place him in exactly the situation he had fled: incarceration. In Washington he met the "extremely charming and idealistic John Collier,"[16] the commissioner of Indian Affairs, who persuaded him to enter voluntarily the camp at Poston, Arizona, which was being built on Indian reservation land.

Collier did not fit the mold of the typical Washington bureaucrat. Ashton likens him to Noguchi as a "fellow visionary."[17] Whether it was Collier who influenced Noguchi in his vision of the model community that Poston could become or vice versa, they shared the same idealistic belief in the benefits of social engineering. Years later, Noguchi wrote about a talk given by Collier at Poston: "'Though democracy perish outside, here would be kept its seeds,' cried Mr. Collier through clouds of dust." But Noguchi added: "It soon became apparent, however, that the purpose of the War Relocation Authority was hopelessly at odds with that ideal cooperative community pictured by Mr. Collier. They wanted nothing permanent nor pleasant."[18]

As a political and social activist, Noguchi viewed situations from the standpoint of an artist. He believed wholeheartedly that art should play an active role in society and that in an egalitarian, democratic society, art had a better chance to flourish than in a repressive one. Hoping to turn the sad plight of his fellow Nisei into a positive experience, he let himself be persuaded to become "a part of humanity uprooted" and to contribute his services as an artist in the camps.[19]

Noguchi was one of the first persons to enter Poston on May 8, 1942.[20] His purpose, according to a WRA official, was to fulfill John Collier's recommendation that he "might contribute toward a rebirth of handicraft and the arts which the Niseis have so largely lost in the process of Americanization." Noguchi hoped to begin "apprentice craft guilds, such as in ceramics, woodworking, etc." Before he entered the camp, Noguchi was provided with an official WRA letter precisely spelling out his status as a volunteer, "not an evacuee," who would not require a permit to travel outside of the restricted military zone. The freedom granted by this letter would prove to be illusory.[21]

Whatever hope Noguchi had of carrying out his vision was dashed by the "harshness of camp life," which brought with it "a feeling of mutuality, of identity with those interned."[22] Noguchi's letter to Man Ray, cited at the beginning of this essay, in which he says bitterly that nothing is of consequence or value in Poston, was written only three weeks after his entry into Poston. The very next day, Noguchi wrote a letter to John Collier. His mood is more optimistic, though his feelings of confinement emerge when he says that he was finally permitted to go outside the camp to bring in clay for ceramics. "It was my first trip outside the camp since coming in and was sure a thrill." He complains about the lack of materials, skilled personnel, a newspaper. He apologizes for his complaints, "due probably to my inexperience in governmental red tape or the military mind—my lack of appreciation that we are war victims for whom even the minimum assistance for economic improvement may be subject to criticism." Noguchi's use of "we" for "war victims" clearly identifies those with whom he sides. We hear a tone of the supplicant when he says: "You see my usefulness here is terribly restricted. I should like nothing better than to be permitted to go to the various camps to enlist a corps of technicians, to start craft guilds here and elsewhere. This might be too great an exception to ask did I not know of Nisei who gained this privilege as politicians."

Toward the end of his letter Noguchi writes: "You are right that I learn a lot here, I am grateful to you for it." If Noguchi's expression of gratitude seems obsequious to us at first, we must examine it further in the light of his darkening circumstances. Collier now represented his only chance for survival or release. Noguchi was no longer a volunteer; he was a prisoner.

About two months later, on July 27, Noguchi wrote another letter to Collier that did not attempt to mask his despair:

> Dear Mr. Collier:
>
> After much hesitation and with deep regret I must finally ask you to do what is necessary to have me released. . . .
>
> I am extremely despondent for lack of companionship. The Niseis here are not of my age [Noguchi was thirty-seven and a bachelor] and of an entirely different background and interest. Also I have become so out of touch with the administration that I do not know of what further use I can be in camp. I am sure they consider me more bother than help.
>
> As you know I sought some place where I might fit into the fight for freedom. This might have been the place were I stronger or more adaptable. As it is I become embittered. I came here voluntarily, I trust that you will not have difficulty in securing this request.
>
> With my sincere best wishes,
>
> Isamu Noguchi
>
> P.S. I might add it's the heat that drives me frantic.

Collier responded immediately to Noguchi's anguished cry, telling him to not feel despondent "because things have not worked out as we had all hoped. There will be a very large field of productiveness and creative activity, outside the Colony." He said that he had spoken about Noguchi's case to Dillon S. Myer, national director of the War Relocation Authority, who would initiate steps toward his release but that it would be impossible to tell when they would be completed.[23] Collier forwarded Noguchi's letter to Myer, accompanied by his own letter. In it he wrote:

> I believe he [Noguchi] has made a sufficiently prolonged and agonized effort at adjustment. When I was down there, I spent a good deal of time with Noguchi. His hopefulness became quite strong, but I feared he would slip. I see no use in his being required to wreck himself trying to do the impossible. And back in New York he could be useful to his people, and to our country, and to culture generally.[24]

Collier's patronizing attitude toward Noguchi conveys no sense of personal guilt or responsibility for the failure of his mission, nor does he offer Noguchi any official means of support. Moreover, his letter to Myer contained no urgent plea to have Noguchi released.[25] As a result, Noguchi's letter requesting release was passed slowly down the chain of command, finally reaching Wade Head, Poston project director, who was asked to submit a report on Noguchi. What transpired was that Noguchi's eventual release became contingent on his "mixed blood," not on his having volunteered for internment.[26] One can only speculate on how Noguchi felt about his freedom being won on the basis of race, his Caucasian genes deemed superior to the Japanese. Identity had always been an issue in his life.

In a July 17 memorandum dictated by Poston legal officer Theodore Haas, there is a hint of the roots of Noguchi's growing frustration and malaise that led to his July 27 letter to Collier asking for his release. It is a record of a conversation between Noguchi and Miles Cary, Poston schools superintendent, on the use of art in the camp. Asked to make suggestions about teaching art in the schools, Noguchi recommends giving pupils art tools and books "with pictures of good Japanese art," which the students would imitate. He also proposes that outside specialists on Japanese art such as Professor Langdon Warner of Harvard University (whom Noguchi knew) be brought to the camp to give lectures that would highlight the virtues of Japanese art without its "warlike aspects." Noguchi suggests inviting Nisei artists from New York who are "well known anti-fascists" to come to speak as role models. The uninflected, objective tone of the memorandum does not give a true sense of the feelings of the participants in the dialogue that it records. Yet one cannot help receiving from it the impression that Noguchi and Cary were not on the same wave length, that Cary's questions were designed to elicit the kinds of proposals Noguchi provided. Noguchi's stress on the unwarlike aspects of Japanese art and the anti-fascist record of Nisei artists indicates that the camp authorities were wary of art no matter how much lip service they paid to it, and that they had to be reassured that it would not be used to undermine their control of the camps or encourage fascist tendencies in schoolchildren.

Noguchi's feelings of being "out of touch" and neglected by the camp administration were undoubtedly justified. Among his camp papers are copies of orders for craft supplies and tools from outside companies. The infrequency and parsimoniousness of these personal orders give the impression that Noguchi was not given much, if any, financial or moral support for his crafts project. Perhaps as consolation for its desultory backing of his plans, the administration put Noguchi in charge of designing park and recreation areas and a cemetery. For his part, Noguchi took these commissions with the utmost seriousness, seeing in them a challenge to his artistic imagination and a way to satisfy his philosophical belief in the public use of art.

The product of these administrative requests was a set of blueprints done by Noguchi of garden oases in the midst of the stockade-like barracks blocks in which the camp inhabitants lived. For the dead, Noguchi envisioned a columbarium (perhaps mindful of the Buddhist practice of cremating the dead), chapel, and gravesites, which in terms of their restrained artistic simplicity would have provided a semblance of dignity to those who died in the desert.

Noguchi's modest and workable plans were never realized.[27] An undated Noguchi memorandum submitted to the Poston community council on the creation of his recreation and arts center indicates why. The WRA, according to the document, refused to allocate labor and money for its construction and equipment. Undiscouraged by this rebuff, Noguchi proposes that the project be built, owned, and operated entirely by the evacuees. In support of this proposal, he writes: "Already members of the athletic and art departments have contributed . . . to constructing the shelter where we will build the adobe bricks." Noguchi's positive, self-reliant (one is tempted to say American "can-do" spirit) is expressed throughout the memorandum: "We feel that the importance of this undertaking to our own development is apparent. [It] . . . will strengthen a spirit of democratic participation" and "will secure a degree of independence from the administration not otherwise possible." Although the internees themselves may have attempted to carry out Noguchi's designs, he nowhere indicates that any part of his vision, which he thought would have to be built in gradual steps, was ever brought to fruition. But the inclusion of these blueprints among the plates of his autobiography testify to Noguchi's recognition of their importance in the development of his career.

Painful though his Poston experience was, it forced Noguchi to confront himself and to ask himself who he was. Some of the answers in this process of self-searching can be found in an unpublished essay that he wrote for the *Reader's Digest* while in camp.[28] In the essay, Noguchi confesses to harboring a "haunting sense of unreality" in his life, "of not quite belonging." By entering Poston he thought he might find "among the Nisei" answers to why he felt that way. For the first time he became aware of a color line he had never known before. Unable to identify with the Caucasian administrative staff, some of whom he had known before camp, Noguchi saw them now as his keepers "whose word was our law." He became embarrassed in their presence. On the other hand, Noguchi could not identify with his fellow Nisei who were so different from him. Not only were they generally much younger than he, but their provincialism and conservatism clashed with his liberalism and urban sophistication. Being Eurasian only added to his inability to fit into the homogeneous camp population. The fact that he was an artist from New York who had entrée to the camp administration also may have created suspicion of his motivations among his fellow internees.[29]

Noguchi's intellectual and emotional isolation in Poston allowed him to observe the Nisei with the keen objectivity of an outsider. To him, as he observes in his essay, the "peculiar tragedy of the Nisei" was that they were "a generation of transition accepted neither by the Japanese nor by America." The internment had shaken their sense of belonging to the country of their birth, but in many ways had powerfully reaffirmed it. However, the Nisei were all too aware that "outside in Washington, D.C., and California a few people are plotting against his [the Nisei's] citizenship."

At one point in his essay, Noguchi allows his own feelings to emerge: "Sometimes an indescribable longing for freedom comes over me." The truth of these words captures with moving simplicity the terrible injustice of the internment. Perhaps it is because of this sentiment that Noguchi, having completed his text, unambiguously gave as title for his essay "I Become a Nisei."

On November 12, 1942, some seven months after he arrived in Poston, Noguchi was finally released from camp, but only on a "temporary basis." In his 1968 autobiography, he writes with deadpan humor: "So far as I know, I am still only temporarily at large."[30] Returning to New York, Noguchi embraced his old life with relief: "Freedom earned has a quality of assurance. The deep depression that comes with living under a cloud of suspicion, which we as Nisei experienced, lifted, and was followed by tranquillity. I was free finally of causes and disillusioned with mutuality. I resolved henceforth to be an artist only."[31]

If Noguchi seems to suggest a total retreat from activism, it was only a temporary respite. Shortly after his release he published an article in *The New Republic* (February 1, 1943) titled "Trouble Among Japanese Americans." It addressed the issue of camp disturbances from his own perspective as a former internee. Noguchi's aim in writing the article was to correct the oversimplified reporting of the camp riots in the press. In succinct fashion he tries to get at the root causes of the disturbances and critically assesses the performance of the WRA, which, he indicates, responded to the real problems of the camps only after the riots. He urges the army to resume Selective Service of Japanese Americans, a practice that had been halted shortly before the evacuation. Such a resumption would have "deeply beneficial psychological effect" on Japanese Americans. Noguchi urges relocation of internees outside of the camps to help overcome the manpower shortage. He recommends that the relocation be done not only on an individual basis but in groups, particularly for the Issei, who would adjust better to the outside world with such a support system. Ever mindful of assimilation, Noguchi sees resettlement as a step toward "speedy assimilation" of Japanese in the "larger American group." For those who would inevitably be left behind in the camps, Noguchi strongly urges the WRA to give them as much latitude for self-government and self-sufficiency as possible, allowing the Issei the leadership roles that the WRA had denied them.

Noguchi's article in *The New Republic* is further evidence that his Poston experience made him a unique spokesman for the uprooted Japanese. In his own struggle to learn who he was, Noguchi discovered what he was: a Nisei and an American.

NOTES

1. A version of this essay was published in *Amerasia Journal* 20:2 (1994). I wish to thank Russell C. Leong, editor of the *Journal*, for permission to republish it in this volume.

2. This epigraph is from a letter dated May 30, 1942, to Man Ray, the modernist photographer and painter. The letter and all following documents cited here are in the collection of The Isamu Noguchi Foundation, Inc., Long Island City, New York, unless otherwise noted. The Noguchi Foundation Archives are not yet catalogued; therefore, documents in this paper are not referenced by file number. I am deeply indebted to the Foundation, particularly Amy Hau, assistant to the director and keeper of the archives, for permission to publish from these materials.

3. Isamu Noguchi, *Isamu Noguchi, A Sculptor's World* (Evanston and New York: Harper & Row, 1968), 25–26, 182–83.

4. My thanks to the Rockefeller Residency Fellowship Fund and the UCLA Asian American Studies Center for funding my research. Also my gratitude to Shoji Sadao, executive director, The Isamu Noguchi Foundation, Inc.; Amy Hau, assistant to the director; and Bruce Altshuler, former Director, Isamu Noguchi Garden Museum, for their generous assistance in my research.

5. See Robert J. Maeda, "From Shape and Shadow: The Mother and Father of Isamu Noguchi," *Amerasia Journal* 22:3 (1996), for a more detailed account of Noguchi's parents' lives.

6. Noguchi, 25.

7. Dore Ashton, *Noguchi East and West* (New York: Knopf, 1992), 67–69. Noguchi was also preparing for an exhibition of his work at the San Francisco Museum of Art.

8. The Los Angeles group was formed with the cooperation of the Hollywood Writer's Mobilization. The earliest dated evidence for Noguchi's group is a letter to Dr. Grace McCann Morley, Director of the San Francisco Museum of Art (February 11, 1942), which Noguchi signed as Chairman of NWAMD, San Francisco. In New York, on December 12, 1941, a similar group of Japanese and Japanese American artists, as "artists and men," issued a ringing declaration of support for the United States and further pledged to "bear arms if necessary to insure the final victory for the democratic forces of the World." Noguchi was acquainted with these artists and would undoubtedly have been a co-signer of their declaration had he been on the East Coast. Documents cited in this note are in the collection of The Isamu Noguchi Foundation.

9. Dillon S. Myer, *Uprooted Americans* (Tucson: University of Arizona Press, 1971), xxiii.

10. In another undated document related to his NWAMD statement, Noguchi made an outline of his organization, listing, probably tentatively, a board of English-language editors for an educational and news bulletin: Larry Tajiri, Togo Tanaka, Taro Katayama, and Bob Tsuda. Shuji Fujii, editor of the Japanese weekly *Doho*, was to be its Japanese-language editor. A similar board for a weekly news magazine was also listed. Of those named, Noguchi was in closest correspondence with Fujii and Tajiri, editor of the JACL's official newspaper, *Pacific Citizen*. A letter from Togo Tanaka, editor of the Los Angeles *Rafu Shimpo* (dated March 28, 1942) acknowledges receipt of Noguchi's proposal and "our wholehearted and sincere approval" of it, but Tanaka does not indicate having been asked to serve on the board.

11. The film was first shown publicly three times on April 6, 1942, to a gathering of an estimated 2,500 people at Koyasan Temple Hall in Los Angeles. This information is from a letter to Noguchi from Kikue Fujii, whose husband Shuji Fujii, provided the Japanese commentary for the film. Ostensibly, the screening was meant to reassure anxious Japanese that their places of future internment such as Manzanar would not be too forbidding, more like their own small towns than camps, complete with United States post office. Mrs. Fujii alludes to these aims when she refers to an army request to delete passages from the film that show "the wind and dust and desolation," because it "would have had a bad effect." In a later letter, the Fujiis wrote to Noguchi that an FBI agent had been present at the screening and later questioned Shujii about the project—who started it, who financed it, etc. Apparently, the FBI was unaware that Noguchi's group had informed the army about the film project and had gained its approval for public showing.

12. Noguchi, "Memo on recording Japanese war relocation, special reference to Film," in Isamu Noguchi Foundation.

13. Carey McWilliams (1905–1980), social and political activist and journalist. Author of *Prejudice: Japanese-Americans, Symbol of Racial Intolerance* (Boston: Little, Brown, 1944). McWilliams, along with Louis Adamic, Tokie Slocum, William Saroyan, Chester Rowell, Pearl Buck, and Archibald MacLeish were named (probably tentatively) to an advisory board for the NWAMD.

14. Noguchi, 25.

15. Lieutenant General John L. DeWitt, commanding general of the Western Defense Command, whose recommendation to evacuate the Japanese from the West Coast led directly to President Roosevelt's Executive Order 9066, issued Proclamation No. 1 on May 2, "designating the western half of the three Pacific Coast states and the southern third of Arizona as a military area and stipulating that all persons of Japanese descent would eventually be removed therefrom." Myer, xxiv. Noguchi's "escape" from California was undoubtedly precipitated by DeWitt's proclamation.

16. Ashton, 70.

17. Ibid. For an understanding of how Noguchi was so easily persuaded to volunteer for internment by the charismatic Collier, see Kenneth R. Philp, *John Collier's Crusade for Indian Reform, 1920–1954* (Tucson: University of Arizona Press, 1977), 208–209. Collier's ideas about the virtues of communal living and the social value of arts and crafts were remarkably similar to Noguchi's.

18. Noguchi, 25.

19. Ibid.

20. Coincidentally, I entered Poston with my family the same day as Noguchi. We were among the internee "volunteers" whom the government allowed to enter Poston early in order to help set up the camp. We drove to Poston in our family car from our home town, El Centro, California, accompanied by a Caucasian friend, who was given our car in exchange for his help. As a cranky, thirsty nine-year-old, I begged for a Coke to drink during the long, hot trip. We were refused service in the restaurant where we stopped to buy the drink.

21. This letter, dated April 27, 1942, and addressed "To Whom it May Concern," was written by John A. Bird, assistant to the director of the WRA. Noguchi, to his dismay, would discover that it gave him little clout with the authorities. Not only could he not travel freely, but it took considerable time and red tape to have his personal possessions returned to him. My thanks to Karin Higa, Curator of the Japanese American National Museum, Los Angeles, for providing me with this letter.

22. Noguchi, 25.

23. Exchange of letters between Noguchi and Collier, Isamu Noguchi Foundation.

24. Ibid.

25. This lack of urgency may have been the result of the ideological and personality clashes between Myer and Collier. Collier had wanted to be WRA director himself, and he had asked Vice President Henry A. Wallace to nominate him for the job. See Richard Drinnon, *Keeper of Concentration Camps: Dillon S. Myer and American Racism* (Berkeley: University of California Press, 1987), 40ff. The enmity between the two men was heightened when both gave speeches unbeknownst to each other at Poston, spaced one week apart, in which they announced diametrically opposed policies to the internees'. I am indebted to Yuji Ichioka of the UCLA Asian American Studies Center for this reference.

26. See Memorandum from Mary M. Kirkland, social worker, to Theodore Haas, Legal Department, Poston, October 9, 1942. According to this document, Noguchi filed a Survey of Mixed Marriage form on July 31, perhaps thinking that doing so might accelerate his release. Certain categories of people of mixed blood and mixed marriage were being allowed to leave camp. Kirkland's memo states that the regional office wrote on August 27 that "it would be possible for him to be released on the grounds that he was a person of mixed blood." Noguchi's original request was made more complicated by his stated desire to go to San Francisco before returning to New York. This move would require special sanction, since San Francisco was in the restricted military area. Noguchi later dropped his request to go to San Francisco.

27. During July 1942, while Noguchi was in Poston, his show at the San Francisco Art Museum, for which he had been preparing before Pearl Harbor, took place. In a review ironically titled "Evacuee Shows Sculptures for Democracy at San Francisco Museum" (*People's World*, July 1942), the anonymous reviewer states that "included in the museum exhibition are plans designed by him [Noguchi] for the U.S. Irrigation Service and landscaping and recreation departments." It is unclear if these were the blueprints discussed here.

28. Noguchi sent a copy of the original manuscript, which is in the collection of the Isamu Noguchi Foundation, to a friend, Mrs. Atherton Richards, in Washington, D.C., telling her in an accompanying letter dated October 25, 1942, that "it's a bit complicated and logwinded [sic] and perhaps a bit too personal."

29.   In his autobiography, Noguchi writes: "There could have been some question of my position, whether on the side of the administration or of the internees" (Noguchi, 25). Noguchi must have been aware that those internees who were seen to be too close to the administration were suspected of being informers (branded as *inu*, or "dogs"). On November 14, just two days after Noguchi was released from Poston, a man was beaten on suspicion of being an informer, and the FBI was called in to investigate. After two young male suspects were arrested, rumors circulated that they would be sent out of the camp. The incident brought out angry crowds demanding their release. See Myer, 62.

30.   Noguchi, 25.

31.   Ibid., 26.

SUE KUNITOMI EMBREY

FROM MANZANAR TO THE PRESENT: A PERSONAL JOURNEY

IT WAS AN INFORMAL INVITATION FROM A STUDENT driving me home one afternoon from UCLA's Asian American Studies Center.

"We're planning a pilgrimage to Manzanar. Why don't you come along?"

I did, and that tentative first step took us on a journey to seek our roots, to confront the monstrous tragedy of the World War II eviction, and to find ways of healing our wounds. It was December 1969.

The year 1969 was pivotal in my personal history, which parallels the history of a community in which so many Nisei grew up. For some, the anti–Vietnam War demonstrations, along with the Free Speech movement, steered us on to the path of activism on campus and in the community. For Japanese Americans as a group, the journey began more than one hundred years ago, when our immigrant parents and grandparents first set foot on America's shores, holding tight to their dreams of riches and success.

My personal story begins long before Manzanar, Poston, Heart Mountain, or Tule Lake became household names among us. It began with a young man signing a two-year contract to work on the plantations in the Hawaiian Islands. Adventurous, draft-age, and unwilling to fight in the Russo-Japanese War, Gonhichi Kunitomi, my father, left southern Japan. When his contract expired, he opted to go to the mainland. He never returned to Japan to claim the land he would have inherited as the eldest son.

He sent for a bride and settled with her in fast-growing Hollywood. My parents worked as domestics until large numbers of immigrant Japanese began starting businesses and living in an area east of downtown Los Angeles.

By Depression-era standards, my father was a successful businessman: he had a Reo stake truck, a family Model A Ford and a pickup truck in which he did a business of "moving and transferring" people and goods. Cash, however, was scarce around our house. Much to my mother's chagrin, my father bartered his services with people he knew had little or no money to pay him.

Eight of us children of Gonhichi and Komika Kunitomi grew up in Little Tokyo, as the area became known. During this prewar period, Little Tokyo stretched from Temple Street on the north to Ninth Street on the south, where the wholesale markets were the centerpieces of the fruit and vegetables grown by Japanese farmers in Southern California. Eastward, the area extended to the foot of the First Street bridge, and on the west side to Los Angeles Street, which bordered Manila Town, where Filipino bachelors lived in run-down hotel rooms and sat on wooden chairs along the sidewalk, watching the traffic go by.

It was a segregated Asian ghetto of poor working people, small businesses, churches, temples, and Japanese language schools. It was a tightly knit community in which life was always busy, and cultural activities filled the evenings and weekends of those who longed for their homeland. For the young people growing up in Little Tokyo, there was a sense of strength and protection from a hostile world.

The most familiar street to most of us was East First Street. At the location of the present-day Japanese American National Museum was the Hongwanji Buddhist Temple, the headquarters of the religion brought over from Japan. Before the war it served as a community center; offices were located on the first and second floors of the building. The most famous of the restaurants in the quarter was the Chinese Far East Café. Parties were held upstairs, where dozens of Cantonese dishes, with plenty of Japanese sake and beer, were served to appreciative Japanese diners, while the children enjoyed the treat of soda pop and eating out. After a funeral and burial at the Evergreen Cemetery, grieving relatives would gather at the Far East and urge their friends to sit and reminisce about the departed.

My most vivid memories from that period are of the rare times when my father felt that he had enough money to order out dinner from the Far East. The food would come in breakable porcelain dishes with matching covers. The waiter would place them on a huge tray and carry it above his head for the four blocks to our house. After the feast we would wash the dishes and put them back on the tray, which my father would return the next day.

A grocery store featuring fresh fish and piles of fresh Japanese vegetables, such as nappa (cabbage), and daikon (white radish), would send fragrant scents out along the street. A clock repair shop, a photography shop, a sushi restaurant that was always packed with people, all stood on the north side, along with a couple of dingy, run-down hotels in which people made their homes.

On the West Side of North San Pedro Street, there was a cultural center, which was used to teach judo and kendo, a sumo ring, and an archery field. South of our rented house on Amelia Street stood a row of factory buildings, which housed the Los Angeles Casket Company, the Railway Express garage, and the White King Soap company, which spewed out noxious smells from its tall smokestacks. A long, loud whistle called its employees to work, to lunch, or to leave at the close of the day. During the week, the nine o'clock whistle at night was our signal for bedtime. We saw white employees every day and spoke to them as they would walk past our houses to catch the red electric cars at the nearby rail station, where the San Bernardino Freeway now stands. It was still the Depression, and everyone took public transportation. We knew that these people lived in the suburbs, which meant little to us, as we seldom left the city limits. We never asked why no one from the neighborhood was employed there. Did we take it for granted that non-whites would not be hired? Had anyone been turned down and not mentioned it?

Some memories are blurred, but the bulk of my recollections is of happy times with family and neighbors. From Central Avenue, where we were born, to Amelia Street, where we lived until World War II, the neighborhood seemed stable. But the second generation was coming of age, and job discrimination would keep most of us out of mainstream opportunities. Little Tokyo was reaching a limit of available jobs for young people within the community. We will never know what might have been, since the outbreak of World War II effectively destroyed Little Tokyo and similar communities along the West Coast.

When it was fashionable in the 1970s to label poor people "culturally deprived," I often wondered what the experts would have said about my childhood in little Tokyo. We were all poor at the end of the Depression. Most people were working hard, but our parents saw to it that we had decent and clean clothes as well as a new pair of shoes each year. Culturally deprived we were not. Growing up in America and yet separated from the mainstream of American society, we lived a mixed life. Dressed in our kimono, we celebrated the New Year with its tradition of special Japanese food, shuttlecock games, and visits to other families, where we tasted their specialties. We also celebrated Christmas, Mother's Day, the Fourth of July with fireworks, and Armistice Day with parades downtown.

Through our public school education we absorbed all the values and principles that are embodied in the American Dream. We never questioned where our loyalty lay, for were we not American citizens, and didn't the public education we were getting emphasize the virtues of our great democracy and our good fortune in living in the United States?

The Amelia Street grade school, housed in a large, two-story wooden building and an adjacent brick building at the northeast corner of Amelia and Jackson streets, had a profound and lasting effect on those of us who attended it. The school is no longer in existence today. It had a large playground area and, in the brick building, an auditorium, a sewing room, and a woodshop. Next to the auditorium were a kitchen and cafeteria for students and teachers. The principal was a woman who, on her first day at work, went from room to room, telling stories and making jokes to get a smile out of us. She said we were the most solemn children she had seen, and she wanted us to smile. She knew that the former principal had been a strict disciplinarian who brooked no nonsense from any of us. The school had no male teachers; even the custodian was a woman who looked like the figure on the Old Dutch cleansing powder can, and wove in and out of the classrooms and down the hall like a ghost, sometimes frightening us when she would silently show up in our midst. The school curriculum was based on progressive education. We had cultural days, when Native Americans came to entertain us and Mexican parents would come and tell us about the history and culture of Mexico. The Nisei students would also be able to show off what we knew of the culture of Japan. Since more than 90 percent of the segregated, minority-population school's student body was of Japanese ancestry, the principal wanted to strengthen our self-esteem and pride in our cultural heritage.

The majority of us attended Japanese language school for an hour after regular public school. The *Dai Ichi Gakuen* was, as its name indicated, the first Japanese language school. Behind the building was a huge lot where the neighborhood children played, as there were no parks or playgrounds in the area. Miss Nellie Oliver, a social worker who spent the bulk of her life and money providing sports activities for the children who attended both the Amelia Street and the Japanese school, owned the property. The Japanese we learned to speak became a uniquely second-generation language, which can be heard to this day.

December 1937 ended on a tragic note for the Kunitomi family. My father missed a curve while driving home from Glendale. His pickup truck ran off the road, turned over, and landed along the railroad tracks. I was home with my mother, cooking dinner and waiting for my father and brothers to return. I was the one who answered the phone call from the police. After I left messages for my brothers at the various places they might stop on their way home, my mother and I took a taxicab to the emergency hospital. Since my mother did not speak much English, I translated for her. My father needed to be moved from the emergency hospital. My mother said that she wanted him transferred to the Japanese hospital. The doctor indicated that my father had suffered massive trauma and was in a coma. He was not sure what the prognosis might be.

With sirens screaming, the city ambulance drove us to the Japanese Hospital in Boyle Heights. I once more telephoned to let my brothers know where my papa was. Several hours after he was admitted, my father died without regaining consciousness. All of us stood around his bed, too stunned to do anything else.

Auto accidents were uncommon then, since there were few cars on the road. The accident made the front page of the *Los Angeles Times*, and there was a photo of the overturned truck. My older sister, who was confined with tuberculosis to the Olive View Sanitarium, read the news in the paper before her husband could get to her bedside to tell her himself.

My father was very popular. His funeral, held at the old Koyasan Buddhist Temple, a converted house on Central Avenue, was filled with friends and others in the community. It was a dismal Christmas and New Year.

My mother, who had not worked outside the home, went out and collected money from my father's customers; my two older brothers dropped out of school to go to work. Meanwhile, shortly before I was scheduled to graduate from Lincoln High School, the chronic pain from my appendix finally convinced the family doctor that he could not wait for graduation to remove the appendix. My mother agreed, although I knew that she did not have the money to pay the doctor or the hospital; few of us had medical coverage in those Depression years.

The year 1941 began with mounting tensions between the United States and Japan. Emissaries were traveling back and forth, and discussions were going on about foreign policy and boycotting Japanese goods. When talk of war began circulating, our next-door neighbors decided to sell their small grocery store and return to Japan with their three American-born children. The couple asked my mother if she would like to buy their business. She grabbed at the chance to become an independent businesswoman. But how would she get the money? She decided to borrow on the insurance policies that she had purchased for my two older brothers. Although the future seemed bleak, she was excited about going into business. She promised me that in two years, after I helped her in the store and after my younger sister graduated from high school,

I would go to college with money saved from her business. With that promise, I took charge of the grocery. We ran the store from early March 1941.

When the mass eviction of the permanent resident alien Japanese and Japanese Americans began in earnest, my twenty-one-year-old brother, Hideo, quit his fruit-stand job and volunteered as one of the one thousand men and women sent in advance to help build Manzanar. When we were told that we would be going to the assembly center at the Santa Anita racetrack, my mother was beside herself. She worried that we would never see my brother again. What a relief for her to learn that the army would allow people to join their relatives as more blocks of barracks were built! When we arrived at Manzanar on May 9, 1942, Hideo greeted us as we got off the bus and escorted us through the registration process and to our barracks in Block 20. We stumbled in the dark, as we were not permitted to carry flashlights, which had been declared contraband. Hideo had already filled the mattress covers with hay, so we did not have to go out before bedtime to do so ourselves, as others did.

A week after our arrival, the Maryknoll Sisters, who had received permission to help internees get adjusted, asked for volunteers to start a school. There were few organized activities for the children, and they were running around loose in the camp. There were no chairs, tables, paper, pencils, books, or chalkboards. The children sat on the rough, unsanded floor. I remember little of what we did with them, but I know that we sang songs and played games outdoors without athletic equipment. My sister-in-law and I left that volunteer job when the camouflage-net factory was completed. Citizens were being recruited for pay to help in the war effort by making nets for the United States Army. In the meantime, sugar beet farmers in Utah, Idaho, and Montana were suffering a labor shortage and begging for help from the government. Arrangements were made for men and women to leave the camps on short-term furlough during harvest time. As more and more people left, there was a labor shortage in the camp itself.

The camp newspaper had begun in mimeographed copy in early April. The editorial staff of older, liberal Nisei published the first issue, ironically naming it the *Manzanar Free Press*. They came up with the idea of thanking General DeWitt* for letting them publish a newspaper. Later, a story made the rounds that the general was pleased when he saw his name on the front page. The paper was short of reporters. My successful application for a job as a reporter marked a turning point in my life. I had always wanted to write. I walked

---

*Commanding General of the Western Defense Command. --Ed.

around Manzanar making notes on gardens being planted, and on the workings of the various government departments that kept operations going. I learned that I had skills I had not been able to use or identify before. I enjoyed writing about activities in the camp and the energy of the hard-working population. People's diligent efforts to beautify their bleak surroundings lifted my spirits.

On the surface, Manzanar appeared to be a stable, growing community of one square mile. But tensions were smoldering between various factions and would soon explode in what has commonly been called a "rebellion." Although it initially involved a small group of people, the event would affect the entire camp.

The first weekend of December 1942 began with a large rally, which was the first sign that Harry Y. Ueno,[1] suspected of beating up a member of the Japanese American Citizens League, had been arrested. People who believed him not guilty were demonstrating for his release. That night, we saw pea-coated, dark figures and heard the tramping of booted feet on the macadam road in front of our barracks. I was cautioned by my mother to stay hidden, as the *Free Press* was looked on as being pro-administration.

My older brother, who was a police officer, came running into our unit saying that the MPs were shooting into the crowd at the front entrance. Then my younger sister's boyfriend ran in, out of breath, shouting that people were being shot; some had been killed. My mother began to tremble with fear. "They'll shoot us all now," she said between chattering teeth, her whole body shaking as we held her to calm her down.

Harry Ueno was a kitchen worker in Block 22. Along with the other kitchen workers, he was frustrated by the lack of kitchen tools needed to cook for 250 people. The workers noticed that sugar was being delivered in smaller amounts than usual. With Harry leading the group, they began to form a mess hall workers union. Complaints to the administration would be filed through the union.

Although he had had no organizing experience or connection with Los Angeles community organizations before his arrival at Manzanar, Harry began to investigate by going from mess hall to mess hall to record the shortage of food, which he reported to the FBI. It was inevitable that Harry would be the object of the administration's suspicions when the JACLer, Fred Tayama,* was beaten.

---

* Fred Tayama was a leader of the Japanese Americans Citizens League, an organization widely believed by camp inmates to be collaborating with the administration.--Ed.

Recalling the crunching of those several hundred feet on the macadam road brings goose bumps to my arms even today. Since 1969, I have walked through the ruins of the former camp-site countless times without fear. Yet one time when I walked from the car I was stopped at the entrance by a sudden vision of the crowd, MPs with machine guns, and fallen men in a pool of crimson. It was gone as suddenly as it had occurred. It was a scene that I had not personally witnessed. But it brought me a fleeting faintness. I did not mention it to any of the students and teachers from the California State University at Fullerton campus who were with me that day.

After the disturbance, the *Free Press* ceased publication until the last week of December, when we were given permission to put out a Christmas issue. The Chalfant Press in Bishop printed it. The *Free Press* staff did the typing, layout, and paste-up of the paper, with its sports section, advertising, and editorial pages. We put the paper "to bed." I was assigned the job of walking the completed paper to the administration office, where it would be handed over for delivery to the printer. The older editorial staff members had been removed from camp the weekend of the disturbance because they were believed to be the target of an anti-JACL group. Pro-administration individuals were said to be on a death list.

As I approached the administration building, I saw a jeep with two soldiers parked directly across the road. I skirted the jeep and started up the cement walkway. I was reaching for the door, when it was flung open and I bumped into a soldier coming out. To my surprise, the soldier turned out to be my former high school social studies teacher, Mr. Green. Now a captain in the United States Army, he was heading the Military Police Unit from Las Vegas, which had been called in after the riot. He was ready to go back, he said. He asked me if I had made any plans to leave camp. When I replied that I did not believe we would be released because of what had just happened, the captain said, "This is no place for you." He had told government officials in Washington that he had taught a number of Nisei students in his classes at Lincoln High School and that he did not doubt their loyalty. Then he climbed into the waiting jeep. As it drove off, I got a salute from the captain.

My chance meeting with Mr. Green raised my hopes for the college education that had been deferred. Almost immediately after the riot, the WRA instituted its program of leave clearance and segregation. From the *Free Press* office window, I could see people leaving several times a week, and I began making my own plans to "relocate." Several nurses working at Madison General Hospital and St. Mary's Hospital in Wisconsin encouraged me to join them. By this time, I was editor of the *Free Press*. We had published our anniversary issue and were working on the pictorial edition. During the summer of 1943, I waited for my clearance to come.

When I got to Madison, where I was sponsored by the YWCA with a month's room and board, I inquired about getting into the University of Wisconsin. To my disappointment, I was told I could not enter because the United States Army was conducting secret war work on campus. My FBI clearance and I.D. card were of no use. The YWCA tried to help, but nothing worked out. Later I learned that a Nisei doctoral student in chemistry headed the "secret" war work project. His sister was my roommate at the YWCA dormitory.

After a year in Madison, I moved to Chicago, where I found a job at the privately endowed Newberry Library, a prestigious research institution with first editions and rare books from around the world. I was referred there by the American Friends Service Committee, which was helping people leaving the camps to find jobs and housing. At the Newberry, I met Mamie, an African American from Texas, and Dottie, an Irish American from Iowa. We became an inseparable trio for lunch and other activities. For me, still longing for a college education, it was a great environment. I got to hobnob with Ph.D.'s and intellectuals who had traveled around the world.

While I was enjoying my independent life in Chicago, my mother had returned to Los Angeles and was seeking the return of our complete family. In 1948, my younger sister decided to get married and live in Chicago, so I packed my bags and headed home. My work experience at the Newberry was the happiest I had had, and I cherish the friendships I made there. When I visited Dottie decades later, in the summer of 1998, she looked down from her six-foot-four-inch height at my granddaughter, Monica, and said, "Did you know that your grandma and I have been friends for over fifty years?"

Soon after my return to Los Angeles, I found myself searching for some activity outside of work. I found it in a group of Nisei supporting the third-party movement of Henry Wallace, Franklin D. Roosevelt's vice president. Roosevelt had rejected Wallace as his running mate for his third election campaign and had chosen Harry Truman instead. Wallace broke from the Democratic Party in 1948 to run as the presidential candidate for the Progressive Party.

The issues that Wallace addressed attracted a number of liberal and progressive Nisei. The early postwar period, when the camps were not yet history, was not a good time for this ethnic group to stand up for ideas that the average American did not embrace: a more liberal immigration policy, citizenship for our Issei parents, and reparations for the victims of the American concentration camps.

Like a true believer, I plunged into my first political activity. I distributed flyers around Little Tokyo, attended fundraisers, wrote articles for the Nisei for Wallace newsletter, and for *The Independent.* Then there was singing—a lot of singing of songs adopted by the Progressive Party, written by folk singers Woody Guthrie and Pete Seeger. For a novice, it was an exciting time. I met many progressive-minded Americans of all ethnicities, strengthening my belief in American democracy.

After Wallace's defeat in the 1948 presidential election, the Nisei for Wallace changed its name to Nisei Progressives and continued its activities. Because of widespread infiltration by the FBI and the House Un-American Activities Committee, which pursued its red-baiting campaign at a fever pitch, people began to drop out. In this repressive period, many innocent people lost jobs, some people went to jail, some who could afford it moved out of the country, and still others committed suicide.

In the aftermath of the Wallace campaign, I met and married Garland Monroe Embrey, an Anglo-Saxon from Waco, Texas, over my mother's strenuous objections. We decided that Gar should get his degree before I went to school, since he had attended UCLA before the war. The 1950s and 1960s were years of personal change. In the summer of 1952, when we were in New Mexico, where Gar was directing a children's camp program, we received word that my youngest brother Tetsuo, who was stationed in Tokyo with the United States Army, had collapsed on the street and died in the army hospital. Tets had last written that his unit might be replacing men returning from the Korean conflict, and he had hoped that his projected return home for his twenty-second birthday would not be interrupted. Our family was devastated. We got very little information from the American surgeon general and could only wait for the return of his body to arrange for funeral services.

During the sixties, while our sons, Gary Kinya and Bruce Takeshi, were in elementary school, I enrolled at Los Angeles City College to take basic courses leading toward the college degree of which I had long dreamed. I had not forgotten my father's admonition that I had two strikes against me: as a woman, and as a Japanese American. College for me, he had said, was "not possible"— he could not afford it. It would be best to take business courses so that I could work until I got married.

My father died in 1938. I carried the burden of his advice until 1972, when I received my master's degree from the University of Southern California. No bells rang, no bright lights flashed; there was only my mother's delight and astonishment that I had gotten the diploma.

It was during my long-delayed college years that I met student activists at California State University, Los Angeles, who, like students on other campuses, were pushing the administration to introduce courses in Asian American studies into the curriculum. It was their interest and concern about the internment camps that provided me with the impetus to study my own wartime experience.

It was a cold and windy December day in 1969 when several hundred of us huddled together against the biting wind at the site of Manzanar to commemorate the human tragedy that had played out on the desert floor of the Owens Valley more than twenty-seven years earlier. The event, the first of what were to become annual pilgrimages to the camp's site, was meant to publicize the beginning of a campaign to repeal Title II of the Internal Security (McCarran) Act of 1950. Under Title II, the president was empowered to exclude and detain anyone considered a threat to national security. It was appropriate that survivors of the camps be in the forefront of the campaign to repeal a law that would threaten the civil liberties of all Americans. The three national television networks were there, even though little advance publicity had been sent out. When the event was carried on Saturday evening's six o'clock news, we were elated. But others were not sure that we should be so visible or vocal.

"Why are they bringing up the past?" they asked.

"Why are they talking about camp?"

"Camp" is what we called it. Camp is what we still call it.

"Camp" refers to shared pain and misery. It refers to denial of civil rights, separation of family, isolation from America. Camp also refers to what happened later when [we] were free to return—to what? There were no homes, no businesses, no farms to return to. There was deterioration of health for many, devastation of the spirit for all.[2]

By 1971, the younger generation of Japanese American college students wanted and needed to know about the camps. Since their parents—former internees—were not talking, the pressure was on to do something. A small ad hoc committee got together under the leadership of Warren Furutani, then JACL National Youth Director, to apply to the State Parks and Recreation Department to designate Manzanar a state historical landmark. We provided the state with historical information, photographs, and maps, along with a proposed inscription for a bronze plaque to be paid for by the state. The original wording read:

From war hysteria, racism, and economic greed, one hundred ten thousand persons of Japanese ancestry were directed by Presidential Order on February 19, 1942 to leave their homes and to relocate to America's Concentration Camps. Manzanar was the first of such camps built during World War II, bounded by barbed wire and guard towers in a mile square, confining 10,000 men, women, and children, of whom the majority was American citizens. This plaque is laid in the hope that the conditions which created this camp will never emerge again—for anybody, at any time. Then may this plaque always be a reminder of what Fear, Hate and Greed will cause men to do to other men. TONDEMONAI!

When the State Advisory Commission to the Department of Parks and Recreation met in Fresno in January 1972 it approved the historic landmark designation. But it raised problems with our text. First of all, because each bronze letter had to be cast separately, there would apparently not be enough space on the plaque for our entire text. Later we learned that the commissioners objected to some of our wording. This was the beginning of a year-long controversy in which the JACL acted as liaison between our organization, the Manzanar Committee, and the state.

An impromptu group from the JACL regional office and several state officials took out the Japanese term "tondemonai" ("incredibly; never happened"), which meant little to most of us. Several commissioners opposed the words "racism" and "economic greed." The State Advisory Commission also invoked the standard argument against the term "concentration camp": the term should refer only to the camps in Europe; "concentration camp" conjures up the horrible memories of Hitler and his countrymen. We must not compare our WRA camps to those in Europe. The Manzanar Committee had never compared America's camps with Hitler's, but it was evident that others would continue to do so.

Under what I believe was pressure from the Advisory Commission to reach a compromise wording, Warren Furutani, the late Amy Ishi, and I flew to Sacramento to meet with the Advisory Commission's president and secretary. The commissioners had said that they wanted the wording approved in time for us to have the plaque for our next pilgrimage, in 1973. We told them that the pilgrimage would take place whether or not we dedicated the plaque. We had not yet removed the words that the commission opposed.

The revised wording that came out of the meeting was to go to the director of the Department of Parks and Recreation, William Penn-Mott. He would not approve the wording, saying that we could put up our own plaque, but that the state bear and the department's name would not appear on any plaque that bore such negative words.

Assemblyman Alex Garcia, who represented Los Angeles' Little Tokyo district, arranged a ninety-minute meeting for us with Director Penn-Mott. We came to the state capitol with several members of the JACL and certain individuals who were prepared to testify about their experiences. We presented the supporting documents on which the director had insisted to justify the use of the term "concentration camp." Yet despite all our efforts, he still refused to approve the wording. At that point, Warren Furutani, our founding chair, who had been quiet up to then, turned to Penn-Mott and said, "One man signed an order that sent all my relatives and friends to the camps; you're one person who's holding up the approval of this plaque wording. You are a racist, nothing but a racist . . ."

Penn-Mott stood up, his face flushed red, and in an angry voice said, "I'm not going to stay here and be insulted and called names. I have to leave; I have a meeting to go to. I don't approve the wording."

Garcia, who was chairing the meeting, reached out and grabbed Penn-Mott's arm. He said, "Well, then this will go to the legislature."

"You can have it all," the director answered as he stalked out of the room. It was an unexpected and stunning victory.

And so it happened that at the 1973 Manzanar Pilgrimage the stonemason Ryozo Kado carefully fitted the plaque into the front wall of the stone guardhouse that he had built more than thirty years earlier. Over fifteen hundred people, many representing other WRA camps, were present for the dedication.

The final version of the dedication, as it appears on the bronze plaque, reads as follows:

In the early part of World War II, 110,000 persons of Japanese ancestry were interned in relocation centers by Executive Order 9066 issued on February 19, 1942. Manzanar, the first of ten such concentration camps, was bounded by barbed wire and guard towers, confining 10,000 persons, the majority being American citizens. May the injustices and humiliation suffered here as a result of hysteria, racism and economic exploitation never emerge again.

During these years, a slow flame began to burn brighter when groups and individuals began to discuss the possibility of asking the United States government for an apology and monetary compensation for violations of the rights of the American citizens and legal residents who were affected by Executive Order 9066. Some members of the JACL's San Fernando chapter asked me to join them in trying to form a committee to canvass our community on its feelings about seeking redress. The initiative would entail a large educational program. When we published a survey questionnaire in a local vernacular newspaper, the responses were overwhelmingly in support of individual reparations. Those who opted for a community fund indicated that they did not want the JACL to handle the funds. The community was still suspicious of the national organization they believed had "done them in."

Redress activists sought resolutions from the ever-friendly church groups, some labor unions, and civil rights organizations. We had to tell our own community that it was not charity we were seeking, but a just settlement that would redress the wrongs committed against us. Many believed it was too late; others did not think we had enough support across the nation. The educational initiative was to be a real test of our patience and endurance.

Throughout the redress campaign, the Manzanar Committee continued its annual pilgrimages and educational outreach. Around 1984, the National Park Service (NPS) completed its survey of the ten WRA camps and nominated Manzanar as a National Historic Landmark because of the large number of recognizable artifacts and remains on the site. The late mayor of Los Angeles, Tom Bradley, who had a number of friends among former Nisei internees, was a strong supporter of preserving Manzanar as a historic landmark. He appointed Rose M. Ochi,* then executive director of the Criminal Justice Planning Office of the City of Los Angeles, as the liaison between Los Angeles and the NPS, and between the city and the Inyo County Board of Supervisors.

On April 27, 1985, Jerry Rogers, Associate Director for Cultural Resources of the National Park Service, came to the Manzanar Pilgrimage and presented the plaque to City Council member Dave Cunningham, who represented the mayor of Los Angeles. Director Rogers declared,

> All nations mark and celebrate the historic places that represent their triumphs, their great leap forward. Even repressive governments call upon the inspiration of history to enforce patriotism. Our nation does that, and properly so. But few nations have the fortitude to do what the United States does here today. Manzanar cannot be celebrated for it is not a triumph, an achievement, and not a great leap forward for the United States. But it must be commemorated, committed to and held in memory as a reminder that Jefferson's words mean as much in our day as . . . in his—"Eternal vigilance is the price of liberty."[3]

---

* Rose Ochi, an attorney who has served in a variety of civic and community organizations, was appointed as Assistant Attorney General for the United States in 1997, and thus became the first Asian American woman to serve in this capacity.—Ed.

By the time of the landmark dedication, much had happened to give the community a sense of optimism. The Commission on Wartime Relocation and Internment of Civilians had published its report. Sansei lawyers had filed three separate *coram nobis* (writ of error) petitions asking the courts to set aside the 1944 convictions of resisters Fred Korematsu, Gordon Hirabayashi, and Min Yasui. William Hohri's class-action suit against the government (an attempt to win redress through the judiciary) was heading for the high courts, and the National Coalition for Redress and Reparations was lobbying Congress.

The National Park Service recommended to Congress that Manzanar be established as part of the National Park System. Behind the scenes, discussions were going on to convince the residents of Owens Valley that development of Manzanar as a national historic site would bring economic benefit to the region. Inyo County is poor. It would need funds to build a new storage facility for its Road Department if the one that it was then using, the former auditorium at Manzanar (still standing today), were to fall under the jurisdiction of the NPS. Ranchers wanted grazing space and water for their cattle. Yet to be decided upon were provisions to safeguard the water rights of the Los Angeles Department of Water and Power.

As these issues were being discussed, some people began to urge us to get a bill into Congress. The Civil Liberties Act had been passed in 1988, although appropriations for the $20,000 in individual redress compensation for which it provided had not been attached to it. We argued that we could not introduce a bill for Manzanar until the redress issue was settled. Two bills in the hopper would not only confuse the representatives; the action might kill both bills. So it was not until 1991 that Representative Mel Levine (D-Los Angeles) was approached to introduce a bill. By the end of the year, we had a large number of sponsors for HR 543, including Congressmen Robert T. Matsui and Norman Mineta, as well as William Thomas (R-Bakersfield), who represented Inyo County. The bill included $1.1 million dollars for replacement costs to Inyo County for construction of a new facility to house its Road Department. The city of Los Angeles would have its water rights; 500 acres would be designated as the Manzanar National Historic Site. In the Senate, Alan Cranston (D-California) was the point man for a similar bill (S 621).

We prepared to testify before the House subcommittee on National Parks, Forests, and Public Lands. Rose Ochi carried a supporting message from Mayor Bradley. Hiro Takusagawa represented the National Japanese American Historical Society of San Francisco, and I represented the Manzanar Committee. In the hearing room we saw a number of familiar faces. Jerry Rogers from the NPS greeted us warmly. His visit to Manzanar was one of the highlights of his life, he said: "It was an honor to be there." A representative from the National Parks and Conservation Association, a powerful environmental group that supported us, was there. JACL Regional Director from Chicago, Bill Yoshino, told us that he had been asked to testify in Washington for Title I of the bill.

"What Title I?" we asked.

Title I had been added to HR 453 by Representative George Miller at the request of a JACL chapter in central California. It would mandate the NPS to do a theme study of places significant to the war in the Pacific, including the ten camps. I told him that a study had already been done. I wanted to know why the JACL had not consulted us before adding the paragraph to the bill. Yoshino had no background information; he had been told only to testify on the bill. Rose and I were worried that the subcommittee would include Manzanar in the theme study and drop its establishment as a National Historic Site. Yoshino assured us that the JACL supported the creation of Manzanar as a historic site but wanted the theme study included in the bill.

Late on Thanksgiving eve 1991, the House, anxious to adjourn for the holiday weekend, passed HR 543. The bill stalled in the Senate, however, because the president of the Los Angeles City Water and Power Commission objected that it did not adequately protect the city's water rights. He had not objected to the House version, but he hinted to me that because he didn't think the bill would pass he hadn't paid it much attention. When asked to write an amendment, he kept sending in the same or very similar wording.

When Los Angles City Councillor Ruth Galanter introduced a motion in the Council to support the House bill, Mike Gage, president of the Water and Power Board, got it sent to the Council Committee on Commerce, Energy and Natural Resources. The following week, Galanter's motion passed unanimously. After getting the resolution sent back to committee, Gage told me that he would offer to make Manzanar a city historic site, to the tune of $2 million, if I would make sure that the bill did not pass in the Senate. The offer, he said, was to remain a secret between ourselves. My supporters waiting in the City Council told me later that they felt sorry for me as the six-footer towered over me, shaking his finger.

The rumor got around City Hall the following week, and an aide to Mayor Tom Bradley called me to ask if I had heard anything about this $2 million deal. I was furious, but I said I knew nothing about it. Of course, there would have been no city park—Gage was just hoping that I would cave in to him. I was not about to do anything to stop the Senate bill, for I knew that the City Council and the mayor supported it.

Memos began going to the mayor as negotiator Rose Ochi and I tried to counteract Gage's persistent efforts to kill the bill. After weeks of delay in the bill's mock-up stage, Bradley ordered, "No more memos." He then personally telephoned Senator Dale Bumpers (D-Arkansas), chair of the subcommittee on National Parks, Forests, and Public Lands, to say that the city supported HR 543, and he urged him to send the bill to the Senate floor for a vote. Rose Ochi and I had testified in support of S 621 in Washington, and we were elated at the mayor's decision.

On February 19, 1992, the fiftieth anniversary of the signing of Executive Order 9066, the bill was brought forward in the House and got a roll-call vote of 400 to 13—a resoundingly supportive endorsement and, for us, the maraschino cherry to top the whipped cream. All that we had struggled for since the 1970s had been won—an impossible dream. And yet the struggle continues.

In 1994, funding was allocated to the Manzanar National Historic Site, and a superintendent was assigned to the location. The best thing that happened to us was that Ross Hopkins, a thirty-year veteran of the National Park System, asked to be transferred to Manzanar from the Death Valley National Monument. Ross was an unusual public servant. He had been superintendent of several other controversial NPS sites. He surely knew what he was getting into when he took over building Manzanar from scratch in a community that was hostile to any development at the site. Those who supported the Park Service were not taking a public stand. Ross became a one-person PR agent, speaking before local organizations, including the veterans' groups, which opposed him personally as well. Both he and his wife were threatened. In the face of that hostility, Ross made friends and allies; he convinced many local residents that the Valley would benefit from developing and preserving Manzanar. With no budget for staff, Ross did a yeoman's job of handling office work, policing the site against vandalism, and building a historic site that successors will more easily be able to oversee and run on a daily basis.

Ross came to Manzanar in 1994, but the land was not transferred until 1997, when the City of Los Angeles' Department of Water and Power agreed to trade Manzanar for land of equal value and acreage. In his last three years before retiring in 2000, Ross not only did public outreach but took care of the routine tasks that were needed to make Manzanar operational. He had a sewer system installed. To organize the Advisory Commission that was mandated in the congressional bill, he recruited volunteers and professionals who studied the new park and discovered unique and interesting features that had long been covered over by the sands and winds of time.*

Finally, in 1997, after some struggle, 313 acres were added to the original amount allotted for the site, bringing the total to 813 acres to be developed and preserved in perpetuity. On April 26, 1997, Deputy Secretary of the Interior John Garamendi attended the pilgrimage to accept the Manzanar land for the federal government and on behalf of the people of the United States.

The Manzanar Committee celebrated our thirtieth anniversary pilgrimage in April 1998. At our request, each camp reunion and pilgrimage group raised a banner of its own creation in a roll call held before the interfaith religious services. It was a fitting memorial on the eve of the millennium.

My narrative ends here, but my journey continues. In the more than three decades of my involvement with Manzanar and my other community activities, I have reaped benefits I never expected. I have met extraordinary ordinary people and participated in wondrous events while traveling across America. Numerous individuals also involved with the preservation of Japanese American history have been my friends and mentors. I have been recognized for my support of working men and women and was one of thirty-five White House delegates to the United National Mid-Decade Conference on Women, held in Copenhagen in 1980. During President Jimmy Carter's term in office, I was invited to a breakfast at the White House.

It has been a long journey of hard work, patience, and endurance, but it has also been one of fun and companionship. As I meet earnest young men and women who feel strongly about our nation and the ideals on which it was founded, I am optimistic about our future. With the vision of these young people, human and civil rights are being strengthened for future generations so that all Americans can share equally in the bounties of our country.

---

* In 2000, the House of Representatives voted to appropriate $5 million for project construction and development of the Manzanar National Historic Site.--Ed.

NOTES

1. Harry Y. Ueno was the pivotal figure in the Manzanar riot. He was supported by a large number of people, much to the surprise of the administration. See Sue Kunitomi Embrey, Betty Mitson, and Arthur A. Hansen, eds., *Manzanar Martyr: An Interview with Harry Y. Ueno* (Fullerton: California State University at Fullerton Oral History Program, 1988).
2. Scott Hagel, "The Gist of It," *Powell [Wyoming] Tribune*, September, 1991.
3. Excerpt from Jerry Rogers's speech during the presentation of the Historic Landmark designation of Manzanar at the 1985 Manzanar Pilgrimage.

ERICA HARTH

DEMOCRACY FOR BEGINNERS

I AM SEQUESTERED BEHIND THE LEAVES OF A LARGE, open book, held upright by my father. I am sitting on his lap, and together we are intoning, "A was an Archer, who shot at a frog—B was a Butcher, who had a great dog." The archer is resplendent in his green hunter's outfit, bow and arrow poised for the kill. The smiling butcher in a blue-and-white striped apron stretched across his broad girth would be friendlier without the formidable mastiff at his side. By now I know and admire these characters. But more than anything I love the letters that magically resolve themselves into meaning. It is 1943, and I am four years old. Six months ago I uttered my first words, which came out in a complete sentence: "No, I don't want any cocoa." Finally persuaded that I am neither mute nor mentally retarded, my parents have leapt into the verbal breach waving the flag of literacy.

Less than a year later I have outgrown my alphabet books. We have left my native city of New York for Riverside, California, where I am in kindergarten, reading away. To describe me, my teacher resorts to a nursery rhyme: "When she is good, she is very, very good, and when she is bad she is horrid." No one has much time to care. There's a war on, after all. My mother is heading up the Traveler's Aid Society for the Riverside USO, and my father is working at the naval air base in nearby San Bernardino.

Our next move, in June 1944, is to a place named Manzanar, in a desert surrounded by high, snow-capped mountains. Although we are still in California, it feels like another continent. My mother is busy with her new job as a counselor with the War Relocation Authority (WRA) in Manzanar's Welfare Section. Inyokern, the naval base to which my father has been transferred, isn't close enough to Manzanar for him to live with us during the week, so he comes to stay on weekends. I miss my father very much, and I am still longing for my nurse-maid, Edith, who wasn't allowed to come with us when we left New York for Riverside.

Books are my consolation. I have *Winnie the Pooh*, *The Wizard of Oz*, and *The Wind in the Willows*. I am only five and already through kindergarten, so what is to be done with me? My parents enroll me in Manzanar's first grade.

In Manzanar's school we had a variety of activities: clay modeling, science, social studies, music and rhythm, and numbers, punctuated by rest and play periods. But what I remember best is reading, at which I excelled. While my classmates struggled to keep up with the antics of Dick and Jane and Spot and Puff, I read with "expression." Clearly no one else could come anywhere near me in skill, so why was Miss Beckwith not calling on me? "She only calls on the Japanese kids," I complained to my mother.

It was Manzanar, I believe, that gave me the long-lasting conviction of my intellectual superiority. I who had caught up and then some with my own developmental lag was now thrown in with a group of kids who, although older than I, were only just opening their books. What an opportunity for me to shine! I was on a roll. Somehow Virginia, the school superintendent's daughter and the one other Caucasian child in the class, didn't count.

The evacuation two years earlier had cost my fellow pupils valuable learning time. While I was being fed alphabet books, they were trying to adjust to the converted horse stalls of "assembly centers." In the fairgrounds and live-stock pavilions where the evacuated population had awaited removal to Manzanar and the nine other wartime concentration camps for Japanese Americans, volunteer evacuee teachers had improvised classes. Without textbooks, supplies, or an established routine, learning was dependent on ingenuity, determination, and good will. Isolated as they now were from the general population, most of my classmates heard more Japanese than they had before the evacuation. Some Nisei children had started the evacuation as native Japanese speakers. Native English speakers like the Sansei, or myself, had an automatic scholastic advantage.

But I had an advantage over both generations of camp schoolchildren. Having just come from the "outside," I understood all the cultural references. For my classmates, the Elson-Gray readers, featuring a nice, white, middle-class family, must have seemed exotic. Pets like Spot the dog and Puff the cat had not been allowed inside the barbed wire, but the rabbits, squirrels, chipmunks, and barnyard animals that were readily available were soon collected

First-grade class at Manzanar, 1944–45. The author is at the left, her arms folded on the desk.

and deposited in the Manzanar "zoo" at the edge of camp. The nearest thing to a household pet for most of my fellow first-graders was a chicken.

My family life was not all that much closer to that of Dick and Jane than my classmates'. I had no siblings, no father trudging home from work every evening, no aproned mother teaching me to sew or cook. But because of my white skin I was possessed of a superior knowledge. In our little white frame cottage in the administrative section of the camp, we had a kitchen with pots and pans in it. Yoshiko Uchida, who was interned at Topaz, Utah, relates in her memoir, *Desert Exile* (1982), that when nursery school children at the Tanforan Assembly Center played house, they always made believe that they were standing in line at a mess hall.

This cultural advantage showed up in other subjects, like social studies, which had been a centerpiece of the camp schools' original progressive curriculum. We were supposed to be learning about the immediate environment, the community, and the world. The program for first grade was the "Home Unit."

(You didn't advance to the "Primitive People Units" until third grade.) Topics in the Home Unit included: "The Family," "Food in the Home," "The Garden," "Animals (Pets, Useful Animals)," "Neighboring Helpers (Milkman, Grocer, Postman)," "Communication in the Home (Newspaper, Telephone, Mail, Radio)," "Manners in the Home," "Transportation at Home (Family Car, Trains, Buses, Boats, Airplanes)."[1] So I was way ahead. No one else (except maybe Virginia) knew about things like milkmen and boats.

WRA educators undoubtedly realized that the environment we were supposed to be studying hardly resembled the barbed wire and guard towers that surrounded us. But they had a plan. Their aim was to "keep alive the faint memory of a home the children brought with them to Manzanar and to create for them the concept of normal, attractive living conditions."[2] Only by pretending that Manzanar was a normal town and the barracks normal homes, only by peopling the desert with milkmen and grocers, by making boats whir through the sand and trains chug up the Sierras would the children be motivated to relocate. Because the campaign for relocation had to be directed at everyone, young and old alike.

As early as 1943, the WRA had begun its big push for resettlement outside the camps, to the east of the West Coast exclusion zones. The campaign was stepped up at the end of 1944, when the Supreme Court decided, in *Ex parte Endo*, that a loyal citizen could not legally be detained. (At the same time, in *Korematsu* v. *United States*, the court supported the argument of military necessity and upheld the constitutionality of the evacuation.) As of January 2, 1945, rescission of the exclusion order that had kept the interned population out of the West Coast would go into effect. So from this time on, our teachers drummed into us refrains from the next life about how we were soon going to do all sorts of unimaginable things like taking a train or eating in a restaurant. We wrote to relocated classmates, and we filled our school newspaper, "The Manzanar Whirlwind," with stories of relocation.

I, of course, had no need to learn about relocation. I had just relocated—to Manzanar—and I liked it! Miss Beckwith would pay for her refusal to bow publicly to my superiority. "Old Duck-Feet," I hissed behind her back. She wore spectacles, a shiny green eyeshade like a newspaperman, and sensible shoes. I mocked her mercilessly.

In mid-year Miss Beckwith administered the Kuhlmann-Anderson intelligence test to our class. (Children in the camps were tested constantly for anything from low body weight and myopia to social maladjustment.) I came out with a higher-than-average IQ for the class and a below-average "mental age."[3] A Manzanar school official who analyzed the scores for our class concluded that Kuhlmann-Anderson was not a suitable test for us. One problem, apparently (although not for me), was that pupils were getting penalized for language difficulties. Blissfully unaware of my test scores, I sailed on through my first year of scholastic triumph to collect a wreath of academic E's (for "excellent"), heralding years of educational success to come.

Yet I who was the exception was nevertheless the norm. The normal world, the one with which I automatically associated the brightly colored pictures in our readers, was mine. No one had to know, least of all myself, that I was Jewish, which was not normal.

And if I was normal, then it was my classmates who were the exception. What was remarkable was not that I had no trouble reading, but that my classmates, with all their impediments, eventually succeeded. Diagnostic tests of 1945 showed that they equaled or surpassed state standards.[4]

If I learned to feel superior (and Miss Beckwith had the wisdom to recognize that in fact I was not), my classmates took away the opposite lesson. If one white child chanced to emerge from Manzanar convinced of her mental prowess, some 30,000 children of the camps' schools were left scarred by feelings of shame and inferiority. In the camps, they had to make up for the months of formal schooling lost in assembly centers in the spring of 1942, to make up for the lack of English at home, to make up for being Japanese American. It was not that Miss Beckwith treated my classmates with what was then called "prejudice" (for she did not), but rather that the curriculum itself was slanted toward the remedial. Wasn't "Americanization"—a word banned from the WRA's lexicon but nonetheless the primary goal of camp educators—itself the remedy for new ethnic groups?

To open our school day we had flag salute, the Pledge of Allegiance, and patriotic songs. In 1943, a Supreme Court decision (*West Virginia State Board of Education* v. *Barnette*) had struck down the compulsory Pledge of Allegiance in schools, but we went on saying it anyway. In the same year, the WRA and the army jointly had subjected internees to a fateful loyalty questionnaire that was to determine which families and individuals would be moved out to be "segregated" as disloyal at the Tule Lake camp in northern California and which would remain at Manzanar. Many of my classmates had witnessed painful arguments at home about how to answer the loyalty questions. The fact that they were still at Manzanar in 1944–1945 meant that they were children of "loyal" parents. They were learning, at home and at school, how important it was to their futures to demonstrate their loyalty in everything from the flag salute to volunteering for the all-Nisei combat team that was earning so many decorations for its costly valor overseas.

They learned their lessons well. A fourth-grader writes in "The Manzanar Whirlwind": "The statue of liberty is big and tall the light in the torch is very bright. It can be seen far out at sea. People say it is very beautiful. I wish I could see it."[5] In another issue of the newspaper, two fifth-grade girls, one of whom was later to publish an account of her time at Manzanar, celebrate the Americanness that we were daily imbibing in the classroom.

Our Flag

Our flag is waving high
Against the light blue sky
We salute to you.

We sing to our Banner
In a gallent [sic] manner
Dear Red, White and Blue
We stand up for you.

We all sing
While liberty reigns
Dear Red, White and Blue
We remove our hat for you.[6]

Proving loyalty, the children were learning, was largely proving that you were not disloyal—that no one in your family was a spy, that your brother or your father would not fight for Japan, and did not prefer to live there. Such proof did not address the question of what you were loyal *to*. If being American meant mastering the English language and gaining the necessary skills for financial and social success in the United States, then "Americanization" was easy to understand. But what if it meant loyalty to the "democratic way of life," to "democracy?"

My parents, who were members of the Communist Party, might have had their own thoughts on loyalty. During the war years after Pearl Harbor, the period of the new Popular Front, they supported Roosevelt, the president who had signed Executive Order 9066 and so made the camps possible. And in April of the year that we spent at Manzanar, my mother wept copiously at President Roosevelt's death during the camp's memorial service. Nevertheless, she who certainly knew of Roosevelt's key role in authorizing the internment told me it was wrong to put the "Japanese" into camps. (It didn't occur to me at the time to wonder what *we* were doing there. My mother's work was always too important and mysterious to question.) Ever since we had arrived in California, the many soldiers who passed through my daily life reminded me that we were fighting a war to preserve the democratic way of life.

But flag salute and patriotic exercises bored me. What I was learning about democracy could not be packaged in ceremony. No one was proclaiming my specialness. Even if once in a while I got to parade my reading ability before the whole class, in the main my talents showed up only on my report card. Miss Beckwith treated me like everyone else.

After school hours, any academic distinctions were forgotten, and my classmates and I ran in packs through the desert. In our exhilaration at being uncaged, we roamed the vast wilderness—the whole one square mile of it. Barracks and mess halls had transformed traditional family life for my companions. Children did not necessarily eat with their parents, and they often scampered from mess hall to mess hall in search of the best food. As for me, for the first time in my life, I was on my own with no nanny to watch over me. And so, in our peculiar freedom, we first-graders forged a bond of friendship and solidarity.

It wasn't precisely what the educators had in mind. In the summer of 1942, a graduate class in Curriculum Development at Stanford University had mapped out a plan for "community schools" in the camps and for a progressive education that was to revolve around the democratic way of life. We—"they" and I, for I had in effect been inducted as a sort of fellow-traveler in this trailblazing—were to be prepared for an eventual return to the democracy outside Manzanar. At the same time, our school would give us the opportunity both to serve the community and to learn from it. Our little barracks room would expand to a school without walls; every corner of the camp would teach us something. John Dewey's ideal—to give the child "an orderly sense of the world in which he lives"—echoes distantly in the Stanford proposal. Grade by grade, our explorations of the world would move us from home and family life to school and neighborhood, to the entire community, and thence back through history and onward in science and technology. To this comprehensive core of general education would be added certain "selective subjects" that would offer the camps' young residents either college preparation or vocational training.

The Stanford class imagined that internees and Caucasian staff would work together democratically to promote the good of the community. Some of the students had made a two-day site visit to the Tule Lake Relocation Center. A glimpse of the unfinished barracks in the sand seems to have quickened their pioneering zeal. To these students, who were personally unaffected by the evacuation order, the spectacle suggested less the trauma of eviction and readjustment than it did the rebuilding of ideals from ground zero. Their vision of the community school appealed to the WRA. Several of its officials, including the first acting head of the Education Section, Lucy Adams (eventually detailed to Manzanar), had come from positions on Navajo reservations, where community schools established during the 1930s were still in place. Meanwhile, WRA officials were aware that evacuee leaders had begun to promote a concept of the camps as "ideal cities" or "ideal communities." The community school would be entirely consistent with the "ideal city," a place where cooperation and accommodation among people of different generations, social backgrounds, temperaments, and tastes would reduce the inevitable tensions of arbitrary imprisonment.[7]

Although internees continued to invoke the principle of "ideal cities" through many crises of the internment, the community school system began to falter within about a year. The progressive credo built on the centrality of the individual child's needs gradually gave way to a more traditional style modeled on that of the children's former schools, located mainly in the Los Angeles area. A high teacher turnover was largely responsible for the change. Who would want to work a forty-eight-hour week in a concentration camp for less pay than in a conventional school? Until 1944, single women—the teachers were overwhelmingly female—felt discriminated against because the administration housed them apart from the rest of the white staff, in evacuee barracks. In the classroom, teachers were pressured to meet the WRA's ambitious goal: "The schools must equip the child with better than average formal education and vocational experience, because the teacher recognizes that the position of minority group members requires them to be better than average if they are to have average opportunity."[8] Not only did teachers have to cope with unusual standards; according to one WRA report, they were frustrated because "they are not master of their classroom situation. They cannot pronounce the difficult and unfamiliar names. All the faces look alike."[9] It was not an atmosphere in which idealism could flourish. As of the 1943–1944 school year, it was education for relocation, a unique goal with no necessary connection to the progressive ideal, that gave the camps' educational system whatever coherence it may have had.

In any case, it was hard to understand what the community was supposed to be. If it was meant to be Manzanar, then "community" was a dubious term at best. It is true that by 1944 the WRA liked to think of Manzanar and the other camps as typical American towns, complete with churches, newspaper (censored by the WRA), barber, hairdresser, baseball games, school teams, and cheerleaders. But the typical American town is not ringed by barbed wire.

Maybe the community was supposed to suggest the larger world to which everyone would soon be relocating. Such, in fact, was one notion offered by WRA educators, especially after 1943. But if so, my classmates' idea of it would depend largely on Miss Beckwith. According to WRA guidelines, the teacher was obliged to "provide the link between the stagnant life within the center and the changing world beyond the barbed wire fence. . . . She must not allow the Japanese-American child to become too absorbed in his own misfortunes and feelings of being the only object of prejudice in America. Children must develop an interest in other minority groups besides their own. Their isolation and treatment has [*sic*] caused them to be self-centered, over sensitive, drained of confidence and poise. This self-pity can be transferred to an interest in other peoples with similar difficulties."[10]

If you could only forget your own "difficulties," you would be receptive to learning about American values. The WRA advised its teachers "to make each classroom as near a miniature democracy as possible."[11] Every school activity was to be evaluated for its social worth according to three criteria: "Does the activity lead to better adjustment in community living? Does it have a wartime value? Does it promote better assimilation into our American society?"[12] The objectives of first grade were: "1) to develop good citizenship through activities related to the general welfare of the individual and the community; to help the child realize his responsibility to the group, whether at home or in school; to create respect for the rights of others; 2) to promote the mental, social, moral and emotional growth of boys and girls; 3) to increase the physical wellbeing and develop a balanced personality."[13]

The WRA liked the idea of the classroom as a "miniature democracy" because from the beginning it had tried to institute a system of democratic self-government in the camps. Strictly defined responsibility was delegated by the WRA administration to elected "block managers" and evacuee community councils. At first only Nisei were allowed to hold office, but since tradition gave authority to the elder males, this restriction caused much tension between Nisei and Issei. Even after the Issei were admitted to office, however, evacuee decision-making was severely limited. Nonetheless, in a policy statement of May 1942, the WRA insisted on its egalitarianism: "WRA offers cooperation, not paternalism, to evacuees." Earlier in the month staffers had held discussions on who should take the initiative for community government, WRA or the evacuees. Those who wanted WRA to take the lead stressed, as the agency's final report tells us, that "the evacuated people as a group were almost wholly inexperienced in the functioning of the American democratic process."[14]

It was this process that we were supposed to be learning in school, where under 10 percent of all the camps' certified teachers were Japanese American. Two-thirds of the teaching staff consisted of (uncertified) evacuee assistant or "cadet" teachers. Many of them had had no previous teaching experience, but their work could be just as demanding as that of the "appointive" (non-evac-uee) certified teachers. Evacuee teachers, both certified and uncertified, were paid on the WRA's pay scale, usually $16 a month.

Whatever the mold—traditional, progressive, or eclectic—our education was by and large geared for Dick and Jane. In this respect, the formal education I received in my "pioneer school" was, for all the abnormality of its situation, not appreciably different from what I would have gotten on the outside. If internees had been seriously included in the planning process, perhaps it would have been. The WRA did seek internees' opinion in the planning conference it held with the Stanford class in the summer of 1942, but because it didn't hear what it wanted to from the people consulted, it decided not to hear them at all. The de-bates it bypassed were several decades ahead of their time. Although no one would have put it this way, the issue was multiculturalism. Some parents wanted the children to learn about their Japanese heritage. Others felt cheated if their child was not being taught by the professionally trained Caucasians who, they be-lieved, would give the pupils the best possible preparation for the society they would eventually have to confront. The other side responded that such feelings only reinforced the racism that had put their children in camp schools in the first place. One internee warned teachers that "added to your routine problems in the classroom will be an undercurrent of antagonism that will, I fear, put you to se-vere test. If your pupils are not going to scorn you outright, they will doubt you. The shattering disillusionment of discovering, in their own minds and from their parents, that democracy was for those of other races and color, but not for them, has left a scar, still tender and open, in these youngsters."[15]

The majority of internees consulted in 1942, though, seemed less interested in educational policy than in getting their children back to something resembling a regular classroom after months of an enforced holiday. It was not, after all, *their* experiment that was being conducted in the camps' laboratory schools. Repre-sentation of Nisei on the teaching staff and inclusion of materials relating to the Japanese cultural tradition nevertheless remained matters of some concern to them. But educating for democracy in 1942 made no room for multiculturalism, and it was left to internees to organize extracurricular instruction in traditional arts and crafts, the tea ceremony, and theater. Such activities flourished, espe-cially among the Issei. After the unrest following the loyalty questionnaire and segregation, a faction of young internee men at Tule Lake began to offer training in the Japanese martial arts. And so it came about that the moral vacuum in which inmates were to be made "ready to hurl as projectiles of democracy into the maelstrom of postwar readjustment," as one WRA educator put it,[16] was eventually filled with activities far removed from the planners' design.

We children—the object of all these educational experiments—sniffed out the absurd in the laboratory. The barbed wire, watchtowers, and guns could slow down any "projectile of democracy." Ours was not, in reality, a school like other schools. Our PTA remained unaffiliated with local PTAs because no one would affiliate with us; our clubs, choruses, and orchestras remained isolated. The only interschool athletic event in which Manzanar participated was a football game with the town of Big Pine in October 1944. Our high school basketball team was scheduled to play against Bishop High in November of that year, but at the last minute the Bishop school board canceled. The president of the Bishop student body wrote to the Manzanar students to express appreciation for the "understanding letter" from the Manzanar High School principal, and continued: "When we were informed that the game with your basketball team had been canceled we did our utmost to change the School Board's decision through a petition signed by the entire student body. It has been taught us in school that a democracy and constitution such as ours guarantees [sic] every American equal treatment. Certain members of the Board, however, refused to acknowledge our efforts."[17]

Older schoolchildren, who had some memory of life before camp, expressed what the younger ones could not say. A sixth-grader writes "A Trip to Death Valley" in June 1943:

Last week my family and I started by car on a trip to Death Valley. Leaving our car, part of the trip was made on horseback.

We saw many pretty wild flowers and bushes. We saw the mystic sand dunes and found some strange ruins.

Everything looked so strange and beautiful that I felt like taking the whole desert home with me and showing it to everyone I met.

At noon we stopped to eat our lunch, and a storm came up just as we were getting ready to go on. This delayed us but after a time, the storm quieted down.

We met Indians, who were friendly and told us much about Death Valley. They told us about the lake we would find if we traveled further. We found it and what do you think it was? Only a mirage!

Traveling so long it began to grow dark and we knew it must be time to go home, but where was our home? We were lost! Which way should we go? We had to spend the night on the lonely desert with the stars and sky overhead. It grew windy, but finally we slept.

Then morning came and where do you think we were?—In our own beds!

This was only a dream.[18]

In his wryly scornful poem, "That Damn Fence," a high school boy calling himself the "mad Mongolian" depicted a much starker view of the internment:

> They've sunk the posts, deep in the ground,
> And they've strung barbed wire all the way around;
> With machine gun nests just over there,
> There are sentries and soldiers everywhere.
> We're trapped like rats in a wire cage,
> To fret and fume with impotent rage.
> Yonder we seek the life of the night,
> But that damned fence is flooded with light;
> We seek the softness of the midnight air,
> But that damned fence is in the floodlight glare.
> They see unrest in our nocturnal quest,
> And mockingly laugh with vicious jest.
> With nowhere to go and nothing to do
> We feel terribly lonesome and blue.
> That damned fence is driving us crazy,
> Destroying our youth and making us lazy.
> Loyalty we know and patriotism feel,
> To sacrifice our utmost was our ideal;
> To fight for our country, and die, perhaps,
> Yet we are prevented because we are Japs.
> We all love life and our country best,
> Yet it's our misfortune to be here in the west.
> To keep us penned up behind that damned fence
> Is someone's notion of national defense.[19]

Once the campaign for relocation was in full swing, WRA policy may even have encouraged such sentiments. During my first-grade year of 1944–1945, the agency made an all-out effort to get the remaining families to leave the camps. In March 1945, "The Manzanar Whirlwind" ran a lead editorial titled "The Gate is Open": "You have surely heard the popular song about fences. When Bing Crosby sings 'Don't fence me in,' does it make you think of Manzanar? If YOU can't stand fences, what should you do? RELOCATE!" Entire issues of the paper were devoted to resettlement. For the March issue, one sixth-grader writes, "I am very anxious to leave here because I want to see new things. I am very tired [of] looking at the same things over and over. I want to see streetcars, automobiles, real houses, with a sink, sofa, icebox and other things in it." A third-grade boy contributed a cover illustration of a train with a smiling locomotive face and the bubble caption "Good-bye Manzanar." One of his classmates looks forward to "a house where there is a bedroom, dining room and a living room with chairs and tables in it. I want two trees in my yard, so I can play with my friends in my own yard."

In the final issue of the "Whirlwind" (April-May 1945) remaining pupils say advance goodbyes. Asked to list what they like or dislike about Manzanar, fifth-graders respond on the positive side: "the mountains, the creeks, the trees and birds, the bright stars, the snow in winter, the good drinking water, the free food, the free electricity and water." And on the other side: "the desert, the sand storms, the hard winds, the cold winters, the fence around camp, a one-room home."

As for me, my deep-rooted suspicion of the "democratic way of life" goes back to these heady days of my earliest personal freedom. Something told me that our community school wasn't in a real community at all. The barracks gave me the creeps. If the barbed wire was my safety net—it kept all my friends inside for me—I nevertheless sensed that although the guns, wire, and watchtowers were not meant for me, they could have been. Why not? It was clear that you didn't have to do anything bad to go to prison.

And yet I did learn something about democracy at Manzanar. In the office hierarchy of my mother's workplace, internees were the underclass. But in my schoolroom the hierarchy was simple: teacher and pupil. Virginia and I enjoyed no special prerogatives under Miss Beckwith's regime of fairness. Perhaps it was from this dispensation of justice in a dismally unjust situation, along with my mother's constant admonitions to avoid "prejudice," that I came to feel a certain moral superiority: wasn't it obvious that you shouldn't be a racist?

My first-grade make-believe classroom glossed over racism. Between the racism that prompted the internment and the postwar return lay the curricular never-never land of "democracy." Soon my young classmates were to face the reality of the "outside": social ostracism, vandalism, beatings, and shootings.

I spent the following school year in San Francisco, where my mother continued to work for the WRA until the closing of the camps. There I got my first personal lessons in racism. With the bells of V-J Day still tolling in our ears, my second-grade classmates were drawing caricatures of Japs. "But the Japanese are my friends," I protested to uncomprehending ears.

I began to lie, at first cautiously, then furiously and indiscriminately. It wasn't that I was swayed by my new classmates' racism, but that I was alone in my convictions. And after that long, luxurious year of camaraderie in the desert, I wasn't used to loneliness. Having landed in the midst of everyday life from an alien world, I did my feeble best to pass for one of theirs. One day, I got ambushed on the blacktop playground by a posse of schoolmates. Claudia, a stocky third-grader in a fake fur coat that made her look like an enormous, evil teddy bear, asked me if I had seen *The Bells of St. Mary's*.

—Oh, yes, I lied.—Remember the elephant?—Yes, I forced myself to grin, ha-ha.—Ha-ha, there was no elephant in it. Gotcha!—caught by one of the oldest tricks in the smart-aleck's bag.

Manzanar was light years away. Perhaps, threatened with imminent dissolution, it didn't even exist anymore.

Back home on the East Coast, when I was in third grade, no one seemed to have heard of Japanese Americans. Now I knew from the inside what it was like to be the minority, for I had turned into a minority of one. I alone guarded the strange, somehow shameful secret that my innocent playmates of old were, from the "outside" view, either hateful or nonexistent. Having succumbed to the army's bulldozers, Manzanar itself was lost forever. Perhaps, after all, it had never been anything more than a little girl's mirage, just like the lake in Death Valley.

Now I am the teacher, and I try to bring Manzanar into my classroom. Once again, I am the best reader in the class. In 1994, while doing research for this essay at the National Archives in Washington, D.C., I go to an exhibit on the internment at the Smithsonian. Three skinny white boys in T-shirts and jeans and ranging in age from about eight to fifteen, probably brothers, straggle into the gallery. They head for the section on the military. The two older boys stick together, and the youngest trots behind in a steady effort to keep up. They look at images of Nisei in American uniform. "Who were the Japanese Americans fighting *for?*" the youngest questions. His companions ignore him; they are riveted by the pictures and mock-ups. "Who were the Japanese Americans fighting *for?*" the little boy insists. No response. He tugs at a bigger boy's arm. Finally I take pity on him. "The United States," I answer. His face expands into a smile of relief, then contracts into wonderment. I have done my job for the day.

NOTES

1. WRA Papers, National Archives, Washington, D.C. Field Basic Documentation, COO53, reels 75, 77. All references to WRA papers in this essay will be to the collection at the National Archives. I am grateful to the Marion and Jasper Whiting Foundation for supporting my research at the WRA archives. My profound thanks to Dorothy Kaufmann for her most thoughtful reading of this essay in manuscript. Aloha South of the National Archives was an invaluable guide to me for the WRA records.

2. WRA Papers, Field Basic Documentation, COO53, reel 75.

3. WRA Papers, Record Group 210, Box 227.

4. Thomas James, *Exile Within: The Schooling of Japanese Americans, 1942–1945* (Cambridge, Mass.: Harvard University Press, 1987), 158. My main sources in this essay for general information on education in the camps are James, and William D. Zeller, *An Educational Drama: The Educational Program Provided the Japanese Americans During the Relocation Period, 1942–1945* (New York: American Press, 1969).

5. "Manzanar Whirlwind" (March 1945), 7. All references to the "Manzanar Whirlwind" in this essay are to the Ralph Merritt collection in the UCLA archives.

6. "Manzanar Whirlwind" (February 1945), 4.

7. On community schools and the Stanford proposal, see James, 36–42; and Zeller, 57–69.

8. WRA Papers, Field Basic Documentation, COO53, reel 75.

9. WRA Papers, Record Group 210, Box 227.

10. WRA Papers, Field Basic Documentation, COO53, reel 75.

11. Ibid.

12. Genevieve W. Carter, "Democracy Behind Barbed Wire," *Nation's Schools* (June 1943), 19.

13. WRA Papers. Field Basic Documentation, COO53, reel 75.

14. *WRA: A Story of Human Conservation* (United States Department of the Interior, War Relocation Authority, 1946), 83. I am grateful to Anne O. Freed for the gift of this WRA report.

15. Zeller, 69–73.

16. As quoted in James, 112.

17. WRA Papers, Field Basic Documentation, reel 77.

18. "Manzanar Whirlwind" (June 1943), 9.

19. WRA Papers, Record Group 210, Box 227.

PART IV

FROM THE PAST TO THE FUTURE

ROSANNA YAMAGIWA ALFARO

ETHNIC EXPECTATIONS:
THE POLITICS OF STAGING
THE INTERNMENT CAMPS

I WAS HAVING COFFEE WITH TWO ASIAN AMERICAN FRIENDS. One said, "I've never seen an internment-camp play I liked. The playwrights were too young to be in the camps, and besides, they don't live and speak Japanese, the way their parents did." The other said, "The trouble is, no one gets worked up about it. The internment camps were the poor man's Holocaust." Extreme views, but the truth is that most internment camp plays are viewed either as case histories—and therefore not entirely artistic, or as issue plays—and therefore not wholly human. The audience comes into the theater bracing itself for an evening that promises to be edifying but not particularly entertaining.

Asian American plays in general make up a minuscule part of the theater scene. In Boston even those of us who have our antennae up see one or two in a good year. The argument has been made that Asian American playwrights with very few exceptions are kept tucked away in their cultural internment camps. Much of the activity is still at companies like East West Players in Los Angeles, Pan Asian Repertory in New York City, the Asian American Theatre Workshop in San Francisco, or at companies that put on Asian American or multicultural festivals like the Magic Theatre in San Francisco or the Group Theater in Seattle.

In this multicultural country of ours the theater audience is almost entirely middle-class and white, which is not at all surprising when you consider the price of theater tickets and the fact that an overwhelming percentage of American plays have all-white casts. Some mainstream theaters have what is perceived as an ethnic slot, much like the ethnic slot in mainstream magazines. Ethnic slots are tricky. They can pit playwrights against each other or make them feel separate and marginal in theaters that actually have no real multicultural leadership or agenda. In some quarters, putting on minority plays is looked upon as a charity or grant opportunity. In a recent *Boston Globe* article, Robert Brustein, then artistic director of the American Repertory Theatre (ART), said he was in favor of channeling foundation money to black theaters "instead of bribing white theaters to do black plays, which is what a lot of foundations are doing."[1] Was he talking here about the American White Repertory Theatre? Was he saying he'd have to be bribed before he'd consider putting on the likes of August Wilson? In an industry dominated by cronyism, ethnic theater doesn't stand a chance of breaking into the mainstream without aggressive advocacy and significant funding.

Along with the impulse to keep ethnic playwrights in their own theaters is the assumption that they should be confined to their own subject matter, that they should "stick to what they know." Half of my plays are non-Asian, which seems appropriate for someone who grew up in the Midwest where there wasn't another Asian for miles around, but this hasn't been without its problems. Some years ago a play of mine about a Latin American dictator was runner-up in a New York competition. One of the judges called and said he'd like to suggest it to a Hispanic theater festival. He said, "You're Latin American, aren't you?" I said, "Well, not really," and that ended that. Another judge recommended it to an Asian American festival at the Magic Theatre in San Francisco. That turned out to be tricky because of the play's Hispanic theme, but this was solved by casting whites as the Americans and Asians as the Latin Americans. When the play was finally produced, one of the reviewers said, "The author does know something about the subject because her husband is Colombian." All this shows how much people still judge the book by its cover, how much they believe that race implies culture, and how many obstacles will always be put in the way of mainstreaming ethnic playwrights.

Sixty years after the internment Asian Americans still have trouble feeling at home in their adopted country. We are caught in a no-win situation. If we assimilate we're accused of hating ourselves. If we emphasize our roots we're told to go back home where we belong. We often feel less like a citizen than a paying guest. At any moment the person across from you might look at you not as a person but as a representative of a group. A woman came up to me after seeing one of my plays about some particularly neurotic and eccentric Japanese Americans. She said, "Thank you for that. I trust you, and now I see what Asian Americans are really like." Ethnic playwrights are unfortunately seen as spokespersons as well as artists. The audience believes that we have some sort of secret knowledge about our subject, and it believes just as strongly that we're limited in our view of the world and can't write about anything else. I do not agree with those who feel that only Japanese Americans should write about the internment camps or that Asian American writers should confine themselves to Asian American themes. If my children were writers, would they write only on Colombian Japanese American themes for an audience of the same? I believe that if you write on what moves you, everything you are will go into your work.

One of the first things people say about internment-camp plays is that they much prefer documentaries on the subject. For them theater seems woefully inadequate compared to actual interviews with the internees or to testimony at the redress hearings. They don't want to be manipulated by the playwright; they want to make up their own minds, draw their own conclusions—which they feel, often naively, that a documentary will allow them to do. They don't want to listen to an actor pretending to be in the internment camp; they want to listen to a real person telling the truth. They are like my friend who felt that no playwright was worthy of the subject who wasn't there and didn't speak the language. But even in interviews with the internees themselves, something is lost in the telling. Words may prove inadequate to describe the experience. Memories over time may become selective, heightened, or distorted. In the editing of any documentary, words and memories can both be transformed when they are answers to leading questions or carefully chosen to fit into the context of a larger story.

As George Tabori, a playwright of the Holocaust, writes, truth is always elusive. In his autobiographical play, *My Mother's Courage*, he tells the story of his mother's narrow escape from a concentration camp. The play is narrated by the son with asides from the mother, who at one moment suggests that he's missed the point. The son asks, "Are you making fun of me?" She replies, "Not at all. Only, well, I told you a story, and now you're telling a story. How can two stories be the same?"[2] A good play, like a good documentary, tries to involve both actors and audience "physically, intellectually, and emotionally" in replicating collective and personal memory.[3] Tabori feels that "true remembrance is possible only through sensual remembrance: it is impossible to confront the past without sensing it again in one's skin, nose, tongue, buttocks, legs and stomach."[4] In this sense, theater, a highly sensual and evocative medium, holds its own with the documentary. An autobiographical play, in the end, must be judged as theater; playwrights should spend as much time imagining an event as documenting it.

To find an audience, internment-camp plays must overcome the prejudice, which runs very deep in this country, that you shouldn't mix art and politics. This prejudice is much less prevalent in Latin America, where the dictator novel is a genre unto itself, or in Europe, where the private world is often portrayed in theater as a metaphor for the public world. Even kitchen-sink plays in London usually have a window open to the world. When Margaret Thatcher stepped down, the word was that the British playwrights were distraught—what on earth would they write about now? American playwrights, on the other hand, are usually reluctant to write about current events because the critics here have a knee-jerk reaction to issue plays, generally finding them earnest, trite, and overburdened.

American critics have a low tolerance for politically correct subjects. There's nothing new here, they complain, it's been done before—the same victims and oppressors, the same theme of racism and injustice. And much of the time, the critics are right. You should be very careful about staging your first thought or even your second because most likely someone has been there before you. Someone else has had a character drop a carton of precious Japanese dishes as he enters a tarpaper barracks. Someone else has described the occasional Nisei preference for fried chicken over sushi. On the other hand, if you try a new tack—something, say, along the lines of the Roberto Benigni's fanciful Holocaust movie, *Life Is Beautiful* (1997)—half of the community will be on your back and the whole enterprise dismissed as unworthy and offensive.

The critics are refined souls, used to sipping fine wine, not taking a drink at the neighborhood fire hydrant. They lump issue plays with sermons or with propaganda, preferring theater that deals with life's many ironies. They detest victim drama without sufficient psychological detail to pull you in. But in the case of most internment camps, the basic issue is crystal clear. At certain moments in history, political and personal issues become one. Life's rich ambiguities fall away before a single overwhelming injustice.

Playwrights David Hare and Howard Brenton once had an agitprop theater in Cambridge, England. When asked what their reasons were for choosing a particular play, they said they hoped to bring down the government—which, when you think about it, is a perfectly valid reason for putting on a play. Art can be a scourge, an instrument for protest and change. There is nothing wrong in producing a play that is also a civic happening. I remember a local theater producer complaining to me about a very angry and powerful South African play in the pre-Mandela years. He said, "Where was the subtlety? Where were the human relationships?" as if all plays should be cut from the same mold. He was one of those easily offended by a "black and white" situation. And yet, as everyone knows, matters of race are sometimes all important and at other times don't matter at all. In most South African issue plays or Japanese American internment-camp plays, race is all important and to miss that is to miss the point.

Theater need not always stand above the fray or forget that it exists in a specific time and space. It can be particularly exciting when theater reacts instantly to an event, implicates its audience, and provides a forum for public inquiry. In April 1989, Tariq Ali and Howard Brenton wrote the play *Iranian Nights* in five days as a response to the Ayatollah's fatwa on Salman Rushdie. When Executive Order 9066 was issued in 1942 it would have been wonderful if someone, Asian American or Caucasian, had produced an agitprop piece written on the spot: an angry, passionate, dangerous play with racism and war hysteria as its target. A flurry of internment-camp plays was produced at Pan Asian Repertory and East West Players during the early 1980s. It would also have been wonderful if a docudrama, based on the eloquent testimony of former internees in the redress hearings, had toured the country in 1983 on a theatrical quest for justice.

Samuel Johnson said that literature should instruct by pleasing. An internment-camp play often instructs by displeasing. It grabs the audience by the lapel and says, "Look, this is what happened in our country. How do you feel about it?" Worse yet, the playwright might even say, "The subject is what's important here. It's important for kids to learn about it. Tour it in the schools." You naturally get worked up about injustices, especially about those against your own people. You become obsessed, reading all the books on the subject in the library. The anger explodes on paper, which can be good or bad. You're full of resentment, which spills over all your characters. After all, what good is memory if you can't hold a grudge? The play is there, the characters are there, all to give vent to your anger. And the critics will, of course, hear the voice of the playwright in every character—shrill and rancorous or didactic and self-congratulatory.

White Americans do not necessarily want to be reminded of the time their government rounded up and imprisoned the Japanese Americans and summarily deprived them of their civil liberties. Does one only imagine a certain resistance in the audience of an internment-camp play, a suspicion that the playwright is a bit neurotic or paranoid, that surely things weren't as bad as all that? I remember that a white friend, after seeing my first internment-camp play, nudged me and said, "But that didn't really happen, did it?" Many Japanese Americans also have a strong resistance to talking about the camps. My parents both taught Japanese at the University of Michigan during the war and were among the fortunate Japanese Americans who were not interned. I can't remember a thing they said to me about the camps except that the internees had taken it very honorably. Perhaps my parents felt that they shouldn't burden me with such a dark event or remind themselves of a time when race was their most important characteristic. During the course of writing an internment-camp play one wonders if anyone wants to be put through yet another evening of isolation and alienation and prejudice. The audience members, after all, are the children of the perpetrators and of the victims, both of whom are drawn back to the scene of the crime, a scene they all would prefer to forget.

The reaction, in fact, of many younger Asian American playwrights is, "Been there, done that." It is as if we have been imprisoned by our ethnicity for much too long and need to mingle with the world at large. In Diana Son's *Stop Kiss*, for instance, nothing in the Public Theater production was made of the casting of a white woman and an Asian woman (with black and white boyfriends respectively) who fall in love. The fact that the women are beginning a lesbian relationship is important; the fact that they are of different ethnicities is not. The playwright Chay Yew, director of the Mark Taper Forum's Asian Workshop, has said that he is tired of the traditional Japanese American internment-camp play. He, like many others, is more interested in the way cultures blur and clash in multiracial America. In his play, *A Language of Their Own*, he, like Diana Son, is more interested in sexual identity than in ethnic identity. As David Henry Hwang (himself only in his early forties) says, "For a lot of writers in my generation it was a new idea to think of ourselves as Asian American, and that's what we focused on. The younger generation sees it simply as one piece in the larger mosaic."[5]

But each piece affects the larger mosaic, and the internment camps are arguably the largest piece in Asian American history. During the redress hearings the internees, silent for so long, took their courage in their hands to bear witness and testify. They wanted to present a charge sheet. Most internment camp plays spring from the same impulse. They study the way people act in the face of racial injustice and reveal the consequences of not questioning and not questioning quickly. Writers of the camps often say they are writing so similar injustices will never happen again. I am not such an optimist. We know by studying history that this sort of thing happens over and over. But at least we should try to ensure that the last word doesn't belong to the oppressors.

If the audience is reluctant to go to an issue play, it also dreads having to sit through a crash course in sociology. It is easily bored with theater that is too expository or too didactic. But internment-camp plays, like most historical drama, must inform and instruct before they can begin to move or entertain. Even today playwrights have the arduous task of explaining to their audiences the most elementary facts about the camps. The event that looms so large for Japanese Americans is generally relegated to a paragraph or two in the history books.

You have to build the foundation before you can make the leap into art. You have to construct before you can think of deconstructing. You have to have a baseline before you can crack a joke. Without historical grounding the audience will never empathize with the internees. In most works about the internment camps, for instance, the 1943 loyalty forms play a critical role. Questions #27 and #28 asked the internees if they would serve in the armed forces and if they would be willing to forswear their allegiance to the Japanese emperor. These controversial questions tore apart friendships and families. Many refused to fight for a country that put their families behind barbed wire while others were eager to prove themselves 200 percent American. Question #28, which implied an obligation to give up their Japanese citizenship, profoundly affected the first-generation Japanese immigrants who were denied United States citizenship by law. If they renounced their allegiance to the emperor they would be without a country. Those who answered no to both questions were heroes to some, traitors to others. The loyalty forms split the family right down the middle in *Behind Enemy Lines*, my first play about the internment camps. Some exposition was crucial, but it wasn't the easiest thing to do without disrupting the flow of the play.

Playwrights of internment camp plays tend to do their homework. After all, ethnic plays are often judged as much on their ideology and accuracy as on their artistic merit. When *The Woman Warrior* played at the Huntington Theatre, the *Boston Globe* reviewed it one day as a work of art, the next day as a sociological document. It chased down various Asians in the audience to see if Maxine Hong Kingston's view of the Chinese American experience tallied with their own. No wonder playwrights make sure all the issues are trotted out. Like *The Joy Luck Club*, their plays contain too many stories. Exhaustive research can produce a play that reads like a dissertation. It's easy to be too comprehensive, to give ten facts where one would do, to end up writing a play that loses its way in historical detail.

Most internment-camp plays are in the realistic vein, and the criteria for naturalistic drama are not the same as those for agitprop theater. A naturalistic play can become theatrically inert when its characters are a representative sociological sampling rather than flesh-and-blood individuals; when they seem to be standing around talking not to each other, but to the audience. In *Behind Enemy Lines*, I succeeded in reducing the members of the Toda family to generic types. The angry and tyrannical father was driven to drink, rage, despair, and suicide. The blinkered mother reverted to making Japanese crafts and tending her Japanese garden. The older son joined the segregated 442nd infantry division, and his rebellious younger brother joined the "disloyals," who did military exercises of their own and demanded to be sent back to Japan. Their studious sister used her admission to Oberlin as a ticket out of the camps. A more schematic cast of characters could not be found, defined by their positions and not by their personalities.

The Toda family may have been a catalogue of internment camp options, but at least they didn't fall into the traditional stereotypes of treacherous, sadistic men and docile, exotic women, created in large part by America's Asian conflicts. In just my lifetime America has been at war in Japan, Korea, and Indochina. No wonder Madame Butterfly is alive and well as Miss Saigon, the prototypical victim of the vanquished country, expressly placed in harm's way to be seduced and abandoned. The United States government defined the internees solely by their shared ethnicity with the enemy, and playwrights should make doubly sure that they people their internment camps with internees who are human, not curiosities or ciphers. They should initiate and terminate actions, not simply be acted upon. It is clear that the actual camps brought out vulnerability in some, toughness and cynicism in others. There were leaders and followers, and those who simply dropped out. The world of the internment camp was not an alien planet. It contained the appealing and the not-so-appealing, idiosyncratic people, as people tend to be when you know them well.

My first play about the camps, *Behind Enemy Lines*, except for its schematic design was straightforward and realistic. *Cowboy Samurai*, my second play on the subject and written sixteen years after the first, viewed the subject through the distorted imagination of a teenager whose parents had been interned before she was born. The first play was written in a burst of anger but had the emotional punch of a high school textbook. The second featured an imaginary cowboy samurai who was assaultive and darkly comic. The first was a reaction to the camps, the second, a reaction to my first reaction to the camps. Perhaps as the playwrights and their audience become more familiar with their subject, they can become less didactic and more experimental. A good example of this is Ping Chong's play, *Deshima*, which juxtaposes the internment camps and Deshima, the island where the Japanese quarantined the Dutch in the seventeenth century, as befitting members of a dangerous, exotic, and barbaric race.

There is obviously no model for the perfect internment- camp play, but there are many I would like to see on stage. One would be a sustained assault on everyone who applauded the idea and execution of the camps, including President Roosevelt, Governor Earl Warren of California, and the Communist Party. The play would be full of bitter, uncomfortable, reproachful questions by, say, a hundred-year-old survivor of the camps, someone with total recall, someone still furious, still unforgiving. It would be an orchestration of anger—

hidden anger, seething anger, anger bursting the dam and flooding over the horror of the camps. Another play would be a promenade piece with the uncomfortable audience following the actors in an area enclosed with barbed wire, standing in lines to the toilets, listening to the older actors talking to them at length in Japanese, and colliding with packs of children running from mess hall to mess hall.

Another play would be deliberately offensive, full of black humor, and played to a segregated audience—Asian Americans on one side of the aisle, and everyone else, including dates and spouses, on the other. The two sections would be labeled "Asians" and "Caucasians (including Germans and Italians)." Caucasian comics would play to one side of the house, Asian comics to the other. There would be soy sauce poured over mashed potatoes as a concession to Japanese culture, the giant hairy fingers of the white prison guard or General DeWitt reaching in and grabbing an unsuspecting child, the voice of a racist commentator blaring over the radio, and buck-toothed cartoons from the tabloids flashed on the walls. It would end with a larger-than-life, three-dimensional Sears Catalogue, the one source of achievable dreams in the camps, with a smiling white housewife inviting the internees into its pages.

Yet another play would be a nonlinear piece—as, in fact, most serious plays tend to be these days. It would mingle the living and the dead and move back and forth in time—a form particularly well-suited to the subject since for many former internees the cloud of the camps hung permanently over the present and affected their plans, or lack of plans, for the future. The set would be a modern kitchen, but dandelions would push up between the floorboards and dust would suddenly fill the air. The FBI would invade the house again and again, overturning the furniture, ransacking the drawers, and taking the father away to parts unknown. The sounds of neighbors quarreling or making love would come through the kitchen walls as if they had turned into rice-paper screens on which were also projected the shadows of their every move. Like schizophrenics distracted from everyday life by voices and music from the camps, the former internees would periodically take out their pent-up feelings on their family and friends. The past would infiltrate and finally blot out the present and the future.

Everyone has his or her prejudices, and there are two types of internment-camp stories in which I personally have no interest. The first has the guilt-ridden Caucasian center stage agonizing over the camps or championing the poor victims. In recent movies the audience identifies more with Ethan Hawke in *Snow Falling on Cedars* (1999) or with Dennis Quaid in *Come See the Paradise* (1991) than with the internees themselves. Really, one thinks, it's not about them. The second is the internment-camp play with a feel-good, life-affirming ending. In camp plays, the temptation is to bring the family back together at the end (as in my first internment play, when the father's death unites the family). But again, it's not about that. Healing and redemption always come at a price; it's not easy to put together a cloth once it's torn, a vase once it's shattered. Things can never go back to life as usual; grave injustices are never completely smoothed over; there is no closure. Something messier is required than a sentimental, well-made play.

Circling back to my friend's comment that the internment camp is "the poor man's Holocaust," I am reminded of a reviewer of *Behind Enemy Lines* who took me to task in 1980 for calling the Japanese American internment camps "concentration camps." I had not intended any comparison to the Holocaust; I used the term because it best described the rounding up and incarceration of a suspect group. These days I use "concentration camps" only in reference to the Holocaust, acknowledging the large difference between genocide and imprisonment, between an unimaginable atrocity and a grave injustice. But there is nothing more damaging than "victim Olympics," or diminishing one injustice by comparing it to another. Every injustice should be treated as absolute, and experiencing injustice should sensitize one to another's suffering. At the end of any internment-camp play the audience should be moved collectively and individually to empathy more than to sympathy. They should see a Japanese American character center stage and say, "That's me. That's my mom. I know who she is and how she feels, how the camps affected her day-to-day relationships and changed the rest of her life."

NOTES

1. Ed Siegel, "The ART of the Matter," the *Boston Sunday Globe*, January 10, 1999: M12.
2. George Tabori, *My Mother's Courage*, in *Theater* 29: 2 (1999).
3. Anat Feinberg, "George Tabori's Mourning Work in *Jubilaum*," in Claude Schumacher, ed., *Staging the Holocaust: The Shoah in Drama and Performance* (Cambridge: Cambridge University Press, 1998), 270.
4. Feinberg, 270.
5. Rachel L. Swarns, "An Outsider Determined Not to Be Someone He's Not," *The New York Times*, Sunday, March 21, 1999: 9.

CHIZU OMORI

THE LIFE AND TIMES
OF *RABBIT IN THE MOON*

THREE AND A HALF YEARS IS A LONG TIME TO A YOUNGSTER, a space in which there is a lot of growing up to do. I spent the years between the ages of twelve and fifteen in Poston, Arizona, one of ten incarceration camps created to hold Japanese Americans during World War II. After the war, these years were more or less repressed in my memory and three decades passed before I had the impulse to look back, to reappraise consciously that troubling, difficult experience. I marvel at the mind's ability to compartmentalize and stuff unpleasant memories into a box that is conveniently warehoused in some rarely visited part of the brain.

I have come to understand why it was necessary for me to forget those years, that it is a natural human reaction to disaster and trauma. In the case of us Japanese Americans, the need to repress was great. No one outside the camps could quite grasp what we had gone through, and it was a subject that made everybody uncomfortable. Moreover, most did not want to know. We hardly had the language to describe these places and experiences, so most of us maintained a distance, a silence.

Since I could not connect those years to anything I had experienced before the war or to my postwar adult life, they remained a strange, surrealistic episode that I was glad to have survived and escaped. The rebuilding—indeed, the reinventing—of our lives took precedence and fully occupied our time. In the last twenty years, however, I have spent much time prying open that box and surveying its contents, as painful as the exercise may be, and I have worked hard at making sense of the period that so greatly affected my life and that of my family and community.

One result of these labors was the making of the film *Rabbit in the Moon*, in collaboration with my youngest sister, Emiko, who also was incarcerated. Because she was a toddler at the time, she has virtually no memories of life in the camps, and so for her the making of the film was a journey of discovery. *Rabbit* chronicles the years of incarceration from a personal point of view, and we labeled it a documentary-memoir. Since we were too young to understand the implications of what was happening to us at the time, making *Rabbit* was an attempt to recover the lost years in our own lives and also to get a handle on the larger story, the story of us all. The need to know had become very great, and then it became a need to tell.

Rabbit premiered in January 1999 at the Sundance Film Festival where it won an award for best cinematography in documentary. During that year, it was screened at numerous film festivals, and in July 1999 it was given a national showing as part of the Public Broadcasting Service series, P.O.V. (Point of View). Though we had hopes that the film would have some impact, its success far exceeded our expectations. As a result of its public exposure, *Rabbit* has won prizes, has been shown at international festivals such as those in Amsterdam and Caracas, and has been selected for use in classrooms all over the country. As a result, it has taken on a life of its own, both within and outside the Japanese American community. General public response has been intense, with much commentary in the press, stacks of e-mail, and spirited comments on various Web sites.

One rarely has the opportunity to lay out one's life in an organized, structured, and public way. We exposed parts of ourselves about which we had rarely spoken. Even close friends expressed surprise and dismay. Repeatedly, the reaction was: "I never knew what you had gone through," "Why haven't we known?" or, "Why have you never talked about this?"

With Japanese Americans, responses ranged from denunciation to grateful thanks, a veritable stew of strong feedback. *Rabbit* has become much like a lightning flash illuminating this convoluted landscape of Japanese American history, both the prominent high points of the conventional story, and the dark parts in between, the fissures and cracks that have usually lain hidden in shadows. We had been nervous about community reaction, and so we were gratified that our film stimulated a reexamination of our collective past. I now view the internment as a great American tragedy compounded of governmental malfeasance, generational conflicts, and our immigrant group's rocky, difficult, sometimes lonely passage to becoming Americans. Internment forced major decisions about identity, self, family, and one's relationship to the country that had been home. It meant discarding parts of the community that couldn't be fitted into our sense of being American, which really meant discarding parts of ourselves, the parts that made us vulnerable. We were divided as a community and divided within ourselves.

We knew that there were cleavages in the community but had little idea of the strength of the feelings that so many older Nikkei harbored in their hearts. These passions were so strong that many, seizing upon one or another particular aspect of our film that had upset them, came up with readings that verged on total distortions. We had clearly touched nerves, and I am prompted to consider why this happened and why we made the film.

Making the film and dealing with the reactions to it have been quite a journey into self and community, a quest that has liberated my sister and me from the burden of the conventional myths, the simplistic public image of our compliance and "loyalty" as "quiet Americans." Perhaps it has done the same for some in the Japanese American community. During the making of *Rabbit*, we learned that prewar Japanese Americans were a vigorous, independent, lively lot. We met many who had not been quiet and docile in the camps. Although many protesters and dissidents paid a heavy price, they willingly accepted the challenges. Their actions made them heroes in our eyes, heroes whose stories had been mostly unknown.

We also understood that because of our youth we two had not experienced the worst effects of the incarceration. We were able to recover and build our lives much as all the young survivors of that terrible war, but as we delved into the historical material, we became aware of those among us who had lost everything, who were too old to rebuild. We talked to people who willingly went to or were forced to go to a defeated Japan at war's end and who were subjected to especially harrowing experiences, adding to the layers of complexity that formed the reality of the internment. We are now helping to break the silence about some of the partially hidden aspects of that experience.

I would like to believe that *Rabbit* will have an impact on internment studies, that it will deepen and broaden the general public's understanding of internment, and that it may render the experience far more interesting by revealing how complex it was. As a political activist who spent the 1980s deeply involved in the campaign for redress for Japanese Americans, I had occasion to learn a great deal about the period of internment. I looked upon redress as a means of educating the public about the camps, but the real payoff for me was learning much that I hadn't known about the history and gaining perspective and a much deeper understanding of that episode.

After the heady victory of gaining redress, it seemed a shame not to use what I had learned in some other form, given the overall public ignorance. Producing another book hardly seemed the answer. There were documentaries and feature films, but there was nothing that covered the history in the way that we wanted it presented, something closer to the actual multilayered experience. How could we break through the public's indifference to our story? How could we crack the myth of us as "quiet Americans," a myth that we ourselves partially created as the price we felt we needed to pay for our entry into American society?

The film project came about quite accidentally. In 1988, I was asked to do a presentation for a small study group that met to consider the issues of the "no-no's," those who responded in the negative to two key questions on the loyalty questionnaire administered by the government in 1943. I could find no book or article that carried the loyalty questionnaire in its entirely. It was my great good luck to be acquainted with Aiko Herzig-Yoshinaga, one of the chief researchers of the internment, both officially for the government's Commission on the Wartime Relocation and Internment of Civilians, convened in 1980 to study the internment, and unofficially as a digger and student in the vast government archives close to her home. She had also done the research for the class action lawsuit instituted by William Hohri and the National Council for Japanese American Redress. When I asked her for a copy of the questionnaire, Herzig-Yoshinaga sent two completed copies. It turned out that there had been two separate questionnaires, one from the military for males of draft age, with twenty-eight questions, called "Statement of United States Citizen of Japanese Ancestry," and another from the War Relocation Authority for all the others over the age of seventeen, with thirty-three questions, called "War Relocation Authority Application For Leave Clearance." The key questions were numbers 27 and 28, having to do with willingness to join the army and to forswear any allegiance to the emperor of Japan.

Along with the questionnaires, Herzig-Yoshinaga sent a number of documents on the formation and effects of the policy: letters, memos, papers from government files. Included among these papers was a grading system used to evaluate the answers of the inmates to the questions. Ostensibly, the questionnaires were used for a winnowing process to qualify those deemed fit to serve in the army and to return to the outer society, but the de facto result was the moving of the "disloyals" to the Tule Lake, California, internment center. An official board, the Japanese American Joint Board, comprised mainly of military officials, was given the job of sorting through the questionnaires. Interestingly, the categorization of individuals was color-coded and divided into three parts: white for those who "passed," black for the "rejects," and brown for the "doubtful" cases.

Though a no to questions 27 and 28 meant automatic disqualification for military service and "leave clearance," it was not the only disqualification. Answers to the other questions were given numerical weights that were then toted up for a quantitative appraisal of a person's loyalty. For instance, you got a –3 for having one or more immediate family members in Japan. In addition, files from all of the branches of military intelligence, the War Relocation Authority, and the Federal Bureau of Investigation were combed for "derogatory information."

The numerical system was soon rejected as too cumbersome, but it turned out that subsequent refinements also presented a bureaucratic nightmare in execution. In the next system, for example, any two of the following constituted disqualification:

1. Residence in Japan over the age of six (1–9 years).
2. Residence in Japan over the age of six for more than ten years though married to citizen wife with citizen children.
3. Seriously objectionable occupation.
4. Objectionable employment (such as official of listed firm).
5. Official of a lesser organization.
6. Contributions to various Japanese war funds where the contributions are substantial in amount or number.
7. Parent or parents in Japan.
8. Intelligence report suggesting dangerous association.
9. Father member of Heimusha Kai or Butoku Kai*.
10. [Qualifying an affirmative answer to question 27 about willingness to serve in the military with] 'Not in the Pacific area.'
11. Two trips to Japan or three trips to Japan if one be accomplished under the age of six.
12. Undisclosed foreign investments $250-$1000.[1]

Suddenly, in poring over these papers, I had a moment of awakening, something like a revelation. The arcing of events that had put us in the camps and kept us there for all those years began to fall into place. My muddled feelings began to coalesce, to sort themselves out, and my own early life came much more into focus as I sorted the information I had in my hands.

Our fate, I learned, hung on arbitrary questions that had little or nothing to do with actual loyalty to the United States, but concerned a group of mostly military men sitting around a table sifting through files for "derogatory information"

---

* Heimusha Kai: Military Men's Society; Butoku Kai: Martial Arts Society.

that was based largely on hearsay and gossip. What had they done to our community? How many lives were ruined as a result? What was meant by loyalty and disloyalty anyway? What were the implications of such procedures for our "democratic" society?

I am a younger Nisei, one of a cohort who were children and adolescents during the camp years. We are now in our sixties and seventies, and soon, most of us who actually experienced the camps will be gone. In my lifetime, I have witnessed and lived through the wild swings of changes in values, attitudes, perceptions, and status to which Japanese Americans have been subjected and have themselves created. We have gone from being labeled enemies, spies, and subversives to being touted as the "model minority," the ethnic group that has "succeeded," the standard and example by which other peoples of color in America are to be measured.

I am very much a part of the postwar generation that sought to recreate itself as eminently qualified for citizen status. For most Nisei, becoming American meant a relentless march toward respectability, particularly through achieving middle-class status. This process usually entailed getting educated, working very hard, getting a good job and a nice home and living a low-profile life.

However, not all of us defined becoming American as melding into the middle class. I myself took a different, more individualistic and political route. I had grown up as an unworldly farm kid. I was used to a racially mixed, relatively amiable environment, mingling with whites and Mexican Americans. I got along with everybody, was well liked by all my teachers, had a happy childhood. I grew up in a dual cultural environment. The striking factor in this upbringing was that we were accepted, and the relative absence of hostility enabled me to grow up without a strong sense of "us" and "them."

Because there was no English spoken in our home, my first language was Japanese, with English added after I started school at the age of five. The rural community I knew was composed of other Japanese Americans, which was somewhat like a village in Japan in that it had its own traditions and social life, networks that formed a web of connections for each farm family. We had a social hall/schoolhouse, where get-togethers were held. I went to our daily Japanese school sessions for an hour after "American" school. Many of the Issei held on to a dream of returning to Japan with enough for a comfortable retirement, though in reality this was a fantasy that helped them cope with the hardships of life in a sometimes hostile country, along with the struggle to make it through the Depression.

The law at that time in California stipulated that land leases were to be restricted to three years, so for Japanese American families it entailed uprooting and moving to a new piece of land from time to time. Many people managed to get around the law by buying property in the name of a citizen son or daughter, or by informal arrangements with a friendly white. I remember several moves to different farms in various towns in Southern California, but the network of social bonds was always present and available for help and reassurance, a source of cohesion and identity. The last farm was in Oceanside, where my father and others had organized and established a cooperative of Japanese farmers. We grew strawberries and other vegetables. Those were Depression days, so few people anywhere were prospering, but the cooperative was taking hold and beginning to do well. In spite of the restrictions, it was a hopeful time.

I was thriving in this environment. A good student, I had happy experiences in every school in all those different towns. In Oceanside, we had a stern, no-nonsense Japanese couple as our Japanese schoolteachers, who demanded Old World obedience from the motley crew of farm kids. As a counterweight, the white schools were friendly and relatively benign. The Japanese were accepted as part of the economic fabric. They were industrious farmers who participated in a network of small businesses, and they were much involved in the commerce of the town. Everyone was working hard in the rhythms of farm life, the seasonal changes, the festivals and holidays, and the get-togethers of fellow immigrants from the same *ken*, or prefectural area of Japan. It was as if the two cultures gave us a richer, more varied existence, one with the emotional security of family, community, *ken* and ties to Japan, the other with the benefits of the American freedom to work hard and achieve, even in the Depression. Some of my relatives were going to college, and at the outbreak of the war I had an uncle at Stanford University. The patriarchal, authoritarian style was the prevailing family mode, but we had a warmer home environment than most.

One feature that the immigrants brought from Japan was an inclination to organize. Thus, we had the prefectural *kenjinkai*, the cooperatives, and the social activities connected with the Japanese schools, even in rural areas. There is a picture of me at age nine or ten, with a group of girls all dressed in kimono, along with some of our mothers, taken at a celebration for the erecting of our combination school-social hall. I remember that party. We were all excited by the prospect of everything that was going to take place in the hall in the future. This building became the community center, where Japanese *chambara* (samurai) movies were shown, kendo and judo classes were conducted, and where the occasional Buddhist service was held when an itinerant priest from some place like Los Angeles showed up.

And yet, the white schools were definitely stamping us with American values, attitudes, and pop culture. As a child, I felt no undue stress in being exposed to and immersed in both streams. I could eat my *mochi* and rice and *tsukemono* along with sandwiches and hamburgers, with no sense that one type of food or one activity was inferior or superior. And though I did observe the patriarchal family style, which was the norm in our community, and also feelings of condescension and contempt for Mexican laborers, I found myself developing Western ideas of fair play and openness.

Our community generally supported Japan in its war against China, sending tokens of support and nodding sympathetically to stories of the brave Japanese soldiers fighting for the greater glory of the emperor and spreading Japanese values throughout colonial Asia.

Our father was an easygoing, amiable man who got along with everybody, and who was very active in the internal affairs of the cooperative. Our mother, a somewhat submissive woman, a Kibei, worked in the fields and ran the household. I remember that when my father bought her a washing machine she insisted that it be returned because it cost too much. I was the oldest of three children, all girls. We bathed together as a family in the *ofuro*, the daily evening hot bath with the fire stoked to keep the water at a steamy temperature, everyone soaking away the day's labors. We were taught to think that the Japanese were an innately superior people, something that we believed with great pride. It was our duty to preserve that status, to behave in such a way to keep from dishonoring the group.

If there was unease about the growing clouds of war on the horizon, I was not aware of it at the time. I didn't know where Pearl Harbor was, so I didn't quite know what it meant when the bombing took place. Going to school the next day was not so different from other days, though there was talk of the war. Some kids spoke of the "dirty Japs" but did not include any of us in that category. I think I went to school until a few days before May 12, 1942, when we were "evacuated" directly to Poston, that strange city of tarpaper barracks in the middle of the Arizona desert.

For me, it was a shock to be trapped in a place where almost everyone was Japanese or Japanese American. My parents, with their good sense, tried not to frighten us and adapted as best they could to the bizarre circumstances in which we found ourselves. But looking back on it now makes me realize what a Kafkaesque existence we lived in the three and a half years that we spent in Poston.

Everyone went through the motions of living a life as close as possible to the one before. Our penchant for organization manifested itself in an explosion of activities, but the extremity of the setting, the artificiality of the "community," the ever-present reminders of our incarcerated status, and the crudeness of the physical conditions made for a very peculiar existence. People from every walk of life, urban and rural, the well-to-do and the farm laborers, all jostled together in flimsy barracks. The communal eating and bathing and the lack of privacy strained usual politeness to the breaking point.

For me, a totally Japanese American setting was not a good fit. Many in the camps lacked my family's positive experiences, and the urbanites with their relative sophistication contrasted sharply with those from the farms. I grew restless and unhappy with life in the camp, observing behavior that seemed particularly narrow-minded and mean, much of it driven by rumor and gossip. One could know almost every intimate detail of one's neighbors' lives, and the enforced idleness of the old folks led to much squabbling and pettiness. Everyone was critically scrutinized by the informal arbiters of manners and morals. I attributed this situation to the Japanese mentality, which stressed conformity and the use of ridicule and shame as means of social control. I began to think that I really didn't want to be part of these people. Still, for many, there were happy times with some genuine camaraderie, marriages and the formation of lifelong friendships.

The splits along generational lines were heightened at this critical juncture in our lives. We younger ones poked fun at others we considered too "Jappy," with poor or nonexistent English and old-fashioned ways, bound up in rituals and customs that clashed sharply with American values and popular culture. Many elders were becoming powerless, slowly losing control, and so they naggingly expressed disapproval of much of what the young people did.

In our family, a rift was developing. When the loyalty questionnaire was administered in Poston, question 28 had been changed for Issei. Mention of the emperor of Japan was dropped, and you were asked if you would be willing to abide by the laws of the United States. My parents could answer yes in good faith to that question. Nevertheless, when the loyalty sorting took place, our parents decided that a future in Japan was preferable to a bleak life as outsiders in America. For reasons unknown to me, our family never went to Tule Lake. The shock of the realization that I might be forced to go to Japan reinforced my determination to become a complete American. It was only after the end of the war that our father and mother realized that it was useless to return to a defeated and desolated Japan. So, in October 1945, we moved back to California.

Even though I lived my early adolescence in camp, my memories are fragmentary, disjointed, fitful, more a series of snapshots than experiences. I have concluded that the whole camp episode was so disturbing and so painful, so unlike my life before and after, that suppression was a survival mechanism. I needed to erase some of the past in order to get on with my life, and I needed to distance myself from Japanese Americans. Today, in spite of a strong desire to uncover those memories, I still have difficulty overcoming the suppression.

After the war, our parents worked for others for a while and then resumed farming. I decided to go to high school in Los Angeles and worked as an au pair. I returned to the family farm for a couple of years after my mother died and then went to UCLA, later transferring to the University of California at Berkeley, where I graduated in 1953 with a degree in English. Left-wing politics occupied much of my time while in college, but getting married to a white, fellow political activist led to a somewhat more settled family life. My "assimilation" took the form of moving within almost totally white, politically liberal social circles, as did my sister, Emiko, who also went to college. She took up a career as a cinematographer. Internment remained a buried matter. Because we had opted out of the ethnic community, we did not encounter the stories, the instances of the muted conflicts, the ostracism of the Tule Lake population, the mental illness, the suicides.

For us and the other Nisei, the scramble to reestablish lives and to become acceptable absorbed most of our time and energy. The ironic fact was that we were accepted, that the "yellow peril" had somehow lost its menace, and that few objected to our becoming their neighbors, their fellow workers, even their spouses. We had neither the inclination nor the resources to approach and examine the internment. Recent literature on the Jewish holocaust suggests that it was downplayed by Jewish organizations after World War II for a number of political and psychological reasons. We were no different. We were aware of the oppression of blacks and Native Americans in our country, which seemed so much worse than what we had endured, and the World War II sufferings of masses of humanity made us grateful to have survived. Because we were for the most part so ignorant of many of the details of our incarceration, I could not justify a prolonged, serious consideration of our case. Yet, like a hidden infection whose presence one is only dimly aware of, there were flare-ups.

For me the feelings came in odd and unexpected ways, the sting of tears, the lump in the throat, and the knot in the stomach when certain questions came up. These small, stabbing pains could not be perpetually denied. Emiko and I were both active in anti–Vietnam War protests and in the civil rights and feminist movements. In the course of dealing with these issues that came to permeate our lives, the internment began to loom larger in our consciousness. Some books were published, like Michi Weglyn's *Years of Infamy* (1976). A televised version of the book, *Farewell to Manzanar,* by my friends Jeanne and Jim Houston, was broadcast in 1978. The internment was resurfacing.

Even though the internment hardly registered in American history books, I began to realize that what had happened to us was not so insignificant. That the internment was a serious violation of the laws and standards of the land was obvious, but minority groups, especially peoples of color, have all been treated badly by whites throughout our history. Yet there was something qualitatively different about our case. The racist bent of the United States government had been made official policy, and a dangerous precedent had been established. Through the loyalty policy, specific lines were drawn as to who was to be considered "American." Our ethnicity was made to be much more suspect than that of anyone else. There had been betrayal, first by the government that had incarcerated us, and then within the group: the protesters felt betrayed by the superpatriots who damned them, and the patriots felt that the dissenters were grievously hurting the image that they wanted to project of us as loyal, patriotic Americans.

We originally titled our film "A Question of Loyalty," and we placed special emphasis on the story of Tule Lake. We spent eight years struggling to put it together. Even though we were unable to convince most funders and others of the film's importance, and despite periods of great doubt about our enterprise, we felt compelled to continue the work. What motivated us to soldier on, in spite of all the hassles and difficulties in raising funds and finding individuals who would talk candidly?

First, we had a passion to tell the story, and then we felt a deep anger coming out of what we were learning and gathering, an anger so great that we often had to take time out before we could continue. The need to know became a driving force. Working together drew the two of us closer in ways that hadn't existed before and also connected both of us to the Japanese American community. We were tapping into common feelings that had lain hidden all these many years.

Underneath our group's apparent assimilation into the American middle-class mainstream, there was a well of pain and hurt. I was struck by the tears that were shed at a 1998 conference of Nikkei who were grant-winners for projects intended to educate the public about our incarceration. These projects were funded by the Civil Liberties Public Education Fund, an agency established by the government as part of the redress legislation of 1988. On the last day of the conference, when we were encouraged to offer some final words, there was an enormous outpouring of emotion and grief by so many that it swept up the entire assembly. What a revelation it was to see that the whole community, not just ourselves, was still carrying a heavy burden from those traumatic years!

Emiko and I knew that we had a great tale to tell about a people forced to make complex, difficult, life-changing decisions, full of dramatic twists and turns, with heroes and villains. It involved the government at the highest levels and also basic questions about legality and constitutional safeguards. It was a story of divided allegiances, frayed families, a story full of ironies and contradictions. What does someone do when faced with a no-win situation? How much were people's responses determined by personal circumstances of family and age?

To get to the truth was daunting and difficult—there was no one truth. And just whom did we want to address? How could we accommodate the millions who knew either nothing or very little about our history, along with those who had great familiarity with the subject? How much could we cram into one film? As we whittled and pared, sorted and discarded, the most important factor became the need to engage the audience on an emotional level.

In the editing process we saw that we needed to create a human story by making it personal. So our family became the small picture within the context of the big picture. We did not feel that we were necessarily typical or that our story had special significance, but there was enough in our perspective to serve as an entry point into the bigger issues. We wanted to show ourselves as ordinary Americans faced with an extraordinary set of problems and situations.

Sundance gave our film five screenings, each one a sellout. After every screening there was a question-and-answer period. We had invited some members of the Utah Japanese American Citizens League (JACL), including a former national president of the organization. We had some trepidation about their reactions to *Rabbit* since we had expressed strong criticism of the JACL's role during the wartime period.

The JACL is the most nationally visible of all Japanese American organizations. Its World War II record was controversial, and its rise to prominence was largely aided by its close associations with the WRA and the Defense Department during the war. It was greatly responsible for the vilification of the draft resisters, the Tule Lake residents, and all the "troublemakers" and protesters. Allied with the veterans of the 442nd, the JACL took a superpatriotic stance that set the tone for postwar Japanese America. We would be seen as attacking some of the pillars of our society.

The feedback that we received from the Utah JACL members and others at Sundance was very positive. In fact, Emiko and I were invited by the Utah JACL to attend one of its district meetings later that year to show *Rabbit* and to join a discussion with leaders from the Western chapters who were also invited. A spirit of dialogue was being established.

In our subsequent appearances at film festivals, panel discussions, meetings, and assorted screenings all over the United States, the questions and discussions have been extraordinary in their variety, quality, and depth of understanding. *Rabbit* exposed many people to information that they hadn't previously known. We became a part of the Television Race Initiative (TRI), an adjunct to public television given to dialogue and interaction among racial groups. TRI prepared a study guide to accompany screenings, which could be used as a teaching tool for facilitators. The National Asian American Telecommunications Association, which had provided some funding, energetically promoted *Rabbit*, even arranging for a showing at the Smithsonian Institution in Washington, D.C., which members of Congress attended.

Rabbit has elicited a firestorm of commentary, both on the Web site that PBS created for us and in letters and in articles in the *Pacific Citizen*, which is the JACL's official newspaper. A particularly sensitive issue has been the draft resisters. It is apparent that loyalty is still a highly inflammatory subject within our community.

Here is a sampling of responses to our film:

[From a person who has close connections to the JACL:] The program while well done was a gross distortion of facts. . . . Mike M. Masaoka* . . . put in perspective the climate, hysteria and actions of that time. These producers of this so-called 'documentary' would not dare produce such fiction when Iron-Mike was still alive. They only jump-on-the-bandwagon after his death. . . . It stinks! . . . This is the worst 'documentary' from PBS that [I] have seen, not just on this subject but from PBS as a whole.

I am a "No-No" boy, a Kibei and a renunciant. . . . [In 1988] I wrote to the *Hokubei Mainichi* [a vernacular newspaper] in San Francisco appealing to the Nikkei community to heal the internal schism created by the loyalty issue. Unfortunately, the schism has not been healed to this day. . . . I continue to see a "rabbit in the moon"** every month when the moon is full, recalling how I used to gaze at the moon behind barbed wire fences in Topaz and later in Tule Lake wondering why there is war and prejudice . . . I lost two childhood friends in battle in that war: one a kamikaze pilot and another a member of 442.

My family was sent to Tule Lake. It was an experience they preferred to forget. . . . Your film helped me to understand more fully their pain. Thank you.

The tragedy is that for many, the lines that were drawn long ago have become so hardened that dialogue seems almost impossible. Until recently, the

---

*   Mike M. Masaoka: wartime leader of the JACL and its postwar Washington lobbyist.—Ed.

**   Refers to a Japanese folk tale of an image of a rabbit making *mochi*—sweet rice cakes—on the moon. Used in our film as a metaphor for Japanese culture.

JACL considered the "no-no's" and the "disloyals" pariahs who tarnished our patriotic image. One manifestation of the great divide was the quarrel over the inscriptions on the monument to Japanese American Patriotism in Washington, D.C. In the planning phase of the monument, the battle lines were drawn over the inclusion of a quotation from the JACL's Japanese American Creed, written in 1940 by Mike Masaoka: "I am proud that I am an American of Japanese ancestry. I believe in this nation's institutions, ideals, and traditions; I glory in her heritage; I boast of her history; I trust in her future."

The quotation, from a person whose behavior has provoked continuing controversy in the community, raised strong protest. Not one word about or from the dissenters and resisters was chosen to appear on the monument—not even from the famous Gordon Hirabayashi, Fred Korematsu, or Minoru Yasui, all challengers whose cases reached the Supreme Court during the war. It is terribly sad that believers in the great American tradition of opposing injustice and tyranny have no place on this memorial.

Once again, we're faced with defining patriotism and loyalty. In *Rabbit*, Emiko and I have tried to address this question, examining the polarization within our group and relating it to American history. It was not our intention to emphasize our victimization, but to show that there were greater consequences resulting from our experience for our community and the body politic.

For the American people, the wartime incarceration of Japanese Americans is a cautionary tale of immense proportions about the capacity of the American government to abuse its own power, particularly during wartime. It was not the first and probably will not be the last such story. For all the seeming assimilation of Asian Americans, the stereotypes of Asians as somehow "other" have not disappeared, and they spring forth whenever relations with Asian countries become strained or threatening. The brutal truth, however, is that no group, no one, can feel totally safe as long as the "loaded weapon"* of wartime incarceration threatens our rights and freedom.

NOTE

1. National Archives, War Department, Record Group 210–17–3.

---

* The phrase is United States Supreme Court Justice Robert Jackson's, from his dissenting opinion in the *Korematsu* case of 1944. The court's decision, which in effect gave legal sanction to the internment, would produce, Jackson said, "a loaded weapon ready for the hand of any authority that can bring forward a plausible claim of an urgent need."--Ed.

VALERIE NAO YOSHIMURA

THE LEGACY OF THE
BATTLE OF BRUYÈRES:
REFLECTIONS OF
A SANSEI FRANCOPHILE

I AM HALF-IRISH, HALF-JAPANESE, ENTIRELY AMERICAN, and fluent in French. As a *hapa* Sansei—a mixed blood, third-generation Japanese American—I have Japanese eyes and an Irish smile, Japanese hair and Irish freckles, Japanese honor and Irish assertiveness. I grew up with rice and potatoes, with teriyaki and corned beef, oblivious to any implications of my ethnic heritage beyond the right to wear green on St. Patrick's Day and the gustatory pleasures of sushi on New Year's Day. I felt white, and passed as white, in the northern Chicago neighborhood I called home. When I was ten, however, I learned that being Japanese in the United States meant something more than eating rice every day. I learned that my father, when he was ten, had lived with his parents and three of his seven siblings in a concentration camp in Arkansas, forced to leave Hawaii because of his father's prominence in the Japanese community.[1] Indeed, over 110,000 other Japanese and Americans of Japanese ancestry were similarly uprooted from their homes, their community, and their livelihoods. Suddenly I realized: it could have been me.

At thirteen, I began reading in earnest about internment; at fourteen, I started learning French. While I pursued both studies with vigor, my passions for Japanese American history and French culture seemed as disconnected from each other as my ancestral homelands of Ireland and Japan. Only after I had long given up hope did I discover that France and Japanese America share

Street sign in Bruyères. Photo by Valerie Yoshimura, 1994.

A Bruyérois spontaneously offers a token of his gratitude to a Nisei veteran in Bruyères.
Photo by Valerie Yoshimura, 1994

an important history that I was particularly well-suited to explore. It was 1994, and reunion festivities were planned for the fiftieth anniversary of the World War II liberation of the French towns of Bruyères and Biffontaine by the all-Japanese American 442nd Regimental Combat Team (RCT)/100th Battalion—the most decorated unit, for its size and length of service, in the history of the United States Army.[2] I marveled at this confluence of my native and adopted cultures and wondered why there would be a special friendship with the small French town of Bruyères among the many battlefields on which the 442nd RCT fought. Who would attend the reunion in France, and why? With my particular combination of interests and skills, what role might I play in these events? As veterans enter the twilight of their lives, will their legacy endure the vicissitudes of time and memory? Indeed, what is the legacy that they bequeath?

Intrigued, I immediately made plans to go to France with the Nisei veterans, and was warmly invited to join the veterans of Company E, 442nd RCT for a mini-reunion in Bruyères in July 1994. Three months later, I also attended the much larger official reunion on the actual anniversary in October, when I was hosted by a local family and was thus made privy to the French perspective.[3] I resolved to conduct oral interviews, in both French and English, with multiple generations of reunion attendees. Both participant and observer, both Japanese American and fluent in French, I helped bridge the two communities, interpreting, inquiring, and listening as we traversed fields of battle and fields of memory. Conducted during the course of and between official events, my oral interviews ranged from the taciturn to the loquacious. I asked all participants why they were attending the reunion, and why a friendship exists and persists with Bruyères. Of Nisei veterans, I carefully inquired about their thoughts upon returning to the battlefield and their impressions of the various memorials in their honor. In some cases, during a 1998 reunion of Japanese American veterans held in Hawaii, I was able to reinterview Nisei veterans and their families about the significance of the reunions in Bruyères. Of the French, I asked why and how they remember the 442nd, and probed for the extent of their awareness of internment. Of those who experienced the 1944 liberation, I sought their memories and queried whether they ever mistook their liberators for Japanese soldiers. I questioned French and American children about their knowledge of the liberation of Bruyères, and about the accomplishments of the 442nd. I spoke with wives and adult children, with senior American officials and Frenchmen who long ago had guided the Nisei soldiers through the thick forest. Of all, I wanted to know whether, and in what respects, the legacies of the 442nd and the Battle of Bruyères may endure.

The Battle of Bruyères ultimately symbolizes a double liberation: while the Nisei soldiers fought with uncommon valor in the Vosges mountains to liberate the French from four horrible years in the clutch of Nazi occupation, they were also fighting a metaphoric battle to free their families from the injustice of life behind barbed wire thousands of miles away in their homeland. Although they succeeded admirably on both battlefields, the Nisei veterans, like all soldiers, brought back more than physical wounds. And so, a half-century later, the profoundly emotional commemorative reunions offer yet another liberation: for veterans burdened with years of silent pain and guilt, for family members who dared not ask too many questions, and for young children who had no idea that their grandfathers were heroes. In turn, the reunions allow the French to express to their liberators their enduring respect, admiration, and gratitude, and to affirm their postwar conviction that they helped liberate Japanese Americans from the sting of prejudice and the burden of internment.

The Battle of Bruyères has an international legacy not because its principals were from different nations, but because it so poignantly restored national identity for Japanese Americans as well as for the French. National identity is most acute when one's community is threatened, and in this unusual case—in stark contrast to the power differential that normally separates soldier and civilian—the threat was shared by liberator and liberated. This uncommon commonality motivates the dedication of official monuments and underlies public discourse, but the monuments and discourse make up only one side of the memorial coin. The reunions commemorating the double liberation of Bruyères highlight the dynamic interdependence of the formal and the personal, of the physical and the discursive, of the historic and the quotidian through which meaning, memory, and identity are forged. Indeed, as the corpus of interviews suggests, the legacy of the Battle of Bruyères finds its critical locus of transmission less in durable stone monuments and lofty language than in the very nexus of community and history: the family.

SECURING AND REMEMBERING THE LIBERATION OF BRUYÈRES: 1944–1994

Surrounded by hills of deep forest, the French town of Bruyères-en-Vosges has long been a critical site in the oft-disputed northeastern region of Lorraine.[4] For the second time in seventy years, German forces on June 21, 1940, occupied Bruyères,[5] an essential crossroads between Germany and the vanquished

France, with strategic roads and supply railway. After four years of German occupation, three and a half weeks of life in basement shelters, and a fierce final assault in pouring rain, the citizens of Bruyères, the Bruyérois, witnessed their liberation by American forces on October 18, 1944. Their liberators, the young men of the American 442nd Regimental Combat Team/100th Battalion, bore American uniforms but Japanese faces. The initial surprise of the Bruyérois at the visible incongruity quickly melted into gratitude, not only for their long-desired liberation but for the kindness bestowed upon them by the Nisei soldiers who treated them with dignity and shared food with them, even giving chocolate to the children. As one Frenchman recalls, "They were very kind towards the people." In the days following the liberation of Bruyères, the French marveled that the Nisei soldiers had come from halfway around the world to restore their freedom; it took many moons, however, before the Bruyérois came to understand the onus of internment that shadowed their heroes, most of whom had volunteered from Hawaii to prove with their blood the loyalty of Japanese Americans to the United States. While their fellow Americans of Japanese ancestry remained incarcerated in desolate concentration camps, the young men of the 442nd RCT/100th Battalion established an outstanding record in Europe as they fought northward in Italy before liberating Bruyères and rescuing the famous Texas "Lost Battalion" in the hills of nearby Biffontaine.[6] The French battles were the most difficult the regiment had yet faced, and it suffered overwhelming casualties.[7]

For over fifty years, the liberation of Bruyères has been remembered in a variety of ways by French and Japanese American alike. In the postwar years, Japanese Americans forwarded care packages to Bruyères,[8] Nisei G.I.'s returned to the town individually, and friendship between the Nisei veterans and the French was nurtured through regular rendezvous at Mama Rosa's café. In 1947, the Japanese American Citizens League (JACL) presented to the French a bilingual plaque affirming that the 442nd RCT proved through the Battle of Bruyères that national loyalty is independent of racial origin.[9] Reluctant to consign the plaque to the walls of the town hall and desirous of a more distinctive expression of their respect for the supreme sacrifice by which their freedom was secured, the Bruyérois enshrined the JACL plaque in a granite monument dedicated on October 30, 1947 in the battle-scarred Helledraye forest above Bruyères. Flowers frequently grace the monument,[10] and every October the Bruyérois honor their liberators with a ceremony at their *monument américain*, which they insist is the first in the world to honor the men of the 442nd.[11] In 1961, a street in Bruyères was named for the regiment,[12] and a sister-city relationship was established between Bruyères (population 3,834) and Honolulu, Hawaii (population 836,231),[13] a relationship that culminated in a 1977 visit by the French to the paradise halfway around the world, which many of their liberators call home. A second granite monument rests deep in the forest of Biffontaine on the site where the 442nd rescued the Texas "Lost Battalion"; it has a pendant cut from the same stone that marks the site of the regiment's battle in Cassino, Italy.[14] Formally dedicated in 1984 to the Thirty-sixth Division, United States Army (which encompassed both the 442nd RCT and the 141st Regiment), the monument is informally a tribute to the 1977 voyage by the French to Hawaii. Mayor of Biffontaine Georges Henri wanted to repay the veterans for their warm hospitality, a gesture of thanks implicit in the monument's form, an irregular granite slab that rises above fragments of cool blue glass, subtly evoking the islands of Hawaii thousands of miles away in the deep blue Pacific.

In a turn away from the genre of the stone monument, a participatory memorial was dedicated in July 1989. As it retraces the path blazed by the Nisei soldiers, the "Peace and Freedom Trail" marks eighty-nine different points of interest in the history of the RCT and of Bruyères. In following the symbol of the regiment (a burning torch) embedded in the sidewalks of Bruyères, individuals pass two other memorials also dedicated in 1989: a street renamed in honor of the United States Army's Thirty-sixth Division and a "Peace and Freedom Fountain" in the heart of Bruyères. In 1994, on the occasion of the fiftieth anniversary of the liberation of Bruyères, Japanese American artist and 442nd veteran Shinkichi Tajiri presented to the French a cast-iron sculptural knot that symbolically entwines the two communities. Offered in appreciation of the French efforts to help secure Japanese American redress (the French had sent nearly 1,500 supportive letters to the United States Congress), the "Friendship Knot" that stands near the American monument in Bruyères and that has a pendant in Los Angeles is the most recent contribution to a long series of tributes from both sides of the Atlantic.

The many official monuments that commemorate the liberation of Bruyères and the rescue of the Lost Battalion by the men of the 442nd are only the most tangible sites of memorialization; far more dynamic and powerful are the interpersonal gatherings during which individuals engage with the memorials and with each other to affirm the 442nd's legacy. Since the thirtieth anniversary of the liberation in 1974, the French have hosted poignant decennial reunions during which Nisei veterans and their families revisit the battlefields and pay tribute to the fallen. The reunions formally revolve around visits to three stone monuments: an obelisk honoring the Bruyérois lost in World War I, the 1947 American monument in the Helledraye forest above Bruyères, and the 1984 monument in the forest of Biffontaine. Military bands play national anthems, flowers are laid, and incense is burned as eloquent speeches by dignitaries and veterans affirm the double liberation of Bruyères and express hopes that the sacrifices of war shall not have been in vain.

Despite admonitions that future generations must remember, the rhetoric of remembrance conceals risks. Most children whom I interviewed—both French and American—knew little about the role of the 442nd in the liberation of Bruyères. A Sansei woman spoke of her commitment to educate her community in Kauai about the Nisei soldiers but conceded that it was like "pulling teeth" to get people to attend the film screenings she organized. In Honolulu, there is scant mention of Bruyères as a sister-city, and no French attended the 1998 veterans' reunion in Hawaii. Many veterans know of the street named after the regiment but not of the street named for the Thirty-sixth Division. Moreover, as I was privy to the French perspective, I realized that the reunions were fraught with local politics and not nearly as consensual as they appear—even the gift of the "Friendship Knot" was in jeopardy.[15] Indeed, beyond the consensus that "we must never forget," the interests and motivations of the reunion participants are clearly diverse, a diversity that threatens to undermine the legacy of liberation and friendship which joins these two communities.

What, then, binds these two communities seemingly destined never to interact? In a celebrated 1882 address, "What Is a Nation?," French philosopher Ernest Renan proposed that national identity is constituted less through valiant victory than through shared suffering: "Shared suffering unites more than joy. In matters of national memory, mourning is worth more than triumph, for it imposes obligations and demands effort in the name of the common cause."[16] When asked why the friendship exists, veterans from both sides of the Atlantic repeatedly cite the particular ferocity of the Battle of Bruyères, during which members of the French Resistance and Nisei soldiers suffered and spilled blood together. The joy of liberation is fleeting and secondary to the miseries of Nazi occupation and battle. More broadly, the two communities each endured the tyranny of racial oppression, becoming inextricably linked as their respective liberations were secured by the very same actions and men. Their shared suffering—whether in cellars, foxholes, or internment barracks—helps explain the genesis of an extraordinary international friendship forged through the fire of war, yet offers little insight into its perpetuation through more than fifty years. Personal interviews and official reunion discourse, however, suggest that the friendship is sustained publicly as well as personally through cyclical demands of obligation and reciprocity.

THE *RAISON D'ÊTRE* OF THE REUNIONS:
A CYCLE OF REPAYMENT

As the anthropological research of Marcel Mauss suggests, gifts implicitly entail obligations of repayment, and reciprocal exchange binds communities together: "to refuse to give, to fail to invite, just as to refuse to accept is . . . to reject the bond of alliance and commonality."[17] Tacit obligations of reciprocity infused with gratitude and pride motivate the French to honor their liberators. The French speak overwhelmingly of their desire to repay *les Hawaïens* for the gift of liberty bestowed upon them in 1944. As one eloquently stated, "Thanks to them [the men of the 442nd], France is not German."[18] One French veteran insists, "the American has done much for us. We will honor him always . . . we are *proud* to know the Americans,"[19] while Mayor Alain Thirion of Bruyères proclaims, "the city of Bruyères is obligated to the 442nd Regimental Combat Team for her liberty returned in 1944; the people of Bruyères know it very well and do not forget."[20] Others evoke the atrocities during four years of German occupation and the horrible weeks in the shelter during the final assault in order to describe by contrast the profound gratitude the Bruyérois feel toward their liberators: "My parents stayed in the cellar for more than a month. And then there were the SS . . . they burned a small village nearby. . . . [F]or us it was a deliverance after five years of war and truly terrible things"; "it was [our] deliverance, joy was profoundly felt in Bruyères."[21] The gratitude of those Bruyérois who participate only passively in the reunion activities is often no less salient. Four years after the reunion, a Nisei woman vividly recalls looking up at residential balconies while marching in a fiftieth anniversary parade through the streets of Bruyères: "We could see these elderly people standing by their homes waving—they must have been young people, young parents. . . . To think that a small French town like that was so appreciative, it was so touching to me."[22]

Official stone monuments and casual conversation alike reflect a profound pride in the very special nature of the Bruyérois' liberators and in the double liberation that Bruyères and Biffontaine represent. When describing the men of the 442nd, for example, the French tend to avoid the term *Américain* (reserving it for general statements like "we knew the Americans were coming"), preferring instead *les petits bonhommes* (the good little men) or, most frequently, *les Hawaïens*. Sometimes, one hears *les Américains japonais* or, rarer still, *les Américains d'origine japonaise*, yet despite increasing sensitivity of the French to the fact that not all of their liberators were from Hawaii, the term *les Hawaïens* persists, prompting some Japanese Americans (including a former president of the

Japanese American Citizens League) to be privately irritated that the French implicitly exclude through their nomenclature the G.I.'s from the mainland.[23]

Although the geographic distance between France and Hawaii was and is a source of admiration for the French, the implications of the term *les Hawaïens* transcend geographic origin. Neither then nor now could one appropriately say *les Japonais*, for the distinction between Japanese and Japanese American is precisely what the men of the 442nd were fighting for. While some Japanese American interviewees express frustration with these varied terms ("why can't we just be called 'American'?" laments one), the term *Américain*, conjuring images of tall, fair men, does not adequately express the specialness of their liberators within the collective memory of the Bruyérois. A more particular term is needed. For some, the French expression *les Hawaïens* may subtly denote "Americans victimized by other Americans," but the frequency with which *les Hawaïens* is used suggests that it functions more as a term of endearment than of exclusion. For the French, the mainland domicile of some of their liberators is a technicality superseded by their conviction that their liberators were truly special, come almost mythically from the ends of the earth to liberate them. Their hyperbolic fantasy was further nurtured in 1961, when the Bruyérois experienced a Hawaiian luau (hosted by visiting veterans in celebration of the sister-city relationship), and again in 1977, when a group of thirty Bruyérois journeyed to Hawaii for a three-week *Visite au Paradis* about which the French still reminisce. Indeed, by clinging to the specialness of their "Hawaiian" liberators (visitors can even purchase postcards juxtaposing images of Bruyères and Honolulu), the French of Bruyères and Biffontaine reveal the extent to which their identity is invested in the metaphoric conflation of liberation and paradise.

Although the French affectionately speak of *les Hawaïens*, they understand that the Nisei are, above all, Americans. At first unaware of the wartime internment of Japanese Americans, in the postwar years the French came to appreciate the investment of the Nisei soldiers in proving their loyalty as Americans by securing the liberty of the French. Knowledge of this double liberation redoubles the pride of the French of Bruyères and Biffontaine to the extent that it has become a trope: the French repeatedly assert that the fiftieth star of the American flag was earned on their soil. This discursive memorial is significant, for the psychological belief that their native France helped *les Hawaïens* secure the epitome of membership in the United States—statehood—enables the French symbolically to repay the gift of liberation bestowed upon them in 1944. Philippe Séguin, former president of the French National Assembly, who hails from the Vosges region, affirmed in an interview that he strongly believes that the claim is legitimate,[24] while E Company veteran and United States Senator Daniel Inouye (D-Hawaii) confirmed, "I think there's much truth to that. What if we had not volunteered? What if the 100th and 442nd had not been formed? Would we have statehood? . . . Would I be Senator? Would the press and the media continue to call us Japs?"[25]

Despite the unity of purpose articulated at the reunion ceremonies, personal interviews betray differences: where the French focus on admiration and repayment, the Japanese Americans emphasize healing and family. The Nisei certainly appreciate the gratitude and gracious hospitality of the French, but their presence at the reunions—as in reunions of other war veterans in general—represents a personal pilgrimage in the face of their own mortality. The Nisei I interviewed speak only tangentially of having secured the liberty of the French and focus instead on the loss of their brothers-in-arms, on their own healing, and on the critical importance of the RCT for the metaphoric liberation of Japanese Americans: "We proved our loyalty to the USA and so doing have made life better for all of us. Our parents were granted citizenship, discrimination is less obvious, opportunities for our younger generations have been greater."[26]

Many journeyed to show their families where they had fought in Europe; some came because they wanted finally to see the town of Bruyères: "We didn't come to window shop [in 1944]."[27] Friendship and camaraderie also motivate attendance: "My goal was just to be with the fellas . . . [and] meet the French people whom I never met." Most, however, testify to an inexplicable need to return to the battlefield of the toughest battle they fought: "I've always had this feeling I need to go back because I feel like I owe it to myself . . . it's hard to explain . . . I don't know what it is that makes old soldiers want to come back."[28] During their pilgrimage back to the battlefield, the Nisei veterans burn incense in memory of their buddies and salute as they stand among overgrown yet still visible foxholes that litter the floor of the silent forest in Biffontaine. The simplicity of the ceremony eloquently evokes their profound pain. A battle-scarred helmet, rusted and punctured by holes of shrapnel, bears poignant witness to the fierce battles that raged in the same hills years ago: it had been found just days earlier. Some descend into the foxholes for photographs; one declines to smile. "Someone could have died here." Rarely articulated but visible on their somber faces, the veterans describe "a sense of guilt, you know, because you're alive and they died, and . . . why them? I don't know."[29]

Clearly, the French and the Nisei share the impulse of repayment. But while the Bruyérois feel indebted to their liberators, the latter feel beholden to those who fell in battle:

My first time to Bruyères was not voluntary, but this time I felt I had to come and say my final good-byes to my many friends, comrades who made the supreme sacrifice, 667 brave men who fell in battle. I wanted to thank all of them and pay homage. Once a year Memorial Day service was never enough. I came back to say I was proud to have served with you, and shared the miseries of combat with you, and at the same time treasured our friendship and our common dedication to our mission. Your loyalty and bravery will never be forgotten. I hope the future generations of Japanese Americans will always remember.[30]

Pride, guilt, and sorrow intermingle in the hearts of the profoundly contemplative Nisei veterans gathered in the forest, their pain all the more palpable for its silence. A Frenchman who has perennially welcomed and honored the veterans articulates his impression of their long shouldered burden:

The most moving, for me, is when they gather before the monument. Because there, I imagine that they think of all those who died for our liberty, of all their comrades, their brothers-in-arms, who like them were eighteen, nineteen, twenty. They saw them killed, wounded, right alongside them, saying to themselves, "we'll never see them again, perhaps tomorrow it will be me." There is such sincerity in this moment of remembrance that it's extraordinary and moving at the same time.[31]

Still, not all choose to return to the battlefield. One E Company veteran whom I interviewed in Hawaii declared, "I have made it a point not to go back to the battlefields. I've been asked to, and I have refused to do it . . . because I can look at that part and say, 'Oh that's where we lost so-and-so, that's where we lost another person.'"[32] Those who do return to Bruyères are profoundly touched that the French have remembered them; of all the memorials, the street name and the 1947 monument above Bruyères are most often mentioned. The effusive gratitude of the French helps them realize that their efforts and their losses were not in vain, and they are moved by the utter warmth with which they are received: "Bruyères, after fifty years, was wonderful. The people haven't forgotten. A street named after the Regiment and a monument too."[33]

A living memorial, the reunions offer a critical opportunity for memories to be shared and therefore validated. For the Nisei veterans and their families to visit Bruyères, to see the monuments, to walk the street named after the regiment, to receive as a gift chocolate like that which they once shared, is to realize that they made a difference that changed not only their own lives, but those of the Bruyérois. An insertion into daily life, the street name symbolizes to the veterans the promise of the future, while the cool solidity of the granite monuments offers each veteran a secret hiding place, a metaphoric confidant in whom he may release the burden of painful memories. The multiple levels of validation that the pilgrimage reunions foster help to break a long silence and heal an indescribable pain. Even my interviews, I was touched to learn, made a difference: "I seem to be more at ease with myself having made the trip," wrote one veteran, "thank you for asking."

FAMILY MEMBERS AND FUTURE GENERATIONS

Rare were the Nisei veterans who journeyed to France alone. Most were accompanied by spouses, children and/or grandchildren who were affected by the reunion in different ways; others were present only in spirit, their widows making the journey in their honor and stead. For spouses, tacit understanding may replace silent ambiguities of fifty years past. A wife of a veteran, describing the reunions as bittersweet, considered the impact of the visit on her husband:

> It's the first time he has been back here after fifty years, and I'm sure he's thinking of the ones that were left behind, and the fact that he came out without a scratch. . . . It's miraculous when you look at this terrain to see how anyone could survive all that hard, intense fighting. . . . He just wanted to go back and see what it looked like; I think it's . . . closure for him—I'm sure it is.[34]

Another wife described the regrowth of the battle-scarred forest as a reminder that life goes on:

> What really touched me was going to Bruyères and my husband said, "you see those trees?" During the war the shells broke the treetops, so now you saw so many trees with double branches or trunks, and how they have grown. And they [the veterans] couldn't get over how the forest was thick again. And I thought, "Gee, just think: fifty years ago they were devastated and yet they've grown back"—you figure, life goes on.[35]

For adult children of veterans, the reality of old war stories becomes manifest:

> [My father] told war stories . . . for years and years and everybody . . . tuned him out. . . . I've gone back and read . . . about . . . these battles I paid no attention to . . . and definitely got a much better appreciation of what it meant to be there and how tough it was and how scary it's got to be to sit in a foxhole in the rain and freezing and shivering and knowing if you stand up you're going to get shot . . .[36]

For others, the serious underside of light-hearted war stories surfaces. One Nisei woman described the impact of the visit on her daughter:

> She said, "Dad only talks about the crazy things they did, like stealing cabbages out of the field . . ." The people of France . . . honor [the veterans] . . . so much that it gave her a different idea: those little rascals . . . were scared.[37]

While sons and daughters of veterans long regretted the awkward silence that followed questions about the war, the emotion of the reunions enables them at last to appreciate their fathers' reluctance to speak: "I now understand what they did and how I can honor and be proud of my father."[38] By validating the veterans' long-repressed feelings, the reunions may release the entire family: one woman, for example, at long last learned how her father had lost his arm.

If spouses and adult children of veterans find understanding, French and American youth are more often mystified by the reunion experience. When I asked one young man (whose Nisei grandfather was decorated by the French government for his wartime heroism) whether he was interested in the reunion, he demurred, "I don't know, my grandpa is supposed to be this big war hero or whatever. . . . He was a hero I guess." Conceding that the reunion ceremonies did not stir him, he explained: "I guess it didn't mean as much to me as it meant to the people who were in the war." French children without a family connection had at best skeletal knowledge of the significance of the American presence. When I asked a group of five French children (ranging roughly in age from eight to twelve) why they were gathered for the parade, they replied that their gymnastic club would be marching in it, but they didn't know the reason for the celebratory procession. Asked if they knew about the 442nd RCT, one knew of the "little street down there," but only because his friend had lived on it. The children were able to associate the regiment with the liberation of Bruyères, but when I pressed them as to whether the 442nd was American, English, or French, all replied "French," except for one boy who deduced from the abundance of American flags that the visitors were American.

In another interview, an adolescent boy similarly mentioned the American flag but was at first uncertain that Bruyères was liberated by Americans;[39] moreover, he described the events of the weekend as "a festival for the old folks . . . they're going to eat."[40] A seventeen-year-old male was better informed. He knew that the visitors were from the United States—from Hawaii, he thought; that they had fought for Bruyères; and that they were present for the fiftieth anniversary of the liberation. Meanwhile, his younger companion blurted out that the visitors were Tahitian. The seventeen-year-old acknowledged that it was important to remember the men who had died for them; when asked if he would participate in the ceremonies, however, he said dismissively, "I don't have the time."

That French and American youth feel alienated from the commemorative events, that they have little knowledge of the liberation of Bruyères beyond that it was secured by Americans, that they can identify the street named after the regiment but not its significance undermines the lofty official discourse of the reunions and threatens the future of the friendship between the French and the Japanese Americans. Indeed, despite their variety, the physical and discursive memorials to the Nisei soldiers are perpetually at risk of failing to evoke the memories they ostensibly enshrine.[41] Ironically, while the stone of which many monuments are carved represents the desire for the memory to endure, enshrinement of memories in stone may seemingly relieve the obligation to remember, as if the memorial itself accomplishes the "remembering." This effect is not necessarily undesired, but it is a double-edged sword: while the investment of sacred memories in stone monuments may relieve the psychic burden of those who suffered, it threatens to alienate those who did not. The obelisk in honor of the men of Bruyères who fell in World War I, for example, is the first to be adorned with flowers during the reunions but is the least evocative emotionally. Discursive memorials such as street names are also at risk, despite—or perhaps because of—their insertion in daily life. Familiarity fosters complacency, complacency replaces remembrance.

Temporal, psychological, and generational distance also facilitate forgetting. Individuals with no personal investment in the events or person commemorated are less likely to derive meaning from a monument beyond its symbolism as a marker of a distant event. Conversely, as long as an individual has a personal connection, the memorial street or monument will be evocative. A twelve-year-old French boy, for example, possesses a striking understanding of the double liberation of Bruyères because his grandfather dedicated much of his life to honoring the 442nd and to maintaining the bonds of friendship. Clearly, personal rather than physical proximity is paramount: those close to the events commemorated have a vested interest in preserving the memory, in passing it down through the generations, while for those who don't have a personal connection, even though they physically pass it every day, a street named after the 442nd RCT is just a street.

THE (INTER-)PERSONAL UNDERPINNINGS
OF MEMORIALIZATION

Though varied in form, the official memorials commemorating the liberation
of Bruyères and of Biffontaine by the 442nd RCT/100th Battalion arose out of
the same impulse to preserve in perpetuity the memory of heroism and sacrifice through which both the French and the Japanese Americans were liberated. Yet despite their physical and metaphoric solidity, memorials are
malleable, subject to the caprice of future generations, the erosion of time, and
the unique interpretation of every individual who encounters them. Not a
static shrine but an invitation to reflect, the memorial fulfills its potential, its
raison d'être, only when mediated by individuals. As James Young writes:

> Public memory and its meaning depend not just on the forms and figures in
> the monument itself, but on the viewer's response to the monument, how it is
> used politically and religiously in the community, who sees it under what cir-
> cumstances, how its figures enter other media and are recast in new surround-
> ings. . . . Memorials by themselves remain inert and amnesiac, dependent on
> visitors for whatever memory they finally produce.[42]

Younger generations admit indifference, but for those who suffered, the
admonition is less "we must remember" than "we can never forget." The
Nisei veterans have never lost sight of the indignity of internment that motivated their great sacrifice; many French whom I interviewed soberly recall the
deportation of their family to German work camps and even to Dachau. More
than a half-century later, the bitterness of the war has not lessened. As one
French woman insists, "it is difficult for those who lived [through the war] to
forget." To her indignation, the Germans had just marched in Paris in celebration of Bastille Day (1994), and she was particularly chagrined that the
German presence in Paris aroused no resentment among her grown children.[43] Similarly, the Japanese American Citizens League was embroiled in
1999 in a controversy over whether to apologize for not having supported
Nisei conscientious objectors during World War II. Initiated and supported
by younger generations, the proposal was vociferously opposed by most Nisei
veterans, many of whom openly expressed their angry resentment in public
fora (for example, in meetings, letters, newspaper articles). By illustrating division within families and within communities, both cases exemplify the purpose and process of memorialization: to reflect on who "we" are in light of
who "we" have been. Conflict, controversy, and collective discussion are inte-
gral to the process.

Still others prefer silent memorialization. One Nisei veteran who had been taken prisoner during the battle in Biffontaine could not bear to speak his pain in an interview. He promised he would write, and he did: a powerful expression of pain and release in just three hundred words. In another interview, a French veteran who had helped dig the Maginot line began to explain the colorful medals that decorated his uniform but suddenly stopped himself: "They are to be seen," he said, "to be seen but not to be told."[44] His emphasis on the visual over the spoken encapsulates the power of memorials as visible reminders of the unspeakable; memorials may be as small as a medal, as unpolished as a rusted helmet, as light as a letter, as intangible as friendship. Whether public or personal, a memorial is ultimately an invitation to remember and to reflect, a stimulus that may propose but never fully control meaning.

Ultimately, legacy lies less in street names and cold stone than in the warm souvenirs of heart and mind. The personal interviews I conducted offered invaluable insight into the profoundly interpersonal underpinnings of legacy. My presence with voice recorder in hand, my questions both planned and spontaneous, and my self-designation as student researcher undoubtedly influenced the narrative choices made by interviewees. But overwhelmingly, those who shared their impressions emphasized detail and personal, familial encounters as they described the significance to them of the liberation and reunions. Stories that are not found in history books were shared with animation; favorite family memories were recited, and new friendships were formed. The physical setting stirred other memories. Nisei veterans shivered among the trees they remember so vividly; when a gentle rain fell, many recalled the thunderous downpour during the Battle of Bruyères. For the Nisei veteran who preferred to write rather than speak, sensory contrasts were most evocative: "How different it was without the din [of] battle, fighting in the streets and in the surrounding hills, rifle shots, machine gun fire and the rumbling of tanks. Cold meals—rain, exhaustion and fear."[45]

The French remember trepidation and relief. The fierce bombings and life in basement shelters are often the first memories cited, after which details emerge.[46] The entry of the Nisei troops was described as "impressive," a mix of euphoria and surprise. Those who were children during the liberation recall most fondly the chocolate bars and food offered by the Nisei soldiers. Another describes how a drink helped her family determine that the atypical soldiers were not the enemy:

> After six weeks of bombing and living in the basement, they woke up one morning and saw before their door small men that they recognized as Japanese—perhaps allies of the Germans. So the [Frenchman] left to get some

mirabelle liqueur, which he wanted to offer to the soldiers. . . . The soldier refused: he was afraid of being poisoned, so the [Frenchman] understood, he went to fetch two glasses, he drank, the soldier drank, and they cried out together, "Vive la France!" So, that's how they knew![47]

Some insist that they knew their liberators were American despite their Japanese features, but most concede their uncertainty over the incongruity:

My father was extremely surprised when he saw them arrive. He did not expect to find soldiers of the Asian race, because . . . he had fought in the great war of 1914, and he saw the Americans arrive in 1917, so he already knew the Americans . . . with their big khaki hats. So he was very surprised [in 1944]: he expected to see—how shall I say it?—Europeans, like he saw in 1917. He was very surprised.[48]

My great-aunt told me that she was very surprised at first, she didn't know if it was the Americans or the Russians, she really didn't know who was there . . . but, seeing the [American] flags, and seeing that they fought the Germans, I think they understood fairly quickly that they weren't the enemy.[49]

Japanese Americans similarly describe a mixed reception: "People in the beginning received us with some caution, because we looked different, for one thing. . . . But then, after they realized we were sacrificing ourselves for them, we became fast friends."[50]

Beyond memories of the war, interviewees describe personal interaction and "fast friendship" as the most meaningful aspects of the reunions. When not at the formal ceremonies, the French and the Japanese Americans visited with each other in the street, in French homes, in restaurants. Gifts were exchanged—often between complete strangers—as the international participants communicated through smiles and tentative but sincere efforts to speak English and French. Sentiment superseded speech: "Although we couldn't communicate that well, the feeling came through, you know?"[51] Formalities of first encounter soon dissolved into heartfelt affection and warm invitations to return. Describing the impact of the reunion on her parents, a Sansei woman beamed: "They loved it, they met the Mayor . . . and they're part of the family *o-hana* [extended family] now . . . they have a big group of friends there now, and I'd like to go and meet them."[52] Small coincidences also foster strong bonds:

When we went in 1984, we didn't know the [Anxionnat family] at all. . . . We stayed in Bruyères and our travel agent . . . went to the bakery and came back with eclairs, we loved it. . . . In 1988, people from France came to California . . . and we had the good fortune to host them. . . . We got to talking, and the [Anxionnats] don't speak English and we don't speak French, and we got through "what sort of work do you do?" and he said he had a bakery. . . . So we said, "that's where [we] got the eclairs" . . . and we brought out our photo album. He said "That's our bakery!" Then we got this special rapport . . . so when we went to Bruyères in 1994, well, we were *good* friends.[53]

Not all, of course, have the good fortune to share repeated visits with their new friends, but the Japanese American visitors are touched and surprised by the warm reception of the French. Even the children are impressed: "I didn't think they'd be this nice."[54]

As they did after the war, the French and the Japanese Americans inevitably part ways when the reunions conclude. But all go home with memories and tangible, portable mini-memorials: souvenirs. Some bring home gifts of gourmet chocolate or precious bottles of wine, but most reunion souvenirs have permanence and practical utility—hand-crafted bookmarks and bags, floral vases and kitchen magnets, T-shirts and caps—all subtle reminders, in the midst of daily life, of the warmth of the international friendship that is one of the legacies of the 442nd. Still, as my father always said, blood is thicker than water. And indeed, although the warmth of friendship between the French and American communities is enjoyed by all, the most profound meaning for reunion participants is grounded in family. Spouses, children and grandchildren of many veterans participate in order to honor and to try to understand the wartime experience that indelibly marks their family history. French participants include the children and grandchildren of those who survived the war: "I came for my grandparents," said one, "because it's important to them."[55] The precocious twelve-year old French boy remarked that his peers didn't know of the history of the 442nd "because they don't have grandparents who participated in the war."[56] Veterans, though glad to be accompanied by family members, clearly derive the most meaning from their reunion with their metaphoric siblings: their brothers-in-arms. Bonds forged through fire and blood, through laughter and tears, prove invincible. Every veteran I interviewed spoke of camaraderie within the family of his company, within the family of the regiment, as a primary motivation to attend. Many had not seen each other since the war; an old friend of my father whom I ran into during the 1998 veterans' reunion in Hawaii was touched that he was so warmly welcomed by his comrades even though it was his first reunion: "I was really gratified in the way . . . they accepted me. . . . I served with them, but haven't participated in their gatherings."[57]

The reunions affirm yet another family: the Japanese American community. As I interviewed strangers, I was often surprised to learn that they knew my family. One veteran remembered my father and his family from the 1930s in Honolulu, while John Togashi and his wife, Yo, attended church with my parents in Chicago in the 1960s; their son remembers playing with my elder brother Joe. A veteran of the Military Intelligence Service revealed to me that he served with my uncle Kiyoshi during the war; others who knew my uncle had worked with him in Hawaii or had attended his funeral. These unexpected relations made me realize that Japanese America is a very close-knit community. We are a family of families who share the burden of internment, the proud legacy of the Nisei soldiers, and the triumph of redress, but through it all, we are a family of *American* families.

In hopes that future generations will always remember, the heroism and sacrifice of the 442nd Regimental Combat Team/100th Battalion are etched in stone, printed in books such as this, and even personified in a G.I. Joe doll. Nevertheless, the memorial reunions that commemorate the double liberation of the Battle of Bruyères suggest that meaning and memory are profoundly personal and all too vulnerable to the vicissitudes of time. Will the Japanese Americans cease coming to Bruyères? Will the monuments in the forests above Bruyères and Biffontaine be relegated to the realm of the forgotten gravesite? Will the French regard them with indifference in another century? We can neither foresee nor control how future generations will interpret the legacy of the 442nd RCT/100th Battalion. But whether the future holds reverential remembrance or amnesiac indifference, the legacy of the Battle of Bruyères for me today is that the Nisei soldiers changed the history of families and of nations. They liberated the French from the oppressive clutch of the Nazis; they helped to clear their fellow Japanese Americans of unfounded allegations of disloyalty; they bequeathed with their blood the freedom the Western world enjoys today. These are legacies more solid than stone.

NOTES

1. Not all of my father's siblings were interned because the family lived in Hawaii, where wholesale evacuation was not ordered as on the West Coast of the mainland. Even though my grandfather only hauled fish from the pier to the market, he was listed as secretary of the small fishing company for which he worked; he

was also a teacher in the Japanese language school and therefore suspect. My grandmother chose to follow her arrested husband, with the four of their eight children who were still minors, to the internment camp of Jerome and subsequently Rohwer, in Arkansas.

2. Brian Niiya, ed., *Japanese American History: An A–Z Reference from 1868 to the Present* (Los Angeles: Japanese American National Museum, 1993), 138. The 442nd/100th fought in eight major campaigns in Europe, earning seven Presidential Unit Citations, thirty-six army commendations, eighty-six division commendations, and 18,143 individual decorations (including one Congressional Medal of Honor, fifty-two Distinguished Service Crosses, fourteen French *Croix de Guerre* awards, 588 Silver Stars, and 9,486 Purple Hearts). Pierre Moulin, *Bruyères: 50è anniversaire de la libération* ([np], 1994), 223. In May 2000, after governmental review of the records of Asian American veterans who had been awarded the Distinguished Service Cross for their wartime valor, nineteen veterans of the 442nd/100th were approved to have their award upgraded to the Congressional Medal of Honor—the highest honor bestowed by the United States. "White House Announces 21 APA Medal of Honor Awardees," *Pacific Citizen* 130:20 (May 19–25, 2000): 1. [By the time of the awards ceremony, on June 21, 2000, a twentieth RCT veteran medalist was added, James Okubo, whose status had been under review in May.—Ed.]

3. With only sixty-four participants, the July mini-reunion enabled more intimate exchange between the French and visiting Japanese Americans; when Bruyères was inundated by eight hundred visitors three months later, family-to-family friendships were more difficult to establish. I am grateful to my hosts, Édouard and Viviane Canonica, for helping me become an exception to the October rule.

4. At the geographic center of a five-pointed star that links Épinal, Saint-Dié, Remiremont, Gerardmer, and Nancy, Bruyères has long been in the midst of political conflict. During the French Revolution, "Bruyères was the starting point for the stagecoaches carrying supplies to Paris"; nearly a century later, during the 1870–1871 Franco-Prussian War, the Vosges region was an important battleground, for Bruyères represented "the funnel for all roads and railways going to Épinal." Pierre Moulin, *U.S. Samurais in Bruyères*, trans. David Guinsbourg (Luxembourg: Peace and Freedom Trail, 1993), 13, 149–51.

5. The Germans had previously taken control of Bruyères on October 11, 1870, during the Franco-Prussian War. Moulin, *U.S. Samurais*, 149.

6. The Rescue of the Lost Battalion is listed as one of the ten greatest battles in American history; a representation of the battle may be found in the halls of the Pentagon (Moulin, 39). Eight hundred men of the 442nd/100th were killed or wounded to save 211 Texans from the 36th Division, 141st Regiment, 1st Battalion; moreover, as Moulin notes, "the 141st Texas is not just any unit: it is the U.S.'s cherished unit, the Alamo Regiment created in 1835 during the Texas Revolution which preceded the annexation of Texas as a U.S. State" (84).

7. Niiya reports that "of the 2,943 men in the 442nd who entered the Vosges [campaign], there were 161 dead, 43 missing and 2,000 wounded" (64–65). Moulin estimates that 1,200 men—half of the strength of the regiment—were killed or wounded in the battle of Bruyères (*Bruyères: 50è Anniversaire*, 49). If one includes French, Germans, and Americans, Moulin suggests that nearly 16,000 men were killed or wounded in the battles of Bruyères and Biffontaine (129).

8. An edition of the 1948 *Chicago JACLer* newsletter acknowledges a ten-dollar donation to this cause. "A Generous Thought," *Chicago JACLer,* 3.1 (February 1948), 1.

9. The full text of the plaque reads:

> To the men of the 442nd Regimental Combat Team, US Army, who reaffirmed an historic truth here—that loyalty to one's country is not modified by racial origin. These Americans, whose ancestors were Japanese, on October 30, 1944 during the Battle of Bruyères broke the backbone of the German defenses and rescued the 141st infantry battalion which had been surrounded by the enemy for four days.
>
> Presented by the Japanese American Citizens League.

> Aux hommes des armées américaines du 442è régiment de ligne, qui ont affirmé ici une vérité historique—que la loyauté au pays ne s'exprime pas par l'origine raciale. Ces soldats américains de race japonaise, ont, le 30 octobre 1944, pendant la bataille de Bruyères brisé l'arrière-garde des troupes allemandes et ont sauvé le 141è bataillon d'infanterie qui pendant quatre jours était cerné par l'ennemi.
>
> Présenté par la Ligue des Citoyens Américains Japonais.

10. Interview with Monsieur Évrard, 14 October 1994; interview with Serge Carlesso, 15 July 1994. Bruyères, France.

11. "In 1947, the town of Bruyères had constructed the small monument in the forest. It was the first monument in honor of the 442nd. . . . Bruyères is the only place in the world where the 442nd was remembered." Interview with Serge Carlesso, 15 July 1994, Bruyères, France. "As there were many Hawaiians who died, we were one of the first to erect a small monument in the forest. . . ." Interview with Viviane Canonica, 14 July 1994, Bruyères, France.

12. *La rue du 442è régiment d'infanterie américaine, libérateur de Bruyères.*

13. According to the 1993 *World Almanac,* the county of Honolulu had a population of 836,231, including the city of Honolulu (pop. 365,272).

14. The 442nd RCT/100th Battalion is also remembered in Pietrasanta, Italy, where a bronze sculpture of Sadao Munemori (long the only Nisei to be [posthumously] awarded the Congressional Medal of Honor) was dedicated on April 25, 2000, in memory of "all Nisei soldiers who fought in Italy." Much as with the memorials in France, the impetus to create a new monument in Italy was infused with the memory of the kindnesses bestowed by the Nisei soldiers. Specifically, the monument was spearheaded by Americo Bugliani, who, as a young Italian boy in 1945, received candy, sundries, and food rations from Nisei soldier Paul Sakamoto. Martha Nakagawa, "Italy to Dedicate Monument in Honor of Nisei Soldiers," *Pacific Citizen* (April 14–20, 2000): 1, 7.

15. As some Japanese Americans deduced, the neighboring communities of Bruyères and Biffontaine were also rivals. Each community had planned its own ceremony and luncheon; that there was no viable coordination between the two became embarrassingly obvious when the second luncheon was essentially identical to the first. More visibly, neither community had invited the mayor of the other to at-

tend its ceremony, while—to the chagrin of many—the residents of Bruyères were specifically discouraged from attending the ceremonies for fear of over-crowding. Additionally, there was tension between the mayor of Bruyères and Japanese American artist Tajiri over the placement of the "Friendship Knot," which the artist was offering as a gift to the town. The conflict reached such an impasse that days before the scheduled dedication, the artist threatened to rescind his gift. The mayor yielded, and the sculpture was dedicated in the place selected by the artist, but word of the conflict rumbled through both communities.

16. Ernest Renan, *"Qu'est-ce qu'une nation?" et autres essais politiques*, ed. Joel Roman (England: Presses Pocket, 1992), 54. My translation.

17. Marcel Mauss, *The Gift: The Form and Reason for Exchange in Archaic Societies*, trans. W. D. Halls (New York: W.W. Norton, 1990 [1950]), 13.

18. Interview with Laurent Carlesso, 14 July 1994. Bruyères, France.

19. Interview with Monsieur Mattlilger, 13 July 1994. Bruyères, France.

20. Interview with Alain Thirion, mayor of Bruyères, 14 July 1994. Bruyères, France.

21. Interview with Madame Maurice Claude, 15 July 1994. Bruyères, France.

22. Interview with Ann Suda, 2 July 1998. Honolulu, Hawaii.

23. "This was a perception that riled [former JACL National President Denny] Ya-suhara, asserting the contingent from the mainland should be credited and re-membered." Harry K. Honda, "Nisei Vets revisit Bruyères, Biffontaine," *Pacific Citizen* (November 1994): 7.

24. "Oui, j'y crois, j'y crois volontiers." Interview with Philippe Séguin, 4 December 1999. Cambridge, Massachusetts.

25. Interview with United States Senator Daniel K. Inouye, 4 July 1998. Honolulu, Hawaii. Indeed, that the valor of the Nisei soldiers on the battlefield positively influenced Hawaiian statehood is suggested by contemporary polls. In 1941, only 48 percent of respondents in a nationwide Gallup poll were in favor of Hawaii joining the Union, but support increased to 60 percent by 1946. Decades after Hawaiian statehood, the successful letter-writing campaign urging the United States Congress to approve redress legislation metaphorically enabled the French once again to return the gift of liberation.

26. Personal letter from Carl K. Saito to the author, 13 August 1994.

27. Interview with Shig Iwamasa, 14 July 1994. Bruyères, France.

28. Interview with Carl K. Saito, 13 July 1994. Bruyères, France.

29. Interview with Carl K. Saito, 13 July 1994. Bruyères, France.

30. Personal letter from Carl K. Saito to the author, 13 August 1994.

31. Interview with Serge Carlesso, 15 July 1994. Bruyères, France.

32. Interview with U.S. Senator Daniel K. Inouye, 4 July 1998. Honolulu, Hawaii.

33. Personal letter from Carl K. Saito to the author, 13 August 1994.

34. Interview with Connie Takahashi, 15 July 1994. Bruyères, France.

35. Interview with Ann Suda, 2 July 1998. Honolulu, Hawaii.

36. Interview with Ann Scheidler, 13 July 1994. Bruyères, France.

37. Interview with Kelly Kuoyama, 2 July 1998. Honolulu, Hawaii.

38. Interview with Tracey Matsuyama, 4 July 1998. Honolulu, Hawaii.

39. At first doubtful about who had liberated Bruyères ("Ben, par les Américains; je ne sais pas, moi"), the boy later affirmed that he knew it was the Americans ("Je sais que la libération est faite par les Américains") but was completely unaware that the liberators of Bruyères were Americans of Japanese ancestry.

40. Interview with Hervé Tissier, 14 October 1994. Bruyères, France.

41. In *The Practice of Everyday Life*, Michel de Certeau observes that physical markers such as memorials may unwittingly efface the very memory they seek to preserve. "Visible, they ['relics,' e.g., monuments] have the effect of rendering invisible the operation that made them possible. These fixations constitute the processes of forgetting." Michel de Certeau, *L'Invention du quotidien, vol. I (Arts de faire)* (Paris: Folio, 1990 [1980]), 147. My translation.

42. James E. Young, *The Texture of Memory: Holocaust Memorials and Meaning* (New Haven: Yale University Press, 1993), xii-xiii.

43. Interview with Viviane Canonica, 14 July 1994. Bruyères, France.

44. Interview with Monsieur Mattlilger, 14 July 1994. Bruyères, France.

45. Personal letter from Carl K. Saito to the author, 13 August 1994.

46. Interview with Monsieur Mauvré, 14 July 1994; interview with Jean-Luc Hollard, 14 October 1994. Bruyères, France.

47. Interview with Madame Maurice Claude, 15 July 1994. Bruyères, France.

48. Interview with Jean-Luc Hollard, 14 October 1994. Bruyères, France.

49. Interview with Jérôme Claude, 15 July 1994. Bruyères, France.

50. Interview with U.S. Senator Daniel K. Inouye, 2 July 1998. Honolulu, Hawaii.

51. Interview with Kelly Kuoyama, 2 July 1998. Honolulu, Hawaii.

52. Interview with Tracey Matsuyama, 4 July 1998. Honolulu, Hawaii.

53. Interview with Kelly Kuoyama, 2 July 1998. Honolulu, Hawaii.

54. Interview with Jeff Takemoto, 15 July 1994. Biffontaine, France.

55. Interview with Jérôme Claude, 15 July 1994. Bruyères, France.

56. Interview with Laurent Carlesso, 14 July 1994. Bruyères, France.

57. Interview with George Eji, 4 July 1998. Honolulu, Hawaii.

ALLAN   WESLEY   AUSTIN

LOYALTY AND CONCENTRATION CAMPS IN AMERICA: THE JAPANESE AMERICAN PRECEDENT AND THE INTERNAL SECURITY ACT OF 1950 [1]

THE SECOND WORLD WAR WAS A TOTAL WAR that did not result in total peace. Americans, many of whom expected an "American Century" of relative stability, peace, and prosperity, were instead faced with a different, but just as threatening, form of conflict: cold war. Although this new clash would differ from the war that preceded it in certain ways, lessons would be drawn from the Second World War and applied to the Cold War by American policymakers. In this manner, methods developed for dealing with the threat posed by presumed internal enemies during the Second World War would be implemented again in waging the Cold War. In this battle against domestic subversion, the incarceration of Japanese Americans under the auspices of Franklin D. Roosevelt's Executive Order 9066 provided a model for dealing with internal threats to security during the Cold War. Indeed, Title II of the Internal Security Act of 1950 has been accurately described as "patently imitative" of the Japanese American exile and incarceration.[2] The movement to repeal Title II that culminated in success in September 1971 presented Japanese Americans, a group that suffered a gross violation of civil rights between 1942 and 1945, with a unique opportunity: these victims of unnecessary and undemocratic federal government power would play a key role in helping to reform government policy and attempting to ensure that their wartime experience would not be repeated in the future against another unpopular minority group.

THE JAPANESE AMERICAN PRECEDENT

Executive Order 9066 developed in the context of a long and often hysterical history of anti-Japanese agitation in the United States, especially in the Pacific coast states. Anti-Japanese sentiment was rooted in both racial and economic concerns and promoted by powerful local and national groups. Racism, fears generated by the upward economic mobility of Japanese Americans, and the external threat of Japanese militarism all provided preconditions for the government's decision to evacuate this population. Indeed, the strong antipathy created by anti-Japanese groups, especially through the promotion of the menacing idea of the "yellow peril," overran potential safeguards, such as an increasing concern for civil liberties, a liberal presidential administration, and the tradition of limited federal government action in the realm of internal security affairs, all of which might have militated against the decision for evacuation and relocation. The emotional anti-Japanese movement, which had previously proven its strength in shaping United States foreign policy and immigration law, would once again demonstrate its influence in the aftermath of the Japanese attack on the Pearl Harbor naval base on December 7, 1941.[3]

In the months following Pearl Harbor, race became increasingly associated with loyalty in the United States. Despite the widely assumed relationship between race and disloyalty, the Federal Bureau of Investigation (FBI) originally arrested only 1,500 alien Japanese, although even this relative restraint resulted in the imprisonment of many who were clearly not a threat to national security. The rights of non-white Americans of enemy ancestry, it quickly became clear, were more likely to be violated in this early attempt at protecting the United States from internal subversion. As hostility grew, especially in the West Coast press, and came increasingly to focus on race and implied guilt, the American government began high-level talks concerning the possibility for mass incarceration.

General John L. DeWitt and the War Department almost immediately became the primary advocates of the mass evacuation and incarceration of Japanese Americans. DeWitt, a jumpy commander prone to panic-ridden responses to even the most obvious false alarms, was clearly a racist. The general referred to all Japanese as members of an "enemy race" and explained to the already anxious American public that "[a] Jap is a Jap.... It makes no difference whether he is an American citizen, he is still Japanese."[4] DeWitt provided the first proposal for mass evacuation within seventy-two hours of the Pearl Harbor attack and justified it with fantasies of a looming Japanese American revolt. Major General Allen W. Gullion, the provost Marshall general, supported calls for evacuation by retreating from his earlier position that the military did not have the authority to detain citizens as long as civilian courts were functioning, and he became willing to seize at least non-white civilians without even a declaration of martial law. Although the cautious DeWitt often shifted ground and seemed unwilling to commit to any single policy recommendation, the War Department adopted the goal of mass evacuation of Japanese Americans and began to use its considerable wartime prestige and weight of opinion to pressure the Department of Justice to exert more vigorous control of this presumed potentially disloyal group.

Despite misgivings, the Justice Department eventually agreed to the War Department's demands for a policy of mass incarceration. Legal objections as well as Attorney General Francis Biddle's personal opposition to exile and incarceration were eventually pushed aside in deference to the War Department's claims of "military necessity." The Justice Department's unwillingness to challenge the military's definition of what was necessary for national security and winning the war, in fact, seems to have been a key factor in its decision to abdicate its important role in the formulation and implementation of internal security policy during the war. The War Department's willingness to accept the administrative duties of evacuation eliminated a final argument put forth by the Justice Department against that policy. Popular civilian demands for a vigorous program designed to ensure internal security may also have helped to move the Justice Department to accede to the Department of War's demands. Other decision-makers were certainly aware of, and perhaps affected to some degree by, an avalanche of mail that fit a discernible pattern of public opinion. "Hello, you lousy Jap lover," began one not untypical letter to the apparently too-timid attorney general. "Why in hell don't you get out of office and let some one in there that's got guts. . . . You and your six freedoms should be put in the garbage can."[5]

The threat of Japanese American sabotage, espionage, and fifth column activities seemed to dominate popular concerns about Japanese Americans on the West Coast. Rumors of such actions, prevalent long before December 7, 1941, found broader circulation and increased legitimacy after alleged details of subversion related to the attack by the Japanese against Pearl Harbor became public knowledge. Indeed, many Americans seemed to connect alleged subversive activities—although none were ever proven—by Japanese Americans in Hawaii with the potential for danger in the West Coast states. Public statements by Earl Warren, the California attorney general, in the months after the Japanese attack on the American naval base in Hawaii both mirrored and reinforced this hysterical perspective. Warren argued that the West Coast represented the most likely Japanese target and ominously warned that the total lack of sabotage thus far provided convincing evidence of a concerted effort to hold back on all subversive activities until the well-planned-for "zero-hour" had arrived. Warren's testimony before the Tolan Committee reiterated these widely shared ideas: "To assume that the enemy has not planned fifth column activities for us in a wave of sabotage," he warned, "is simply to live in a fool's paradise."[6] Such a coordinated attack, he contended, was inevitable. DeWitt's racist comments, because he was West Coast commander, lent verisimilitude to such warnings. Many accusers supported the general's position by pointing to "arrows" that had been constructed by traitorous Japanese Americans in a variety of ways, such as the strategic planting of flowers and tomato plants or stacking of hay, as clear evidence of plans to guide Japanese pilots to American defense plants and military bases. Warren added to this panic by suggesting that Japanese Americans congregated, quite intentionally, near defense plants, apparently ready to storm such plants after Japanese air raids. Daily newspaper reports of contraband seized from the Japanese American community added to the hysteria. These perceptions resulted in increasing editorial support for the removal of the Japanese American population as well as the argument that evacuation was necessary to maintain public morale. Everybody would feel safer, the argument went, if all Japanese Americans were locked up in concentration camps.

The ties of Japanese Americans to Japan were often cited as proof of their disloyalty. That most adult Japanese Americans had supported Japan's military aggression in the 1930s was cited as proof of the Japanese American threat. Race obviously remained an implicit component of this argument. For example, the *Sacramento Bee* discussed only Japanese Americans, and not Americans of German or Italian descent, when it contended that "[t]hey cannot help but sympathize with their own country."[7]

The institutions of Japanese Americans were also singled out as a subversive danger because of their close ties to the Japanese government—prefectural associations, language schools, and the Shinto and Buddhist religions were all identified as institutions that promoted an unbending allegiance to Japan. The flimsy evidence used to support these conclusions was accepted by a largely uninformed American public. The perverse logic of the times is shown by the argument that Japanese Americans clearly remained loyal to Japan because no Japanese American had ever informed on a subversive Japanese American.

Racism remained at the heart of most of the arguments designed to prove Japanese American disloyalty. Such feelings led to statements like "Once a Jap, always a Jap," and "You cannot regenerate a Jap, convert him, and make him the same person as a white man any more than you can reverse the laws of nature."[8] Cultural considerations also played into the anti-Japanese hysteria that was seizing the American public. Japanese American culture simply made, some hypothesized, for an inferior Americanism. Education in the late-afternoon language schools fashioned students who were, for all intents and purposes, Japanese. Japanese religion also served as a deterrent to the development of 100 percent Americanism.

Burdened with such racial and cultural liabilities, Japanese Americans faced the ultimate "catch–22" when the federal government decided to send them into exile. Loyal Japanese Americans, many Americans argued, would willingly cooperate with all government decisions. Any who disobeyed were, by definition, disloyal. Thus, Japanese Americans who had acculturated politically and believed in the Constitution and the civil liberties that it was supposed to protect had to give up their freedom without protest. The alternative was clear: if one was not loyal enough to cooperate quickly with the government and move quietly to a concentration camp, one obviously belonged in such a camp as a disloyal person.

The War Relocation Authority (WRA), the civilian agency created on March 18, 1942, by Roosevelt's Executive Order 9102 to administer the concentration camps, quickly became aware that those camps bred frustrations, fear, and bitterness. Thus, by mid-1942, the WRA, fearing the permanent institutionalization of Japanese Americans, decided to initiate a process to release many of its prisoners. To do so without freeing disloyal and perhaps dangerous Japanese Americans, the WRA required a loyalty oath before release. This decision raised considerable controversy in the camps and resulted in 6,000 who refused to declare their loyalty to the United States and 3,000 who qualified their answer or chose not to answer (out of about 40,000 responses).[9]

Morton Grodzins, a prominent early critic of the government's policy of evacuation, argues that various motives moved this substantial minority to answer no to the loyalty questions. Some did so to protest or to demand their rightful equal status. Others felt that loyalty to the nation meant disloyalty to the family. The fear of being removed from the camps and thrust back into what was perceived as a decidedly hostile environment led some to refuse to declare their loyalty. A final group answered no to express a preference for Japanese culture and to prepare for living in Japan. Living conditions, which varied considerably from camp to camp, also influenced decisions on this issue.

The results of these loyalty questionnaires probably reinforced some attitudes about Japanese American disloyalty. However, Grodzins points out that "few, if any, would ever have openly declared themselves not loyal to the United States [if not faced with a forced, direct choice]."[10]

Executive Order 9066 was almost immediately endorsed by Congress and, in 1943 and 1944, by the Supreme Court. Congress accepted the War Department's claim of "military necessity" without question, never pausing to examine critically the situation and the issues involved. What little study Congress undertook has been described by Grodzins as full of "misunderstanding and irrelevancy."[11] The Supreme Court's approval relaxed its standards for civil liberties. In the *Hirabayashi* decision in June 1943, the court, grounding its racist decision in the prevailing popular conception of racial guilt, upheld the legitimacy of emergency curfew regulations that affected only ethnic Japanese, aliens and citizens alike. The Supreme Court would not rule again on the constitutionality of the government's actions until December 1944. In *Korematsu*, a no-longer-unanimous court sustained, in effect, the legality of the forced exile of citizens of Japanese ancestry. The serious dangers of 1942, the court continued to maintain, justified these policy decisions. The *Endo* decision was handed down on the same day as *Korematsu*. While *Endo* did assert that loyal citizens could not continue to be held in concentration camps, the case did not result in a repudiation of the evacuation. The Supreme Court faulted only the administrative processes of the WRA, not the decision to implement a program of exile and incarceration, in its ruling.

Grodzins argued soon after the war that the national government had succeeded in one of its main tasks, winning the war, but had failed in an equally important task, protecting democracy at home. He argued that American policies toward the Japanese American population had been the antithesis of democracy, more closely resembling the directions one might find in "the totalitarian handbook." Japanese Americans, he continued, had been victimized by a pervasive racism as well as by economic and political goals that had become intertwined with and ultimately inseparable from the issue of patriotism.[12] The arguments for evacuation reflected these mixed motives but seemed to focus on the underlying issue of race and disloyalty.

THE INTERNAL SECURITY ACT OF 1950

The exile and incarceration of Japanese Americans during the Second World War was not an action entirely without precedent in American history. Richard Drinnon argues that the reservations established for Native Americans were precursors of the Second World War's concentration camps.[13] However, the government's concentration camp program for the Second World War was unprecedented as an act of mass incarceration of American citizens. The wartime camps, furthermore, were built with a very specific and unprecedented purpose: to house a group of people assumed to be guilty of disloyalty solely on the basis of ancestry. Indeed, considerations of race, and not individual actions, drove this determination of guilt.

Although the decision of mid-February 1942 to incarcerate Japanese Americans on the mainland faced little initial opposition, a growing number of critics began to question both the merits and the future implications of this policy as the war progressed. It was becoming increasingly apparent to some that the evacuation had set what would later be described as "a dangerous precedent—some might call it a loaded gun—awaiting only an appropriate crisis."[14] Morton Grodzins noted the potential future ramifications of the Japanese American incarceration as early as 1949, warning that wartime actions against this group could be repeated against other unpopular minority groups: "The process of government is a continuing process; what it produced for Japanese Americans it can also produce for other Americans."[15]

Grodzins' 1949 warning would be realized the very next year with the passage of the Internal Security Act of 1950, also known as the McCarran Act.[16] The anti-Japanese hysteria of the early period of American participation in the Second World War was followed by the anti-Communist hysteria in the early years of the Cold War, which peaked between 1945 and 1954. This hysteria, intensified by the triumph of the Communist Revolution in China in 1949, would help to foster widespread fears of communism as well as broad support for a variety of anti-Communist rhetoric and legislative action. Americans in this era, Richard Fried has argued, "developed an obsession with domestic communism that outran the actual threat and gnawed at the tissue of civil liberties."[17] This climate of opinion helped to convince Congress to pass a bill that would reestablish concentration camps for use in times of an internal security emergency. The concentration camp bill clearly mirrored government actions taken towards Japanese Americans in the Second World War in dealing with perceived threats to the internal security of the United States.

Congressional debate in August and September over the various anti-Communist proposals that became the Internal Security Act of 1950 focused on the immense threat posed by communism to the United States. The stridently anti-Communist rhetoric that had permeated the Eighty-first Congress even prior to this debate outweighed objections to the concentration camp clause of the Internal Security Act of 1950 contained in Title II. Frequent evocations of both a domestic and a foreign Communist threat (seen in the Alger Hiss case and the Korean War) argued for the necessity of internal security legislation. A Communist registration law, Representative John S. Wood (D-Georgia) contended in late August 1950, was required as an act of simple self-preservation, a badly needed defense against a "cancer on the body politic."[18] The Communist Party of the United States, most seemed to agree, was not a normal political party because it was controlled by a foreign dictatorship. The government's successful prosecution of eleven Communist Party officials in 1949, furthermore, had suggested that "Communism, for top Party officials at least, was now apparently illegal."[19] Staffed by "miserable curs" and "traitors," the Party, Congressman John Jennings, Jr. (R-Tennessee) charged, sought "to destroy by conspiracy, by perjury, and by treason."[20]

The rhetoric used to justify the necessity of the Internal Security Act of 1950 often paralleled that used to support the incarceration of Japanese Americans during the Second World War. Both groups, for example, were accused of being loyal to an entity outside of the United States. Neither group, it was widely believed, thought for itself; instead, orders from without were unquestioningly followed. The Communists, much like the Japanese Americans before them, lurked menacingly within the United States, enjoying the benefits of citizenship while fiendishly plotting internal subversion designed to overthrow the government. All Communists, simply by their association with communism, were potential troublemakers. This conjunction represented a particularly threatening situation, especially because the Communist mind, much like that of the Japanese during the Second World War, was considered to be inscrutable: "I cannot," lamented Representative John McSweeney (D-Ohio), a hardened but harried veteran of the Un-American Affairs Committee, "understand a Communist. . . . I find there is a basic similarity among all of them, and yet I have not been able to formulate a definition which will cover all of them."[21] Communists were also considered guilty by association by most supporters of the new legislation. Simply put, membership in this ideological group, like previous Japanese American membership in a racial group, meant disloyalty. Faced with such an enemy, concentration camps, Senator Edwin C. Johnson (D-Colorado) reasoned, made considerable sense, at least if limited to a time of national emergency.[22] This qualification generally represented the strongest reservation in Congress about the inclusion of Title II in the Internal Security Act of 1950.

Congressional rhetoric concerning internal security in 1950 placed Communists (and, in a slight variation of the rhetoric of the Second World War, any opponents of the legislation) in another "catch–22" situation, similar to the one with which Japanese Americans had earlier become all too familiar: "An American who is loyal to his country," Congressman Gordon Leo McDonough (R-California) reasoned, "can have no objection to stating his loyalty. . . ."[23] Thus, anyone who resisted the legislation, even on the grounds that it was unconstitutional or un-American, proved him or herself beyond any reasonable doubt to be un-American. Any true patriot, Congressman Thomas Albert Jenkins (R-Ohio) claimed, would wholeheartedly support any anti-Communist legislation that was drafted. Finally, Representative Charles Wesley Vursell (R-Illinois) branded anyone who opposed registration as at best a dupe of the Communists: "The delay in the passage of this legislation," he concluded, "is an indication of the tremendous influence these [Communist] groups are able to yield."[24]

In the late summer of 1950, Republicans and Democrats fought to outdo one another in crafting and passing the strongest anti-Communist legislation. President Harry S. Truman had joined the fray on August 8, submitting a measure designed to deal more harshly with espionage and aliens. Senator Patrick J. McCarran (D-Nevada) moved only two days later to present even more repressive legislation, combining his bill, which dealt with alien Communists, with another bill requiring the registration of Communists. Truman's proposal was obviously "weak tea next to these strong spirits."[25] The House of Representatives' companion bill to McCarran's more potent measure was introduced on August 21 and quickly garnered widespread support, passing the House of Representatives on August 29 by a vote of 354 to 20.[26]

Liberal Democratic Senators Harley M. Kilgore (West Virginia), Paul H. Douglas (Illinois), Hubert H. Humphrey (Minnesota), Herbert H. Lehman (New York), Estes Kefauver (Tennessee), and Frank P. Graham (North Carolina), not wanting to be outdone on the issue of anti-communism, soon offered what they presented as a fairer but even more potent anti-Communist proposal that authorized, in times of emergency as declared by the president, the detention of those likely to engage in sabotage or espionage. Liberals claimed that the concentration camp bill represented an improvement over the incarceration of Japanese Americans during the Second World War because it provided a clearly defined procedure that allowed for hearings and at least the possibility of release. The "concentration camp bill," as it came to be called, was also proposed in an attempt to "to set a backfire against the more comprehensive McCarran legislation. . . ."[27]

In promoting their own proposal while denigrating the opposition's, both sides thus continued to engage in a contest of "bizarre posturing" in attempting to present their legislation as the toughest. This posturing reached a climax when Hubert Humphrey, in praising the strictness of the liberals' detention bill, dismissed McCarran's legislation as a "cream-puff special."[28] The compromise that resulted was a logical if unhappy one: the McCarran bill, with emergency detention now attached by the Senate as Title II. The amended bill was passed by the Senate on September 12 by a vote of 70 to 7.[29]

After a conference, the internal security bill with Title II attached was brought to a vote in both houses on September 21, 1950. Not surprisingly, given the tenor of the times and the strong anti-Communist rhetoric in Congress, it passed easily despite Truman's threats to veto it. The House of Representatives approved the bill by a vote of 312 to 20, the Senate by a count of 51 to 7. Each house encountered only limited resistance to passage by a small group of Democrats. Truman immediately made good on his threat and vetoed the act, pleading for congressional support and focusing his arguments against Title I and its provisions on registration and immigration. Truman's veto on September 22 was swiftly overridden, however, in large part because many congressmen ignored the bill's perils in order to avoid the impression of not being tough enough on communism. Although a few more Democratic representatives rallied to support Truman, the House easily overrode the veto on the same day that it was issued by a vote of 286 to 48. In the Senate, after an abortive attempt to filibuster by a group seeking to uphold Truman's veto, the act was repassed after an all-night session by a vote of 57 to 10, four Democrats joining the six originators of the concentration camp bill in seeking to uphold Truman's veto.[30]

The Internal Security Act, as finally enacted on September 23, 1950, consisted of two sections. Title I, proclaiming that Communist organization was a clear and present danger to the United States but that Party membership was not a crime, required officers or members of Communist groups to register with the attorney general. A Subversive Activities Control Board (SACB) was established to decide which groups were covered by the law. Title I also barred covered individuals from government and defense jobs as well as American passports. Espionage and immigration laws were tightened to crack down on potential subversives. Title I ultimately resulted in considerable litigation, but no Communist group was ever registered under its mandate.[31]

Title II (or the Emergency Detention Act), based on the model of Executive Order 9066, "mandated detention of likely spies and saboteurs during an internal-security emergency declared by the President."[32] The act clearly followed the precedent established by the Roosevelt administration during the Second World War. It could be activated by the declaration of an internal security emergency by the president, who would then transfer oversight of the program to the attorney general. The attorney general, in turn, would issue warrants for detention against anyone reasonably believed to be likely to conspire to engage in sabotage or espionage against the United States.[33]

The right to appeal, a key concept for the liberals' "fairer" approach to American concentration camps, was established in the act and a system of administrative review was created. Hearings officers would meet with detainees to inform them of the reason for their detention as well as their right to legal counsel. At the official hearings, the detainees would be allowed to present evidence and cross-examine witnesses on their own behalf. The rights of detainees were limited, however, by the attorney general's right to withhold evidence or sources deemed potentially dangerous to national security. After the hearing, the detainee would either be released or held. A detainee who did not obtain release had the right of direct appeal to a bipartisan Detention Review Board, which had to hear the case within forty-five days of the appeal. The board, however, had no time limit imposed on its decision.[34]

The debate in Congress leading to the passage of the McCarran Act made it clear that Communists were assumed to be the most likely group to be rounded up in the context of a Cold War emergency. Title II was never invoked, and no internal emergency was ever declared. However, appropriations were made by Congress between 1952 and 1957 to ready six detention sites throughout the country: Florence, Arizona; Wickenburg, Arizona; Avon Park, Florida; Allenwood, Pennsylvania; El Reno, Oklahoma; and Tule Lake, California. The selection of Tule Lake, the location of one of the Second World War camps, as one of the sites for future concentration camps is another reminder of the parallels between Title II and the Japanese American experience during the Second World War. It also provided a rallying point for Japanese Americans in their campaign to repeal Title II in the late 1960s. Funding for the camps was not renewed after 1957, however, and the camps were eventually sold, leased, or given to state governments (except for the facility in Allenwood, Pennsylvania, which became a minimum-security federal prison). Although the camps had thus been abandoned by the federal government by the late 1950s, the survival of Title II on the law books would continue to nag at some civil libertarians.[35]

The anti-Communist hysteria of the 1950s was so pervasive that criticism of the concentration camp bill would remain muted until the late 1960s. Indeed, even some liberal critics of Executive Order 9066 did not immediately argue against Title II. Morton Grodzins, a critic of the policy of Japanese American exile and incarceration after the war, turned to an emphasis on the threat of communism in the mid-1950s. Although Grodzins did not support current loyalty programs or the use of concentration camps in 1956, his book

The Loyal and the Disloyal paid particular attention to both the appeal of communism and its dangers. Grodzins was especially concerned that David Riesman's "other-directed" man suffered from a "relatively soft" loyalty that, while not likely to breed traitors, was likely to create "the easy collaborator."[36] Alienation, Grodzins warned, could fashion a revolutionary predisposition for creating a new world. Once a person joined a revolutionary group like the Communists, the social scientist concluded, the individual's loyalty to the group would be unlimited. Like common assumptions about Japanese Americans during the Second World War, the disloyalty of Communists, it would seem, could easily be determined by group association during the Cold War. "When conformity to the deviant group is established," Grodzins concluded, "the basis for overt disloyalty has been laid."[37] This assertion certainly suggested that all American Communists ought to be considered dangerous as potential subversives.

Grodzins' scholarly analysis of loyalty and disloyalty did not overtly support anything remotely like the draconian Internal Security Act of 1950. In fact, the author argues that strict loyalty-security programs like the ones adopted by the United States government in the 1950s engendered more disloyal actions than they prevented or exposed. However, his argument that internal communism represented the greatest challenge to democratic nations certainly supported the widely held notion that something like the Internal Security Act of 1950 was necessary. The jump from the rationalizations for concentration camps in the 1940s to those of the 1950s was a small one. Ideology simply replaced "race" as the basis for determining group disloyalty.[38]

THE CAMPAIGN FOR REPEAL

A concerted movement for repeal of Title II did not begin until the late 1960s, at the height of the civil rights and anti–Vietnam War protests. At this time, rumors began to circulate of government plans for concentration camps to incarcerate various groups of dissenters. One key event that seems to have fueled such reports and drawn renewed attention to Title II and its undemocratic provisions was a 1968 report that originated in the House Un-American Affairs Committee. Titled "Guerrilla Warfare in the United States," the report contained a suggestion that Title II could be used to create concentration camps for the new and threatening breed of subversives. This report, in addition to rumors of the reopening of camps, sparked a revitalized interest in Title II. Japanese Americans would take advantage of this receptive environment to begin to lead an active campaign for repeal of Title II.[39]

The Japanese American Citizens League (JACL) had shown a passing interest in combating the McCarran Act when it was first passed and had joined with the Leadership Conference on Civil Rights in the battle to sustain Truman's veto in 1950. That battle lost, it virtually ignored Title II. Mike Masaoka has suggested, not too convincingly, that the JACL decided to focus on other issues at least in part because Title II was viewed as relatively benign unless an emergency was declared. The JACL adopted repeal of Title II as its primary legislative goal in August 1968, but did so only after a vigorous grass-roots campaign in favor of repeal had been waged, according to JACL chronicler Bill Hosokawa, by a number of "young boat rockers."[40] The JACL would become more active in the late 1960s, producing a pamphlet that starkly warned of concentration camps in America and assuming leadership of the repeal movement as "[t]he most prominent organized interest [group] spearheading change. . . ."[41] Nisei activism in favor of repeal may have helped to set a precedent for the later movement for redress. The JACL must certainly have learned the importance of government lobbying as well as public relations in its campaign for the repeal of the Internal Security Act of 1950.

The first bills aimed at the repeal of Title II were presented in Congress in April 1969 by two Hawaiian Japanese American legislators, both of them decorated veterans of the renowned 442nd Regimental Combat Team/100th Battalion. The movement against the Emergency Detention Act became increasingly popular the more the issue was discussed. Senator Daniel Inouye's repeal bill had 23 co-sponsors while Congressmen Spark Matsunaga's identical House version had 157. By the end of the year, the Nixon administration had recommended that Title II be repealed because it was so widely (and, from the administration's point of view, unfortunately) misunderstood and seen as threatening by Japanese Americans.[42]

The momentum for repeal was momentarily stalled by Richard Ichord of Missouri, who suggested that repeal was not the proper response to the problems inherent in the Emergency Detention Act. Ichord instead proposed that Title II should simply be revised to provide "expeditious personal hearings."[43] A repeal measure went through Congress and was signed into law on September 25, 1971, by Richard Nixon.[44]

The bill that eventually became law in 1971 represented more than simple repeal of Title II. The law included what political scientist Richard Longaker has identified as "a positive prohibition of detention."[45] That is, Congress not only repealed Title II, but also amended Section 4001 of Title 18 of the United States Code to begin: "No citizen shall be imprisoned or otherwise detained by the United States except pursuant to an act of Congress."[46]

Longaker argues that this language prohibits detention without a specific act of Congress. The power of the president to act unilaterally as Franklin D. Roosevelt had in 1942 seems to have been circumscribed by this language. It is important to note that Congress still reserved to itself the power to authorize detention. Longaker has argued that this loophole is relatively unimportant, contending that "the cumulative legislative history [of the 1971 act] leaves no room for doubt that Congress intended to prohibit rather than permit, even under its own authority, the use of detention."[47]

Longaker views the repeal of Title II in very positive terms. The 1971 law, he asserts, ended detention in concentration camps as an accepted principle of law, even in times of emergency under unlimited presidential authority. "While this single legislative act," he argues, "does not point conclusively toward further growth of constitutional liberty it does, at least, say something significant about forces at work in that direction."[48]

Historian Roger Daniels takes a less optimistic view of Title II and its 1971 repeal. He has no confidence that the legislative intent of Congress will necessarily prevail in some future emergency. Daniels points out that the three key Supreme Court decisions upholding the constitutionality of the Japanese American exile and incarceration remain unchallenged and unrevised precedents despite the so-called *coram nobis* cases of 1983.[49] This is an important point and reminds us on the sixtieth anniversary of decision for exile and incarceration that, in the words of Grodzins, the legacy of the evacuation " . . . betrayed all Americans."[50] Even the extended language of the 1971 repeal does not necessarily preclude a repeat of the Japanese American experience during the Second World War. Although a simple executive order may no longer be a legally permissible route to the establishment of concentration camps, some future perceived emergency and an acceptable target group make the threat of concentration camps a very real one.

The positive progress achieved by the repeal of the Emergency Detention Act should not be minimized, but it is important to note that the danger of concentration camps has not, even today, disappeared completely. The high hopes for the repeal bill were very clearly expressed in House Report No. 92–116: the law was designed to restrict detention "except pursuant to an Act of Congress" and to repeal Title II of the Internal Security Act.[51] Although the "internal security emergency" needed to trigger Title II was never declared and so the standby concentration camps were never used, many Americans were concerned in the late 1960s that the act might be used against antiwar or black nationalist groups. (Today almost certainly the target group would be terrorists.) All such groups were, by definition, disloyal and thus seen as a serious threat to the internal security of the United States. Title II of the Internal Security Act of 1950 was "beyond salvaging": it served no useful purpose, might have been found unconstitutional, and mandated the creation of decidedly undemocratic concentration camps.[52]

Despite the positive aspects of the repeal of Title II, the potential for the future establishment of concentration camps in the United States remains. The threat of such camps has been in no way completely eliminated. While the 1971 act does make it more difficult for camps to be established, it is still quite possible to imagine a situation, given a very specific and deeply felt sense of emergency as well as an unpopular target group, in which concentration camps might once more appear on the American landscape. Although the 1971 law requires congressional approval for the establishment of concentration camps, it is important to note that Congress strongly supported concentration camps for Japanese Americans during the Second World War. The Supreme Court likewise bowed to political considerations, wartime emergency, and "military necessity" in allowing the concentration camps to continue.[53]

Thus, while concentration camps and new prisoners of the home front may seem an impossibility today, especially in light of the end of the Cold War and the elimination of the Communist menace, the danger of a repeat of the Second World War Japanese American experience remains. The fluid transfer of guilt by association from a racial to an ideological group in the 1950s suggests the readiness of Americans to find new enemies in times of perceived emergency. Given this predisposition, the repeal of Title II in 1971 and the caveat placed in Section 4001 of Title 18 of the United States Code are but poor protection should a new and serious threat to internal security, either real or imagined, arise in the future.

NOTES

1. The author would like to thank Erica Harth and Roger Daniels for their assistance with this project. This essay benefited greatly from their suggestions at various stages.
2. Roger Daniels, *The Decision to Relocate the Japanese Americans* (Malabar, Florida: Robert E. Krieger Publishing Company, 1986), 57.
3. The material on the Japanese American precedent presented in this essay is drawn from the following sources: Daniels, *Decision*; Roger Daniels, *Concentration Camps USA: Japanese Americans and World War II* (New York: Holt, Rinehart and Winston, Inc., 1972); Roger Daniels, *Asian America: Chinese and Japanese in the United States since 1850* (Seattle: University of Washington Press, 1988); Morton Grodzins, *Americans Betrayed: Politics and the Japanese Evacuation* (Chicago:

University of Chicago Press, 1949); Morton Grodzins, *The Loyal and the Disloyal: Social Boundaries of Patriotism and Freedom* (Chicago: University of Chicago Press, 1956); Francis Biddle, *In Brief Authority* (Garden City, New York: Doubleday and Company, Inc., 1962); and Audrie Girdner and Anne Loftis, *The Great Betrayal: The Evacuation of the Japanese-Americans During World War II* (London: The Macmillan Company, 1969).

4. As quoted in Grodzins, *Americans Betrayed*, 362.

5. As quoted in Ibid., 419.

6. Ibid., 401–402; U.S. Congress, House Select Committee Investigating National Defense Migration, *Hearings*, 77th Congress, 2d Session, Part 29, 11011–11012.

7. As quoted in Grodzins, *Americans Betrayed.*, 405.

8. As quoted in Ibid., 407.

9. Audrie Girdner and Anne Loftis, *The Great Betrayal*, 122; Morton Grodzins, *The Loyal and the Disloyal*, 110.

10. Morton Grodzins, *The Loyal and the Disloyal*, 118, 105–30. Grodzins was a political scientist at the University of Chicago. His previous work on the Japanese American exile and incarceration during the Second World War had emphasized the egregious violations of civil rights that had occurred. See "Morton Grodzins, Political Scientist," *New York Times*, March 10, 1964: 34.

11. Grodzins, *Americans Betrayed*, 364.

12. Ibid., 372–74.

13. Richard Drinnon, *Keeper of Concentration Camps: Dillon S. Myer and American Racism* (Berkeley: University of California Press, 1987), xxii-xxiii.

14. Daniels, *Decision*, 56.

15. Grodzins, *Americans Betrayed*, 1.

16. 64 *Stat.* 1019. The text of Title II of the McCarran Act may also be found in *Congressional Record*, 81st Cong., 2d sess., 1950, vol. 96 pt. 18: A7126.

17. Richard M. Fried, *Nightmare in Red: The McCarthy Era in Perspective* (New York: Oxford University Press, 1990), 3. See also Ellen Schrecker, *Many Are the Crimes: McCarthyism in America* (Boston: Little, Brown and Company, 1998), xiv.

18. *Congressional Record*, 81st Cong., 2d sess., 96 pt. 10, 29 August 1950: 13730, 13733 [hereafter cited as *CR*].

19. Fried, *Nightmare in Red*, 93–94.

20. *CR*, 81st Cong., 2d sess., 96 pt. 10, 29 August 1950: 13731, 13734.

21. *CR*, 81st Cong., 2d sess., 96 pt. 10, 29 August 1950: 13732, 13747; *CR*, 81st Cong., 2d sess., 96 pt. 11, 12 September 1950: 14622–14623.

22. *CR*, 81st Cong., 2d sess., 96 pt. 11, 12 September 1950: 14621, 14624; *CR*, 81st Cong., 2d sess., 96 pt. 10, 29 August 1950: 13739.

23. *CR*, 81st Cong., 2d sess., 96 pt. 10, 29 August 1950: 13747.

24. Ibid., 13741–13742.

25. Fried, *Nightmare in Red*, 116.

26. "Congress Passes Bill to Curb Reds by Heavy Margin," *New York Times* (September 21, 1950): 1, 13.

27. Richard Longaker, "Emergency Detention: The Generation Gap, 1950–1971," *The Western Political Quarterly* 27 (1974): 395–96; Fried, *Nightmare in Red*, 116.

28. Fried, *Nightmare in Red*, 116–17.

29. "Congress Passes Bill to Curb Reds by Heavy Margins," *New York Times* (September 21, 1950): 1; *Legislative History Collection: Documents Pertaining to the In-*

ternal Security Act of 1950, H.R. 9490, S. 4037, P.L. 81–831, 81st Congress, 2nd Session (Washington, D.C.: Atomic Energy Commission, 1951).

30. "Congress Passes Bill to Curb Reds by Heavy Margin," *New York Times* (September 21, 1950): 1, 13; "Red Control Bill is Vetoed, Repassed at Once by House; Congress Votes Big Tax Raise," *New York Times* (September 23, 1950): 1; Longaker, 396–97. The text of Truman's veto may be found in *Congressional Record*, 81st Congress, 2d sess., vol. 96, pt. 11, 22 September 1950: 15629–15632.

31. "Red Control Bill is Vetoed, Repassed at Once by House; Congress Votes Big Tax Raise," *New York Times* (September 23, 1950): 1, 6; "Red Bill Veto Beaten, 57–10, by Senators," *New York Times* (September 24, 1950): 1, 57; Fried, *Nightmare in Red*, 117. The FBI had begun to compile lists of allegedly dangerous individuals as early as 1939, although it had no mandate for such actions. The Security Index, as the list assembled by the FBI for its "custodial detention plan" came to be called, grew quickly after the Internal Security Act of 1950 authorized its existence, rising from 12,000 names in 1950 to 26,000 in 1954. The FBI also compiled another list of "slightly less dangerous individuals," accumulating more than 430,000 files on groups and individuals by 1960. See Schrecker, *Many Are the Crimes*, 208.

32. Fried, *Nightmare in Red*, 117.

33. Longaker, 397–400.

34. Ibid., 400.

35. Fried, *Nightmare in Red*, 117–18; Longaker, 400.

36. Grodzins, *The Loyal and the Disloyal*, 14–16.

37. Ibid., 132–52.

38. Race and ethnicity have continued to serve as markers for disloyalty. Chinese applying for entry to the United States, for example, were suspected in the early 1950s by at least some government officials of being part of a potential fifth column. Furthermore, as the government began an active campaign against illegal Chinese immigrants in 1956, rumors began to circulate in the Chinese American community of plans to round up Chinese Americans en masse for either deportation or removal to concentration camps. See Mae M. Ngai, "Legacies of Exclusion: Illegal Chinese Immigration during the Cold War Years," *Journal of American Ethnic History* 18:1 (1998): 10, 15.

39. Longaker, "Emergency Detention," 400. Mike M. Masaoka of the JACL recalled rumors about reopening the camps. See Mike Masaoka with Bill Hosokawa, *They Call Me Moses Masaoka: An American Saga* (New York: William Morrow and Company, 1987), 303. In 1969, Harry H. L. Kitano wrote that "[m]elancholy traces of the evacuation remain today. Rumors that the evacuation camp at Tule Lake was ready for 'enemies' were afloat during the McCarthy period and occasionally are heard today." See Harry H. L. Kitano, *Japanese Americans: The Evolution of a Subculture* (Englewood Cliffs, New Jersey: Prentice-Hall, 1969), 46.

40. Bill Hosokawa, *JACL: In Quest of Justice* (New York: William Morrow and Company, Inc., 1982), 323; Masaoka and Hosokawa, *Moses Masaoka*, 304; Raymond Okamura, "Background and History of the Repeal Campaign," *Amerasia Journal* 2 (1972): 76–79.

41. Longaker, 401; Masaoka and Hosokawa, *Moses Masaoka*, 304. The JACL pamphlet "Concentration Camps in America?" can be found in the Sumiko Kobayashi Papers, Box 7, File 10, at the Balch Institute for Ethnic Studies.

42. Deputy Attorney General Richard D. Kleindienst's letter of December 2, 1969, to the Senate Judiciary Committee announcing the administration's decision is reprinted in Daniels, *Decision*, 131–32.

43. Masaoka and Hosokawa, *Moses Masaoka*, 304–305; Okamura, "Background," 86.

44. Hosokawa, *JACL*, 323–24; Masaoka and Hosokawa, *Moses Masaoka*, 303–307; *CR* 92nd Cong., 1st sess., 117 pt. 24, 14 September 1971: 31781; *CR* 92nd Cong., 1st sess., 117 pt. 24, 16 September 1971: 32143–32145; *CR* 92nd Cong., 1st sess., 117 pt. 26, 29 September 1971: 33828. The repeal bill was approved by the House in a vote of 356 to 49 and by a voice vote in the Senate. See Longaker, 405.

45. Longaker, 405.

46. *United States Code: Congressional and Administrative News*, 92nd Congress, 1st sess., 1971, vol. 1: 363.

47. Longaker, 405–406.

48. Ibid., 406–408.

49. Richard Drinnon sees the two United States District Court Decisions in the 1980s that overturned the indictments and convictions in *Korematsu* and *Hirabayashi* as part of a lifting of the "'legal cloud' that has hung over Japanese Americans for decades" (Drinnon, *Keeper*, 260n). The Supreme Court did not, however, rule on either of these cases and thus still has not overruled the precedents it established in the 1943–1944 Japanese American cases of World War II. The *coram nobis* plaintiffs' lawyers in these cases hoped for a Supreme Court rehearing that might reverse the half-century-old precedents, but the Reagan administration blocked this move by refusing to appeal after losing in the lower courts. See Daniels, *Asian America*, 281;and Daniels, *Prisoners Without Trial: Japanese Americans in World War II* (New York: Hill and Wang, 1993), 99–100. For an account of the cases, see Peter Irons, ed., *Justice Delayed: The Record of the Japanese American Internment Cases* (Middletown, Conn., Wesleyan University Press, 1989).

50. Daniels, *Decision*, 56–57; Grodzins, *Americans Betrayed*, 374. See also Roger Daniels, *Prisoners*, 107–14.

51. *United States Code: Congressional and Administrative News*, 92nd Congress, 1st sess., 1971, vol. 2: 1435.

52. Ibid., 1436–1438.

53. Daniels, *Asian America*, 281.

JASON KOHN AND CARA LEMON

NINETEEN IN '98:
A CONVERSATION ON
STUDYING THE INTERNMENT

*The authors wrote this essay during their sophomore and junior years at
Brandeis University. In their freshman year they studied the internment in
my freshman seminar, "Not for the Fainthearted." Their dialogue began as a
taped conversation with Ariel Ahram, a fellow undergraduate at
Brandeis.*—Ed.

JK: Studying the Japanese American internment immediately raises questions of
relationship. Where were my grandparents when Executive Order 9066 was
passed? Did they know about it intimately, in passing, or even at all? Was there
any explicit connection between this American wartime atrocity and the mess of
cultural and national identities that constitute my family? Attempting to understand my lineage and family history in this context, I begin to reevaluate my historical perspective; do I view history as an American, South American, Jew . . . ?
My brother and I are first-generation American citizens. My mother and father
were born in Brazil and Argentina respectively, and most of my great-grandparents were Eastern European, so I never identified myself as an American or "typical American," as my mother says. There were always too many prefixes and
languages to sort out. Discussing my relationship to the internment probably
marks the first attempt I have ever made to understand an American historical
event in terms of a shared national experience.

CL: My experience as a Southern middle-class kid growing up in the suburbs carried me to the study of Japanese American internment with a very different perspective on American history. My ancestors immigrated to the United States so many generations ago that their arrival dates and even information about their countries of origin have been lost or confused. I have often taken my American identity for granted, and until late in my public school education, I also took the history that I read in textbooks for granted. My position in a predominantly white, Protestant environment didn't present discrepancies with the mainstream American history taught in school. I had not given history enough attention to realize that it was not written by a machine, but by people who had the ability to expand or collapse events in history, even choosing to omit some entirely.

JK: I grew up on Long Island, and I don't remember having any friends who didn't know when their families came to America. For the most part, we were all the children or grandchildren of Jewish, Asian, or Italian immigrants. The European stories were mostly the same: we were immigrant families who crossed the Atlantic sometime before World War II and then, sometime after Vietnam, moved down the Long Island Expressway from Brooklyn and Queens to Nassau County. My Asian and Indian friends were almost exclusively first-generation Americans, but everybody was mixed into the multicultural "salad bowl." Above all else, we were the suburban, middle-class children of parents who commuted to the city.

    In an attempt to counteract the influences of an extremely homogenizing environment, many parents supplemented our public school education with additional religious or cultural schooling. Like the Nisei children whose parents obliged them to go to Japanese school after their day in American school, I was forced to go to Hebrew school. As did Japanese school for the Nisei, Hebrew school emphasized an awareness of religious, cultural, and historical differences. I was supposed to identify with a group of Jewish children with whom I shared no outward common interests or religious convictions. We were taught about "our" history and were expected relate to each other through a shared tradition in a long line of tragic events. There was an understanding that history was a personal and cultural tie rather than an attempt to understand an event objectively or impartially. Hebrew school was an imagined community where words like "Holocaust" and "genocide" were used so frequently to assert one's religious affiliation that Jewish identity bore a very loose relationship to custom and belief. Instead, it seemed a kind of guilt-ridden attempt to overcompensate for the secularizing effects of an affluent New York suburb. Studying the Japanese

American internment, though, revealed to me a culture with a very interesting historical connection to Jewish history during World War II. Japanese Americans, having been locked away in camps and robbed of their freedom, fought the same war in which millions of Jews were sent to death camps.

CL: As a college student, I find war a distant concept. Because it has never been an imminent threat to us or to our families, our generation has had the privilege of being future-oriented. We can plan our careers and our families with reasonable assurance that we will not confront major warfare. I think that wartime produces its own mentality. Citizens of a country that is sending soldiers off to war by the millions have a far different outlook from that of our generation. The only real experience that we have had with war was the Gulf War of our childhood. Even this conflict gave us only a glimpse of war's potential devastation, as there were relatively few troops sent and very few American casualties. We don't have any notion of what it feels like for war to be a threat to our individual lives, much less a threat to the survival of our nation. As a result, at first it was difficult for me relate to the experience of the Japanese American internment and the political agenda of a nation that would find such an action necessary.

JK: Even more, we have never had to stand in line for food or supplies. A toothbrush or a loaf of bread have never been scarce commodities, and our lives have never been complicated by a shortage of simple goods. It is easy to be future-oriented, since our generation of middle-class Americans has been provided for without interruption. I asked my grandmother about some of her experiences during the war while she was a girl growing up in Brazil. She told me stories about standing in line with her entire family all night to receive rations of flour, sugar, and noodles. The domestic repercussions of war undoubtedly have drastic effects on one's values. To sit and meet with survivors of the internment, with people who faced the most severe domestic repercussions of war, gave me a personal as well as historical appreciation of Japanese internment.

CL: After Professor Harth introduced the possibility of participating in this collection, we had the opportunity to interact with other Americans who had personally experienced the internment. Through Professor Harth, we met three people who had been in the camps. The experience of hearing the actual voices of people who had spent time in the camps was a lot different from watching films or reading books about the internment. Listening to their experiences, in the form of personal and family histories and anecdotes, brought the reality of the internment into the present for me and gave it a very human element that did not necessarily surface in my research. These stories highlighted the sense of confusion, betrayal and alienation that accompany being forcibly removed from one's home without cause and detained as a prisoner. The understanding of an event as it affects individuals' lives is remarkably different from viewing it as a set of historical facts.

So Professor Harth and her friends were our first link to eyewitness experiences of former internees. The screening of Emiko and Chizu Omori's film, *Rabbit in the Moon* at the Museum of Fine Arts in Boston provided us with another. After the film, there was a panel discussion and question and answer session with Emiko Omori, with the head of the local chapter of the Japanese American Citizens League, and with members of the audience. Omori, as well as many other members of the audience, shared their stories. There was a fairly broad representation of people who had been in internment camps themselves or who had family members who had been there. Each person told a very different account of his or her past experiences, which not only exposed us to the range of experiences but also illustrated the interrelatedness of those experiences. Many of these stories were sparked by other stories told during the discussion, forming a sort of chain of common experience.

JK: Not having done extensive studies in American history, especially contemporary American history, I remember having been very impressed by the quantity and accessibility of physical evidence. Watching new films and original documentaries, reading primary sources not fifty years old, and speaking with so many people who were directly involved with the internment, including our professor, were extremely valuable. It becomes increasingly difficult to understand how the internment is so underrepresented in education and in popular conceptions of American history when there is so much information at hand. For the most part, Asians appear in textbooks only as enemies—in World War II, Korea, and Vietnam, or as competitors—in the narratives of the Japanese economic resurgence in the 1970s and 1980s. Popular thought in fact denies Asian Americans a position in the social and racial matrix of domestic American life.

CL: Although they are not readily accessible in the body of mainstream American history, many available primary resources relate the experience of being Asian American during World War II. In reading firsthand accounts, histories, and narratives of the Japanese American internment, I had to reevaluate my perceptions of the United States as a diverse and welcoming nation. Although I don't have a naive notion that America offers a utopian alternative for anyone who wants to come here, I do think that our generation believes it is a safe place for immigrants, for people who are seeking asylum and trying to escape overwhelming atrocities in their home countries. While I have recognized that racism is still very much a concern, I have believed that immigrants are able to come to the United States in search of a home. The fundamental premise of the internment contradicts that notion. The internment interrupted the process of creating a home and achieving the American Dream by uprooting, ostracizing, and imprisoning innocent people involved in the everyday course of maintaining their families and hoping for an improved future. This drastic measure administered by the United States government absolutely conflicts with the American ideology of freedom and human rights.

JK: Public schools teach Manifest Destiny and the massacre of Native Americans, the slave trade, and Jim Crow, yet leave out an event that is still so resonant, especially because it involved people who are still alive. People today still have an opportunity to learn about the internment firsthand as we did. But after all, this is an event that carries scary implications for immigrants and minorities. With so much media attention given to Islamic terrorism here and abroad or to the expanding nuclear capabilities of developing nations, the relative closeness of an event like the Japanese American internment sheds light on America's often dubious relationship with its citizens and residents. It still seems too easy to blame immigrants and their children for perceived problems with their native countries. I find it troubling that the United States, a country founded and populated by immigrants, is so unaware of the wartime incarceration of Japanese Americans.

CL: Although the internment can be grouped with other American atrocities, it feels different from some of those other incidents of injustice because it cannot be isolated in centuries past. It seems that we view the massacre of Native Americans and the slave trade with a sense of distance and separation, as if there has been an evolution of social justice in our country. Although the Japanese American internment seems foreign in concept, it feels uncomfortably close in time. Many of the victims, perpetrators, and witnesses are still living. The internment challenges the attitude in our nation that we can overcome an event and then deny it a historical function. We attempt to break with selected events from the past and claim that we have moved onto another plane where social injustice is obsolete. Because the Japanese American internment happened so recently, it forces us to reconsider our distance from achieving the American ideals of freedom, equality, and non-discrimination.

JK: But our social perspective on World War II can be just as distant as it is on earlier injustices. As students electronically connected to anything and everything, we find it easier than ever to assimilate this "uncomfortable closeness" into notions of a past considered archaic. We are in the midst of the "technological revolution," which is a new and very explicit marker in cultural history. Our generation has seen the end of the Cold War and the beginning of a new digital, globalized world market. In that sense, the war is already part of a bygone period, the twentieth century. Perhaps this is why the personal interaction with survivors was so important to our research. Our fears, goals, and expectations have all changed. The idea of a national enemy is all but gone. Whether it was Germany, Japan, the Soviet Union, or even Cuba, our parents and grandparents always knew who they were fighting against. I remember watching the Berlin Wall fall when I was twelve. Coming into a new historical era, our generation now faces the interesting position of living without fear of war, real or illusory. The last political remnants of the Second World War having disappeared, it becomes increasingly difficult to understand concepts of mass bloodshed, totalitarianism, and national sacrifice as tangible rather than merely hypothetical or historical situations.

CL: One of the reasons the internment is able to maintain its obscurity is the absence of education and general knowledge about it. The fact that I had absolutely no knowledge of the internment when I entered college is a testament to how little attention the subject has received. Because in Texas I lived so much closer than other students to where the Japanese were interned, I would expect that more information on the internment would have been available to me. Depictions of the Second World War in American public schools still often present United States efforts in the war as sacrificial and heroic. The American role in the war is often portrayed as representative of democratic reason battling totalitarian regimes and ensuring justice for the future. Because of the United States' victory in the war, it is easier to remember it in that role. As a consequence, education about the Japanese American internment has received little attention.

JK: The first thing I remember learning about the internment was that very few people knew anything about it at all. Less than half of our class raised their hands when asked if they had even heard of the internment. I had a general idea that such an event had occurred only because of a few news broadcasts in the early 1990s reporting the $20,000 in compensation for survivors. It's an interesting contrast to the treatment of the Holocaust in German schools. The

United States, especially in relation to the Second World War, has always maintained its historical distinctiveness as the standard-bearer of freedom, "the arsenal of democracy," the winner in the ultimate battle of "good" versus "evil." To learn about the wartime politics of racism and issues of domestic social injustice is extraordinarily troublesome. The Japanese American internment forces the essential question, "What were we fighting for?" In this context, the standard responses of patriotism, democracy and national security become questionable.

In 1943 Arthur Koestler wrote, "In this war we are fighting against a total lie in the name of a half-truth." He describes the battle between the lie of Nazism's New Order—the social "might is right" and reduction of "Sociology to Zoology," which turned "Civil Law to Jungle Law"—and the myth of liberal Western democracy. Koestler continues:

> We fight against Racialism and yet racial discrimination is far from abolished in the Anglo-Saxon countries; we fight for Democracy and yet our mightiest ally is a dictatorship where at least two of the four freedoms are not operating. But such is the sticky, all-pervading influence of our climate that even to mention these facts, undeniable though they are, has the effect of a provocation.

The history of the internment is at once a reminder of the deficiencies in a contemporary democratic nation and an example of how we have faced them: the transformation of more than 120,000 innocent people's imprisonment into a footnote of American history.

CL: If racism was not the sole motivation for the internment, it at least facilitated the imprisonment of Japanese and Japanese Americans. Germans and Italians, who were not easily distinguished from the average white Americans, had the advantage of blending into the majority. It was easier for the government to isolate, gather, and relocate a group of people with distinct physical features, and to take action against a group of people who could be identified by the general populace as "other." In this way, the government itself was an agent of "assimilation" in deciding who did and did not qualify as American.

JK: It's interesting to see how by the outbreak of the war, Germans and Italians, as whites, had for the most part already been assimilated into American culture. German and Italian Americans were depicted as good American soldiers by Hollywood in World War II combat films, while the simultaneous depictions of buck-toothed Japanese men wearing thick, round, black glasses demonstrated an American inability to separate race and ethnicity from nationality. I went to an exhibit on the internment at Ellis Island in 1998 where I read war pamphlets on how to distinguish Japanese men and women from Koreans and Chinese. It listed facial and body distinctions as well as differences in the sound of languages and manners. One government pamphlet also listed ways of detecting the difference between the Issei and Nisei generations, which of course boiled down to a quantitative measure of respective threat. It was all so explicitly racist and yet so ridiculous that I had trouble seeing it as historical text and not as kitsch. At the same time it is difficult not to remember the same brand of racial tactics employed by the Nazis. It's not hard to believe that many Americans who would like to maintain certain traditional notions of our role in the war would feel uncomfortable with this similarity. I would venture to guess that there was no government pamphlet on the subtle differences in Northern European languages that would enable one to detect a native-born German, or how to distinguish an Italian from a Greek.

CL: This racism becomes all the more evident when we examine the American government's inconsistency in dealing with people of German and Italian descent living in the United States during the war. This entire population was not forced out of its homes into prison camps as were the Japanese immigrants and Japanese Americans. Such a profound instance of racism demands an explanation. How instrumental was widespread racism in facilitating the internment? Did the government actively use propaganda to stir up anti-Japanese feeling during the war? Were the American people proponents of the internment or did American policymakers simply make decisions without considering the wishes of the people? Were the American people looking for a reason to put the Japanese and Japanese Americans in camps, or were they convinced that it was necessary? All of these questions are very difficult to answer because it is almost impossible to determine when racism is a structure imposed on people by a dominant system and when racism is a sentiment felt by a large number of people and subsequently transferred to government policy. It is most likely a combination of the two. Still, the Japanese American internment cannot be completely removed from the context of the war, because people are more likely to allow governments to take extreme measures in circumstances where they feel threatened. At the same time, I believe that the motives for the internment must be questioned because of the inconsistency in government policy toward other immigrant groups during the Second World War.

JK: In this sense, the term "total war" must be seen as inappropriate. How can we use the words "total war" when the victims, or at least the American victims, were so arbitrarily selected? I should think that a total war would have entailed at least *some* consistency, some action taken towards first- and second-generation German and Italian Americans. There was no shortage of support for the rising Nazi powers among German American communities in the 1930s, yet we chose our total war at home only against Japanese American citizens and their resident parents (resident because of the legal restrictions against naturalization of immigrants from Japan).

CL: I am very curious about older generations' perceptions of the Japanese American internment. I remember one conversation in particular that I had with several family friends in my parents' generation at a dinner party. I asked them for their memories and impressions. They relayed only a vague sense of having heard about the internment in childhood. Distance from the event seems to be a common response. I haven't gotten an impression of guilt or responsibility when I've spoken to older Americans about the internment. Often they simply admit to not having given it much thought. It might be different talking to people outside of Texas or Boston, who lived in communities from which Japanese Americans were removed for internment, but it seems that collective guilt does not exist. Many people are of the opinion that the American government was carrying out necessary measures during a time of war, and the racist implications of such an action are not addressed.

JK: Again, it's interesting to see the contrast with Germany. Although camps in Europe and the United States implemented similar means—segregation and incarceration—to very different ends—genocide rather than detention—it's difficult for me to understand the two events independently. In Germany, there exists a real sense of guilt and collective responsibility. When speaking with Germans, even today, you can hardly mention World War II and the exploits of the Third Reich without a weird sense of unease. But in America there's really no sense whatsoever that the internment was our responsibility. Nobody is willing to accept that our direct ascendants were responsible for destroying so many people's lives. Although there are many reasons for this lack of acceptance, from deficiency of education to continuing racial discrimination, one of the simplest may have to do with the misleading label "internment camp." It has a very benign sound, but in fact the Japanese Americans were concentrated into small camps and forced to live and work there for an average of two to four years.

It seems that the problem of calling internment camps "concentration camps" has much less to do with our understanding of concentration camps than with a common misunderstanding of the differences between concentration

camps and extermination camps. It would not be inappropriate to call the relocation centers concentration camps, whereas they were definitely not extermination camps. There is no denying that concentration camps as they existed in
Germany were far worse than the ones in the United States, yet their relative impact here and abroad, personally and socially, may be better understood by the
use of the same term. In *Rabbit in the Moon*, it was amazing to see that Japanese
Americans felt guilty coming out of the camps, not because what they went
through was horrible, but because it wasn't as horrible as what the Jews were
going through in Germany. How could they complain when the Jews had it so
much worse? We can acknowledge that the relocation centers were concentration camps, because in America, the reputed model democracy, our camps represented the same racial bias as did those in Germany. The Third Reich was a
regime of destruction and death. But in America, the idea of locking up innocent
citizens is completely abhorrent.

CL: In a historical context, the term "concentration camp" is so loaded that we
hesitate to use it to describe the Japanese American internment camps. It
brings with it a sense of destruction, death, and absolute horror. These images
are not representative of the experience of being incarcerated in the United
States. At the same time, I too believe that it is not completely inappropriate to
use the term concentration camps for the internment camps in the western
United States, because it is an acknowledgment that the internees were un-
justly imprisoned. Although there is most certainly a distinction to be made between the American and the European camps, the principle of denying basic
human rights is the same in both instances. The admission of a large-scale,
government-imposed denial of personal freedom is an important step toward
educating the public and preventing a similar injustice from happening in the
future. I think that the measures taken by the government to correct the damage caused by the internment were inadequate. The money granted to survivors over forty years later did not begin to compensate for lost land, property,
time and freedom. There was no attempt to restore people to their former
lives. For many older people, it was too late to start over. I believe that regardless of the issue of guilt, there should have been an effort to help them rebuild
their lives after having taken them away.

JK: Although complete restitution for losses would have been an ethical and
appropriate compensation for Japanese American survivors, it seems that the
broader issue of education is far more pertinent and crucial to current national
and international problems. Within the past ten years, ethnic conflicts in

Rwanda and the former Yugoslavia have proven that racial nationalism and its violent consequences are hardly irrelevant issues in contemporary political and social thought. And while it is easy to point fingers overseas, there is obviously no shortage of racial problems domestically as well. Although it may be somewhat naive to suggest that any of these problems have simple or even foreseeable solutions, by denying events like the Japanese American internment a place in popular education, we are clearly perpetuating the same half-truths of Western liberal democracy that Koestler spoke of almost sixty years ago.

CL: Our generation faces a danger very different from the dangers of World War II. It is all too easy as an American student to feel removed from war, insulated from the rest of the world and its conflicts, and complacent about large-scale, racially motivated injustices. Reading about ethnic conflict in the newspaper does not carry the same weight as considering it a part of everyday life in your home country. Americans often think of the United States as a place with relatively equal opportunity and equal treatment. The Japanese American internment is a reminder that we are not as far removed from racially motivated policy as we might pretend. Unfortunately, this important reminder has not reached many American citizens, especially the younger generations. The danger of not knowing about the Japanese American internment and its consequences is the inability to prevent the occurrence of a similar event. This is a danger that we should take extremely seriously by educating our present and future generations.

APPENDIX

CHRONOLOGY OF EVENTS

December 7, 1941: The Japanese attack the United States naval base at Pearl Harbor, Hawaii, killing some 2,300 Americans and catapulting the United States into the Second World War. At home, the attack galvanizes decades of hostility toward the Japanese immigrant group and their citizen offspring. What to do with the "Japanese?" military and government officials ask. Army brass succeed in persuading the Department of Justice and President Franklin D. Roosevelt that "military necessity" requires drastic action.

February 19, 1942: President Roosevelt signs Executive Order 9066, authorizing the secretary of war and military commanders to designate military areas "from which any or all persons may be excluded." No one is fooled. "Any or all" means "Japanese."

By this time, martial law has been declared in Hawaii. Delos Emmons, commanding general there, resists War Secretary Stimson's urgings for a large-scale evacuation from the islands. The roughly 158,000 ethnic Japanese in Hawaii form more than 35 percent of its total population and so are vital to the local labor force. In the end, a total of 1,875 Hawaiian ethnic Japanese will have been removed to internment camps on the mainland.

March 1942: The forced removal of over 110,000 persons of Japanese descent from the West Coast states and part of Arizona begins. They are allowed to take with them only what they can carry by hand. First stop, "assembly centers," or holding pens improvised from fairgrounds, racetracks, and the like. Several months later the "relocation centers" are ready, and the incarcerated population is transferred to ten concentration camps scattered throughout the western and southern states from California to Arkansas. Accommodations in the camps are a grade above the malodorous horse stalls of the assembly centers: barracks, one family to a twenty-by-twenty-five-foot room, without private plumbing facilities and with little protection against the extreme rigors of climate in the remote regions where the camps have been built. The camps are ringed by barbed wire; searchlights swing from the watchtowers manned by armed military guards.

March 18, 1942: President Roosevelt, through Executive Order 9102, creates a civil administrative agency for the camps, the War Relocation Authority (WRA).

In the camps: periodic restiveness, factional infighting among internees, sporadic violence. Perhaps the best known of the disturbances is a "riot" that erupts on December 6, 1942 at Manzanar, leaving two internees shot dead by the military guards. Hospitals and medical care are rudimentary, and inadequate or improvised service leads to much suffering and a number of unnecessary deaths. Some inmates can obtain "leave clearance" after an elaborate screening process and are allowed to leave the camps temporarily (for seasonal agricultural work) or permanently, provided that they do not return to the exclusion zones—that is, to their homes. Conditions for temporary workers are no improvement on those in camp.

February 1943: Recruitment for volunteers to an all-Japanese American army unit begins. It involves "registration," or filling out a long questionnaire with two key questions on loyalty. Those inmates judged disloyal are "segregated" at the Tule Lake (California) camp, and the "loyals" at Tule Lake are moved to other camps. After disturbances at Tule in the fall of that year, the military is called in.

January 1944: The draft is reinstituted for Nisei, who had been reclassified 4-C (enemy alien status) after Pearl Harbor. A draft resistance movement gains strength at the Heart Mountain (Wyoming) camp.

July 1, 1944: Congress passes a bill permitting voluntary renunciation of citizenship. By March 1945 over 5,000 citizens have renounced their citizenship. After many years of court actions initiated by attorney Wayne Collins, those in the overwhelming majority who later change their minds are allowed to regain their citizenship. (By the end of 1945 over 20,000 requests for repatriation have come from camp inmates, but in the end only about 8,000 nationwide actually leave the United States.)

December 18, 1944: The Supreme Court finds for Mitsuye Endo in ruling that the WRA has no right to detain a loyal citizen. In the *Korematsu* case, handed down on the same day, the court upholds the constitutionality of the mass incarceration.

January 2, 1945: The Allies are clearly winning the war. Following the War Department's lifting of the general exclusion orders for the West Coast (December 17, 1944), the incarcerated population is allowed to resettle there.

August 10, 1988: The Japanese American community's movement for redress culminates in President Ronald Reagan's signing of the Civil Liberties Act (HR 442), which provides for a national apology and $20,000 in reparations to each individual survivor of the camps. The amount is symbolic. Under the terms of the Japanese American Claims Act (1948), Congress finally appropriated approximately $37 million in settlement of some 26,500 claims of property loss totaling about $148 million. One estimate puts uncompensated property loss at between $41 and $206 million and total loss in income between $108 and $164 million in 1945 dollars, and the combined total loss of property and income somewhere between $810 million and $2 billion in 1983 dollars. [Figures are from the 1982–1983 Report of the Commission on Wartime Relocation and Internment of Civilians, *Personal Justice Denied.*]

By 1988 the convictions of wartime resisters Gordon Hirabayashi and Minoru Yasui for violation of curfew orders (1943) and that of Fred Korematsu for violation of exclusion orders (1944), which were all upheld by the Supreme Court, have been overturned following the reopening of the cases in 1981 by a team of lawyers.

At the expiration of the Civil Liberties Act in 1998, President Clinton settles a class-action suit with the award of $5,000 in compensation to each of 1,200 surviving Japanese Latin Americans who were among the roughly 3,000 ethnic Japanese, Italian, and German residents of Latin America deported to the United States at the request of this government. Over two-thirds were Japanese nationals and their families, and over 80 percent were from Peru. In the spring of 2000, further redress legislation is introduced into Congress. Among the provisions is the increase of compensation for Japanese Latin Americans to $20,000. Canada incarcerated its own ethnic Japanese during the war. So the wartime incarceration of ethnic Japanese expands into an international American story.

In the course of the redress movement, early in the 1980s, researcher Aiko Herzig-Yoshinaga uncovered a document showing that in 1942 the government had intentionally suppressed important official reports that found no evidence of disloyalty among the population that was to be incarcerated. Not one case of sabotage or espionage among the Japanese immigrants and Japanese Americans has ever been proved.

CONTRIBUTORS

ROSANNA YAMAGIWA ALFARO has written numerous plays on the internment and other subjects, which have been produced in the Boston area where she resides, in Los Angeles, San Francisco, New York, Philadelphia, Edinburgh, and elsewhere. She was runner-up for the Weissberger Award with her play *Barrancas* and a recipient of a 1995 Artist Finalist Grant from the Massachusetts Cultural Council.

ALLAN W. AUSTIN is an assistant professor of history at College Misericordia in Dallas, Pennsylvania. He received his doctoral degree in 2001 from the University of Cincinnati with a dissertation titled "From Concentration Camp to Campus: A History of the National Japanese American Student Relocation Council, 1942–1946."

GEORGE F. BROWN spent two years of his childhood, from 1943 to 1945, in the Gila River Relocation Center in Arizona, where his parents held appointed staff positions with the War Relocation Authority. He is a public health physician and former vice president of International Programs at the Population Council, an international research organization. His work has taken him to various parts of the globe. Currently he lives in New York City.

SUE KUNITOMI EMBREY was interned at Manzanar. She is a retired adult education teacher and lecturer in Ethnic Studies at the University of California at Santa Barbara. She edited *The Lost Years* (1972), and co-edited *Manzanar Martyr: An Interview with Harry Y. Ueno* (1986) and *Reflections in Three Self-Guided Tours of Manzanar* (1998). Her essays and poetry have appeared in a variety of newspapers and anthologies. A longtime activist and community leader, she is the founder of the Manzanar Committee.

ERICA HARTH is Professor of Humanities and Women's Studies at Brandeis University. She is the author of several books and numerous essays and articles in her academic field of training, early modern French studies. In recent years, her personal essays on the year of her childhood that she spent at the Manzanar Relocation Center in 1944–1945 have appeared in *The Massachusetts Review*, *Soundings: An Interdisciplinary Journal*, and elsewhere.

PATRICK S. HAYASHI was born in the internment camp at Topaz, Utah. He is Associate Vice Chancellor for Admissions and Enrollment at the University of California at Berkeley. As chief admissions officer for the campus since 1988, he has been responsible for Berkeley's affirmative action policies. He is the author of publications on affirmative action and admissions.

STEWART DAVID IKEDA is currently Editor-in-Chief and Director of Content Development for the iMinorities.com Multicultural Villages online network. His award-winning novel, *What the Scarecrow Said*, was released in 1996 by HarperCollins-Regan Books. His poetry, fiction, and essays have appeared in numerous publications, including *Ploughshares*, *Story*, and the anthologies *Voices of the Xiled* and *Yellow Light: The Flowering of Asian American Arts*.

JASON KOHN is an alumnus of Brandeis University, where he majored in European Cultural Studies, with a minor in Film Studies. He is from New York City.

CARA LEMON is an alumna of Brandeis University, where she majored in French. She is from Fort Worth, Texas.

ROBERT J. MAEDA is Emeritus Professor of Fine Arts at Brandeis University. He is the author of *Two Twelfth-Century Texts on Chinese Painting* and other work on Asian art. His current research is on Isamu Noguchi, and an article of his on Noguchi has appeared in *American Art* (1999).

MARNIE MUELLER was born in Tule Lake Japanese American Segregation Center. Mueller is author of the novel *Green Fires* (Curbstone Press, 1994), which won a 1995 American Book Award and the 1995 Maria Thomas Award for Fiction. *Green Fires* appeared in German translation in 1996. *The Climate of the Country*, her novel about life in the Tule Lake camp, was published by Curbstone Press in 1999. Mueller's latest novel is *My Mother's Island* (forthcoming from Curbstone Press, 2002).

DONNA K. NAGATA is an Associate Professor of Psychology at the University of Michigan, Ann Arbor. She has studied and written about the long-term impact of the internment for over ten years. Her publications include *Legacy of Injustice: Exploring the Cross-Generational Impact of the Japanese American Internment* and a range of articles and chapters in books.

CHIZU OMORI is a writer living in Seattle. Her work includes articles and book and film reviews for local and national newspapers and magazines. She is a longtime political activist, whose involvement in the Japanese American redress movement led to the making of *Rabbit in the Moon* (1999), a co-production with her sister, Emiko Omori, a filmmaker. This documentary has won many awards, including an Emmy for Outstanding Historical Programming. Omori continues to educate the public about the wartime incarceration as a lecturer and discussion leader in schools and other institutions.

TOYO SUYEMOTO was born in 1916, grew up in Sacramento, and lived in Berkeley until internment. In Topaz, where she was interned, she wrote for the camp publications *Trek* and *All Aboard*. Her poetry has appeared in a wide variety of journals, including *The Yale Review*, *Amerasia Journal*, and *Common Ground*, and also in numerous anthologies, most recently the *Longman Anthology of World Literature by Women, 1875–1975* (1989) and *Only What We Could Carry: The Japanese American Internment Experience* (2000). An academic librarian, she was head of the Social Work Library and assistant head of the Education/Psychology Library at Ohio State University until her retirement in 1985. Her editor, Susan B. Richardson, is an Associate Professor of English at Denison University in Granville, Ohio.

JOHN TATEISHI was born in Los Angeles in 1939 and at the age of three was interned at Manzanar, where he spent the duration of the war. He received his graduate degree in English literature and taught at the University of London, England, and at the City College of San Francisco. In 1978 he headed the successful national redress movement for the World War II internment. Subsequently he established Tateishi/Shinoda & Associates, a management consulting firm in San Francisco and Dallas. He is currently serving as the National Executive Director of the Japanese Americans Citizens League, the nation's largest Asian American civil rights organization. He is the author of *And Justice for All* (University of Washington Press, 1999), an oral history of the internment.

JENI YAMADA is the author of *Laura: A Case for the Modularity of Language*. She has also written short stories and essays, one of which will appear in a forthcoming anthology. During her graduate studies at UCLA, she was a spokesperson for Women Against Violence Against Women, a group protesting images of violence against women in the media. She started a Social Responsibility Committee at her children's school in Massachusetts and has lectured on racism, human rights, and the internment camp experience in schools, colleges, and community forums. Currently she is writing and illustrating short stories.

MITSUYE YAMADA is the author of *Camp Notes and Other Writings* (1998), a combined new edition of her *Camp Notes and Other Poems* and *Desert Run: Poems and Stories*. She has co-edited anthologies of writings by multicultural women and is founder and coordinator of MultiCultural Women Writers. She is a former board member of Amnesty International USA and is an active member of Interfaith Prisoners of Conscience Project. She teaches in the Asian American Studies program at the University of California at Irvine.

VALERIE NAO YOSHIMURA has a Ph.D. in French literature from the University of Michigan at Ann Arbor. In her academic career, she received numerous academic awards and scholarships. Her publications include scholarly articles on French literature as well as essays on Japanese American issues. She has lectured widely on the internment and related matters, and has curated exhibits and headed research projects on Japanese American history. In 1997 she was a delegate to the Forty-ninth Japan-America Student Conference. She is a former president of the Detroit chapter of the Japanese American Citizens League.

SUGGESTIONS FOR FURTHER READING

(The following represents a limited selection of some of the most significant contributions to the extensive literature on the Japanese American internment. Only scholarly works and memoirs are included.—Ed.)

Armor, John, and Peter Wright. *Manzanar.* New York: Times Books, 1988.

Bosworth, Allan R. *America's Concentration Camps.* New York: Norton, 1967.

Burton, Jeffery F., Mary M. Farrell, Florence B. Lord, and Richard W. Lord. *Confinement and Ethnicity: An Overview of World War II Japanese American Relocation Sites.* Tucson, Ariz.: Western Archeological and Conservation Center, National Park Service, U.S. Department of the Interior, Publications in Anthropology 74, 1999.

Conrat, Maisie, and Richard Conrat. *Executive Order 9066: The Internment of 110,000 Japanese Americans.* San Francisco: California Historical Society, 1972.

Daniels, Roger. *Concentration Camps, North America: Japanese in the United States and Canada during World War II.* Rev. ed. Malabar, Fla.: Krieger, 1977.

———. *Prisoners Without Trial: Japanese Americans in World War II.* New York: Hill and Wang, 1993.

———. *The Politics of Prejudice.* Berkeley: University of California Press, 1977.

Daniels, Roger, Sandra C. Taylor, and Harry H. L. Kitano, eds., *Japanese Americans from Relocation to Redress.* Rev. ed. Seattle: University of Washington Press, 1991.

Dower, John. *War Without Mercy: Race and Power in the Pacific War.* New York: Pantheon, 1986.

Drinnon, Richard. *Dillon Myer, Keeper of Concentration Camps.* Berkeley: University of California Press, 1987.

Eaton, Allen H. *Beauty Behind Barbed Wire.* New York: Harper, 1952.

Embrey, Sue. *The Lost Years, 1942–46.* Los Angeles: Moonlight Publications, 1972.

Fujita, Stephen S., and David J. O'Brien. *The Japanese American Experience.* Bloomington: Indiana University Press, 1991.

Gesensway, Deborah, and Mindy Roseman. *Beyond Words: Images from America's Concentration Camps.* Ithaca: Cornell University Press, 1987.

Girdner, Audrie, and Anne Loftis. *The Great Betrayal.* New York: Macmillan, 1969.

Grodzins, Morton. *Americans Betrayed: Politics and the Japanese Evacuation.* Chicago: University of Chicago Press, 1949.

Hansen, Arthur A., ed. *Japanese American World War II Evacuation Oral History Project.* 5 vols. Westport, Conn.: Meckler, 1990–1992.

Hosokawa, Bill. *JACL in Quest of Justice: The History of the Japanese American Citizens League*. New York: William Morrow, 1982.

Houston, Jeanne Wakatsuki, and James Houston. *Farewell to Manzanar*. New York: Bantam, 1974.

Ichioka, Yuji, ed. *Views from Within: The Japanese American Evacuation and Resettlement Study*. UCLA: Resource Development and Publications, Asian American Studies Center, 1989.

Irons, Peter. *Justice at War: The Story of the Japanese American Internment Cases*. New York: Oxford, 1983.

Irons, Peter, ed. *Justice Delayed: The Record of the Japanese American Internment Cases*. Middletown, Conn.: Wesleyan University Press, 1989.

James, Thomas. *Exile Within: The Schooling of Japanese Americans, 1942–1945*. Cambridge, Mass.: Harvard University Press, 1987.

Kikuchi, Charles. *The Kikuchi Diary*. Edited by John Modell. 2nd ed. Urbana: University of Illinois Press, 1993.

Kitagawa, Daisuke. *Issei and Nisei: The Internment Years*. New York: Seabury Press, 1967.

Kitano, Harry H. L. *Japanese Americans: Evolution of a Subculture*. Englewood Cliffs, New Jersey: Prentice-Hall, 1969.

Leighton, Alexander H. *The Governing of Men: General Principles and Recommendations Based on Experience at a Japanese Relocation Camp*. Princeton: Princeton University Press, 1945.

Levine, Ellen. *A Fence Away from Freedom: Japanese Americans and World War II*. New York: G. P. Putnam's Sons, 1995.

McWilliams, Carey. *Prejudice: Japanese Americans: Symbol of Racial Intolerance*. Boston: Little, Brown, 1944.

Maki, Mitchell T., Harry H. L. Kitano, and S. Megan Berthold. *Achieving the Impossible Dream: How Japanese Americans Obtained Redress*. Urbana: University of Illinois Press, 1999.

Muller, Eric L. *Free to Die for Their Country: The Story of the Japanese American Draft Resisters in World War II*. Chicago: University of Chicago Press, 2001.

Myer, Dillon S. *Uprooted Americans: The Japanese Americans and the War Relocation Authority during World War II*. Tucson: University of Arizona Press, 1971.

Nagata, Donna K. *Legacy of Injustice: Exploring the Cross-Generational Impact of the Japanese American Internment*. New York: Plenum, 1993.

Okubo, Miné. *Citizen 13660*. [New York, 1946] Seattle: University of Washington Press, 1983.

Sone, Monica. *Nisei Daughter*. 2nd ed. Seattle: University of Washington Press, 1979.

Spicer, Edward H., Asael T. Hansen, Katherine Luomala, and Marvin Opler. *Impounded People: Japanese-Americans in the Relocation Centers*. Tucson: University of Arizona Press, 1969.

Takaki, Ronald T. *Double Victory: A Multicultural History of America in World War II*. Boston: Little, Brown, 2000.

Takezawa, Yasuko I. *Breaking the Silence: Redress and Japanese American Ethnicity*. Ithaca: Cornell University Press, 1995.

Tateishi, John. *And Justice for All: An Oral History of the Japanese American Detention Camps*. 2nd ed. Seattle: University of Washington Press, 1999.

Taylor, Sandra. *Jewel of the Desert: Japanese American Internment at Topaz*. Berkeley: University of California Press, 1993.

Thomas, Dorothy S. *The Salvage*. Berkeley: University of California Press, 1952.

Thomas, Dorothy S., and Richard S. Nishimoto. *The Spoilage*. Berkeley: University of California Press, 1946.

Uchida, Yoshiko. *Desert Exile, The Uprooting of a Japanese American Family*. Seattle: University of Washington Press, 1982.

United States Commission on Wartime Relocation and Internment of Civilians. *Personal Justice Denied: Report of the Commission on Wartime Relocation and Internment of Civilians*. Seattle: University of Washington Press, 1997.

United States Department of the Interior, War Relocation Authority. *WRA: A Story of Human Conservation*. Washington, D.C., 1946.

Weglyn, Michi. *Years of Infamy: The Untold Story of America's Concentration Camps*. New York: Morrow, 1976.

Yamamoto, Eric K. et al. *Race, Rights and Reparation: Law and the Japanese American Internment*. Gaithersburg: Aspen Law and Business, 2001.

Zeller, William D. *An Educational Drama: The Educational Program Provided the Japanese Americans During the Relocation Period, 1942–1945*. New York: American Press, 1969.

INDEX